D1531716

DATE DUE

WID

DEMCO 38-296

The Practitioner Inquiry Series

Marilyn Cochran-Smith and Susan L. Lytle, SERIES EDITORS

ADVISORY BOARD: Rebecca Barr, Judy Buchanan, Robert Fecho,
Susan Florio-Ruane, Sarah Freedman, Karen Gallas, Andrew Gitlin,
Dixie Goswami, Peter Grimmett, Gloria Ladson-Billings, Roberta Logan,
Sarah Michaels, Susan Noffke, Marsha Pincus, Marty Rutherford,
Lynne Strieb, Carol Tateishi, Polly Ulichny, Diane Waff, Ken Zeichner

WRITING TO MAKE A DIFFERENCE
Classroom Projects for Community Change

Chris Benson
Scott Christian

with

Dixie Goswami and Walter H. Gooch

EDITORS

Teachers College, Columbia University
New York and London

Published by Teachers College Press, 1234 Amsterdam Avenue, New York, NY 10027

Copyright © 2002 by Teachers College, Columbia University

All rights reserved. No part of this publication may be reproduced or transmitted in any form or by any means, electronic or mechanical, including photocopy, or any information storage and retrieval system, without permission from the publisher.

Library of Congress Cataloging-in-Publication Data

Writing to make a difference : classroom projects for community change / Chris Benson, Scott Christian, with Dixie Goswami and Walter H. Gooch, editors.
   p. cm.
  Includes bibliographical references and index.
  ISBN 0-8077-4187-6 (acid-free paper) — ISBN 0-8077-4186-8 (pbk. : acid-free paper)
  1. English language—Rhetoric—Study and teaching—Social aspects—United States. 2. English language—Rhetoric—Study and teaching—United States. 3. Community development—United States. 4. Community college students. 5. Community and college.
6. Computer networks.
I. Benson, Chris, 1956– . II. Christian, Scott, 1962– .
PE1405.U6W77   2001
808′.042′071173—dc21   2001041572

ISBN 0-8077-4186-8 (paper)
ISBN 0-8077-4187-6 (cloth)

Printed on acid-free paper

Manufactured in the United States of America

09   08   07   06   05   04   03   02   8   7   6   5   4   3   2   1

CONTENTS

ACKNOWLEDGMENTS

We wish to express sincere gratitude to teachers and students whose imagination, insights, and hard work are visible in their own communities and neighborhoods and in this collection. We are also thankful to Robert Barr and Robert T. H. Davidson, Trustees of The Bingham Trust, for their generous support of Clemson Writing in the Schools and Write to Change, Inc.

Other important supporters of teachers' work in writing for the community include James Maddox, director of the Bread Loaf School of English, and his staff; Robert Becker, director of the Strom Thurmond Institute at Clemson University; Peter Stillman, executive publisher of Calendar Islands Publishing and author of *Families Writing* (1998); Art Young, Campbell Professor of Technical Communication at Clemson University; and Carl Lovitt, director of the Pearce Center for Professional Communication at Clemson University. Each of these individuals has provided essential support to teachers and students who practice literacy as a means to social action and change.

Leslie Owens, director of numerous writing for the community projects, established long-standing networks of teachers and students whose writing served to inform and educate others. Caroline Eisner, director of the Writing Center and member of the faculty at Georgetown University, designed and edited the *Guide to Writing for the Community* that has been distributed to hundreds of teachers since 1994. The *Guide* was co-edited by Marjorie Kleinneiur Morgan (who has contributed a chapter to this book) and Margaret Cintorino, two exceptional teachers who, with their students, have helped shape and define our notions of writing for the community since the 1980s. Special thanks to Carolyn Benson, administrative assistant to Write to Change, who has expertly guided and directed writing for the community projects for a decade. We are also indebted to the work of Dr. Janice Redish and her team on the Document Design Project that produced *Writing for the Professions* and *Guidelines for Document Designers* (American

Institutes for Research, Washington, DC, 1981), two texts whose principles support the models, methods, and motives of the projects described in this book.

We are deeply grateful to Lou Bernieri and Hazel Lockett, co-directors of the Andover Bread Loaf Writing Workshop at Phillips Academy, Andover, Massachusetts, who have provided hundreds of teachers, children, and young people in urban communities with chances to participate actively in the life of their communities and to acquire the habit of service by engaging in research, writing, and publishing that lead to active, transformative literacy.

Finally, we must acknowledge the wise and faithful support of the late Fred Hechinger, for many years *New York Times* education editor and a senior member of the Carnegie Council of Adolescent Development's team at the Carnegie Corporation. Fred Hechinger's (1992) important book, *Fateful Choices: Healthy Youth for the 21st Century*, showed us that much can be done to prevent health and education casualties if we give young people a chance to learn firsthand about the "fateful choices" before them and if they have the chance to contribute to public discourse about these issues.

Preface

WRITING FOR THE COMMUNITY

Dixie Goswami

In the early 1980s, I worked for the American Institutes of Research (AIR) in Washington, D.C., as a member of the Document Design Project team led by Dr. Janice Redish, a distinguished linguist and an international leader in document design for government and industry. Our goal was to develop a research-based process model for designing and field-testing documents intended for use by large and diverse public audiences: a highly political goal then and now. We conducted research in hospitals, social service agencies, fire departments, federal agencies, among many other sites, and also in corporate settings. As you probably know, if you have occasion to read or use a public document, we did not solve the problem of poorly written documents, but we learned a lot, and the project produced *Guidelines for Document Designers* (Felker, Pickering, Charrow, Holland, & Redish, 1981), a text that continues to provide professional writers and other researchers with tools for clear and effective writing. In 1985, Lee Odell and I edited a collection of essays, some of which drew on document design research questions and methods (Goswami & Odell, 1985). Karen Shriver's article, "Document Design from 1980 to 1989: Challenges That Remain" (1992), provides an excellent analysis of still-relevant issues and research questions. Elizabeth Tebeaux and Linda Driskill (1991) present a more recent perspective in "Culture and the Shape of Rhetoric: Protocols of International Document Design."

Another of our tasks as members of the Document Design Project team was to develop a curriculum guide for college writing programs based on the document design process model, an approach that required students to create or revise and field-test documents in actual use: an inquiry-based approach to the teaching of writing that took students and teachers out of the classroom and into settings where written documents had real consequences for writers and readers. The guide, *Writing in the Professions* (1981), was field-tested with good results at several universities.

Insights and materials from the Document Design Project, from the action research movement that promotes inquiry-based programs, and from constructivist teaching practices that invite students to build knowledge for themselves through hands-on experience and problem solving contributed significantly to the Writing for the Public program that was established in 1991 at Clemson University, with generous funding from The Bingham Trust, and that continues today as Writing for the Community, a program of Write to Change, Inc., a nonprofit organization associated with the Literacy and Community Service Networks at the Thurmond Institute at Clemson University. Dr. Tharon Howard's Usability Testing Facility and Multimedia Authoring Laboratory, also at Clemson University, are sites where important research and applications of document design theories and principles take place in the context of Clemson's graduate program in professional communication.

Writing for the Community is a powerful method or approach to teaching writing, one that links an informal network of teachers, students, and out-of-school partners from a dozen states who are engaged in community writing projects that involve students as managers, researchers, teachers, editors, and publishers: These projects recognize that young people are highly productive when they have opportunities to tackle real communication tasks. Increasingly, we use electronic communication technology for writing, publishing, and staying in touch. Please visit our Web site: www.strom.clemson.edu/teams/literacy/index. html. We are working on software that will be helpful to those involved in community writing projects. Write to Change will collaborate with a number of groups that plan to establish community writing and publishing centers in the coming years.

Writing for the Community projects take place in classrooms, agencies, neighborhood associations, extended day programs, and summer programs—anywhere literacy and service are important and young people are seen as resources to be developed rather than problems to be solved. The core principles include the five elaborated on below.

Becoming Researchers

The writing process model, an important part of writing for the community projects, requires students to become active researchers, introducing them to the methods and purposes of inquiry. Young people gather, analyze, and apply information from a variety of sources (electronic and print). They discover the history and origins of documents and the way they function in social contexts as well as features of documents themselves, including language, meaning, organization, format, design, and comprehensibility. Documents may be electronic or print; primarily text, visuals, or film; and, increasingly, multimedia.

Becoming Writers

Writing for the community projects stress writing and publishing for different audiences and purposes as well as relationships among critical reading, clear thinking, and effective communicating. As young people move through the process, they become sensitive to the rhetorical situations and to the complex ways in which their writing is (or should be) shaped by subject, audience, intentions, and constraints, resulting in a heightened sensitivity to diversity and to the real needs of readers. Multimedia authoring and emerging technologies are creating exciting possibilities, resources, and challenges.

Collaborating

Writing for the community promotes cross-cultural and cross-generational work, with young people at the center, making decisions and solving problems with the help of others. To communicate effectively with the public, and especially with those who are in their own age group, young people learn to manage long-range writing and design tasks, raising questions at every stage about how members of a research and writing team must function to get the job done.

Mastering Basic Skills

Writing for the community projects embody basic skills that appear in educational standards and assessment frameworks but go beyond the basics to help young people achieve critical literacy, broadly defined in the context of public service.

Connecting with Communities

Communicating with the public helps young people make connections among academic activities, community service, and the world of work. Projects invite young people to see themselves as capable of changing and improving communication and thinking about their future in the present Information Age.

Like all communities, we have our stories and heroes, including many who are not represented in this book: Leslie Owens, who directed writing for the community projects for several years; Caroline Eisner, the superb editor of the *Guide to Writing for the Community* published informally in 1994; Lou Bernieri and Hazel Lockett, co-directors of the Andover Bread Loaf Writing Workshop for urban teachers, who established writing for the community projects in a dozen schools; Margaret Cintorino, Gary Braudaway, and Marjorie Kleinneiur Morgan, gifted teachers, who with their students, established and documented writing for the community projects that showed us how children and young people can learn to be confident, resourceful, and productive researchers and writers.

Taken together, the chapters of this book are intended to help us imagine how we might create genuine communities of learning for young people, where they will develop their abilities to read and write because they need to read and write to accomplish tasks that mean something to them and their communities. This book is an argument for providing teachers, children, and young people with chances to participate in the life of their communities and to acquire the habit of service that leads to active, transformative literacy.

REFERENCES

Felker, D., Pickering, F., Charrow, V. R., Holland, V. M., & Redish, J. C. (1981). *Guidelines for document designers*. Washington, DC: American Institutes for Research.

Goswami, D. (1981). *Writing in the professions*. Washington, DC: American Institutes for Research.

Goswami, D., & Odell, L. (1985). *Writing in nonacademic settings*. New York: Guilford.

Shriver, K. (1992). Document design from 1980 to 1989: Challenges that remain. *Technical Communication, 36*, 316–339.

Stillman, P. (1998). *Families Writing* (2nd ed.). Portland, ME: Calendar.

Tebeaux, E., & Driskill, L. (1999). Culture and the shape of rhetoric: Protocols of international document design. In C. H. Sides (Series Ed.) & C. R. Lovitt (Vol. Ed.), *Exploring the rhetoric of international professional communication* (pp. 211–251). Amityville, NY: Baywood.

Write to Change. (1994). *Guide to writing for the community*. Clemson, SC: Write to Change.

In memoriam
Walter H. "Rocky" Gooch
1951–2001

This book is dedicated to Walter H. "Rocky" Gooch, a tireless supporter of students and teachers across the nation. Rocky was telecommunications director for the Bread Loaf Teacher Network and the secretary of *Write to Change,* a nonprofit organization promoting greater literacy in many communities and schools. Rocky trained hundreds of teachers and students to use technology that enabled them to form informal networks and intentional learning communities. All who knew him were guided by his wisdom, patience, and kindness.

Chapter 1

AN INTRODUCTION

Chris Benson

As Dixie Goswami points out in the Preface of this book, writing for the community, as it is presented in the following pages, began at a specific time and place and involved specific people. For Dixie, the pedagogical benefits of writing for the community were apparent soon after she began working for the American Institutes for Research in the late 1970s. When she began teaching at the Bread Loaf School of English in 1979, and then later became coordinator of its writing program, she began to share the philosophy of writing for the community with scores, if not hundreds, of teachers, who came from secondary and middle schools across the United States for summers of study at Bread Loaf.

With small grants obtained from the Bread Loaf School of English, many of these teachers went back to their communities and schools and initiated projects that involved students in researching, writing, and reporting to their communities about vital issues. At about the same time, in 1984, the Bread Loaf School of English created one of the first, if not *the* first, electronic network for teachers of English. This network enabled teachers who had worked together at the various Bread Loaf campuses (there are currently four: Vermont; Oxford, England; New Mexico; and Alaska) to communicate with relative ease via computer conference throughout the academic year. Summers of study at Bread Loaf and the ongoing correspondence online among teachers during the schoolyear gave rise to a network of teachers who experimented with writing for the community, discussed issues related to this method of learning to write, and met periodically with each other and their students to present the fruits of their writing projects. These projects varied widely in ambition and scope. Some teachers just beginning to experi-

Writing to Make a Difference. Copyright © 2001 by Teachers College, Columbia University. All rights reserved. ISBN 0-8077-4186-8 (paper), 0-8077-4187-6 (cloth). Prior to photocopying items for classroom use, please contact the Copyright Clearance Center, Customer Service, 222 Rosewood Drive, Danvers, MA, 01923, USA, telephone (508) 750-8400.

ment with the method conceived of projects with limited goals. Other teachers, seeing the power of the method to motivate students, instituted writing for the community as an ongoing part of the way they teach writing.

What is writing for the community? It has much in common with many of the increasingly popular community-based, "service-learning" projects that teachers are familiar with. What's different is its emphasis on literacy, action research, and "real-world" writing and publishing. Some teachers use writing for the community instead of traditional approaches to business, vocational, or practical writing courses. Others use the approach to integrate work across the disciplines. Still others want their students to gain information about workplace literacy and develop skills that will help them find and keep good jobs. And still others are most interested in getting students involved in research and writing about issues that are important to them and their particular communities, issues as varied as avoiding teenage health risks, preserving oral histories, fighting racism, investigating environmental hazards, decreasing instances of teen pregnancy, and more.

Writing for the community is closely linked to the idea of public or community service. Youngsters are by nature idealistic and socially interactive, so they usually discover a strong sense of motivation in a project that asks them to engage collaboratively in public life and community problem solving. In such a project, students and their teacher— usually in a writing class, though any teacher with interest in writing across the curriculum can guide students—identify an issue of vital concern to the community where they live. Teachers can be very instrumental in guiding students' interest in identifying these concerns. Some students may immediately look to the "fluffier" issues that are limited to their own adolescent sphere simply because they aren't used to being active in larger issues of vital concern to the community. But teachers can and should guide them to critical issues in the community, such as those mentioned above. There is no reason for students not to have a stake in their community's discussion and treatment of such issues.

Though the topics in writing for the community projects vary widely, the process doesn't; it is based on a process model of writing instruction. That is, once students select a topic that is relevant for them or for their community, they set to researching it, compiling information, and organizing data. When they have a thorough knowledge of the issues, they analyze the needs of their audience (their community) and their purposes for the writing. Then they draft and revise a document for the community. One important step in the writing for the community process is field-testing the document on a real audience of readers. In field-testing, students gather more information about how readers actually use—and misuse—their document, and the students then use this information to improve the usability of the document through more revision. Eventually, the document is presented or distributed to the community. The design for this process of writing that we suggest comes out of the *Guidelines for Document Designers*, compiled by Janice Redish and colleagues for the American Institutes for Research. (See Figure 1.1.)

Writing teachers will recognize the steps included in the prewriting and writing phases in Figure 1.1. What distinguishes writing for the community from the basic process model of writing instruction is its focus on a specific audience and the postwriting steps. If students are researching the effects of environmental pollution in a small creek behind their school, for example, they will naturally keep the community audience in mind as they research and write about the subject. In such a project students will address specific audience concerns; for example, identifying the creek's location and its proximity to the school and other community activities, listing the types of pollution found in the creek's waters and on its banks, determining the source of the pollution, and recommending solutions for cleanup and maintenance of the environment. In a writing for the community project, each of these topics would be addressed keeping in mind the needs of the specific audience.

The postwriting steps of writing for the community, however, take the process one step further. Field-testing the document on a targeted audience for the purpose of improving the document's effectiveness gives students a much-needed lesson in how language can and should be used to make meaning for others. In the creek scenario described above, the middle school students wrote the information in a fact sheet for the community. Before they distributed the fact sheet, they asked members of the community of various ages and backgrounds to be research subjects and read the fact sheet. Students observed their subjects reading, timing how long they needed to read the document completely. They then quizzed their subjects on the facts to see which information was retained, which wasn't, and which created confusion for the readers. With this field-test information from various potential readers, students then went to work on revising the document for final publication.

Some teachers of writing might ask, "Why go through this final field-test?" Isn't it enough to have students simply review and revise their drafts, perhaps with the aid of a peer-editing process? Teachers whose writing appears in this book believe in the field-test because it brings subtle issues of language and meaning into focus for writers. The field-test teaches acute editing skills, and it certainly results in more

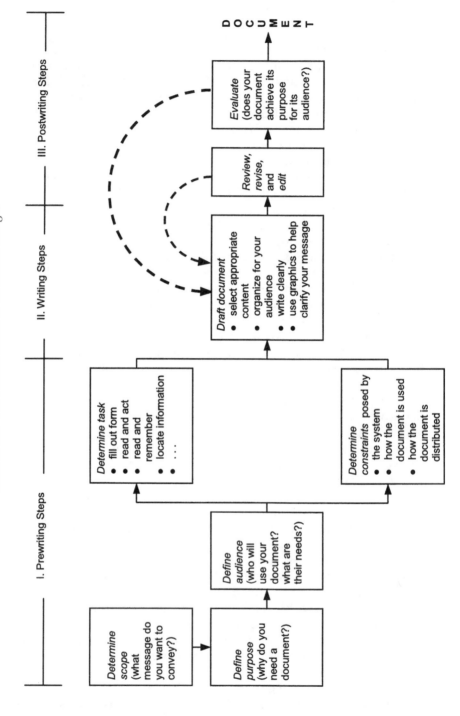

FIGURE 1.1. The Process Model of Document Design.

effective documents, which are especially crucial when dealing with issues related to health and environment.

But there is another reason to use writing for the community. The method gives students a voice in their community: They determine the key issues and how to address them for an audience they want to persuade or inform. The method therefore links writing with activism and advocacy, which have never been strange bedfellows except in schools. Writing is the motor that pushes activism and advocacy. Without articulate writing or speaking, activism and advocacy amount to no more than wish-making.

Writing for the community projects are especially valuable for students who come from families that are disenfranchised in their own communities because such projects promote interest in literacy. While the goal of all English teachers is to introduce and empower their students in the use of standard English, many teachers have successfully used writing for the community models to build on the students' native nonstandard dialects. Through the process of engaging with real audiences with wider and wider demographic bases, students begin to gain experience in using standard English effectively. The power and authority to speak about important community issues can do much to offset the disheartenment, even hopelessness, that hamstrings poorer communities.

Methods for teaching writing for the community require no special equipment or resources other than ample time. In such projects, research is not limited to texts or library sources, as it might be with traditional writing projects. Writing for the community may require special field-trips or visits from or to experts in certain issues. The students who investigated the creek behind their school eventually found themselves in the state capital to meet with an outreach committee of the Department of Health and Environmental Control. A flexible schedule and curriculum are likely the two greatest assets to a group of students engaged in writing for the community. The methods of writing for the community can be adapted for students of any age, and this book of chapters describes projects by elementary through college-age students.

Finally, this book shows how writing can be used to broaden the definition of *community*. As teachers refer to it in this text, *community* is a term that includes learners in the classroom, learners at a university, people living in a single geographic area, and communities of learners that are now being created with the use of electronic networking.

In Part I, "Writing for the Community," Marjorie Kleinneiur Morgan and Lauren Kocks write about projects at the middle school level.

For many years, Margie's middle school students in Dallas, Texas, have completed writing for the community projects, working with various local organizations including the American Cancer Society, the Society for the Prevention of the Cruelty to Animals (SPCA), and local health organizations. Her students have worked with these agencies to conceptualize, design, and revise public service documents. Most recently, her ninth-graders worked with the SPCA to design and write a summer newsletter for teens who own pets.

Scott Christian's middle school students on the Kenai Peninsula in Alaska embarked on a 2-year intensive, interdisciplinary study of their community: They documented oral history, wrote creative place-based literature, studied and cataloged the local flora and fauna, and generated and analyzed statistical information about local wildlife on the peninsula. This information was documented, revised, and published for the local community in a book titled *Away from Almost Everything Else: An Interdisciplinary Study of Nikiski.* The book is an important community reference guide.

Carol Collins, a drama teacher at the college level, participates in outreach drama projects with elementary students under the auspices of a special program called Writing and Performing Across Communities. In her chapter, Carol describes how she and an elementary teacher provide students with opportunities to use drama as a collaborative tool to improve students' attitudes toward and practice of writing. Carol and her colleague create classroom community by having students write, perform, and revise their own scripts. Then students take their production on the road to other schools, further expanding the notion of literate communities of learners. Carol's focus on the genesis of one script, "Why Snakes Don't Have Legs," depicts a successful project from beginning to end.

Part I also includes two chapters about students at the college level. When Bernadette Longo found herself as a new professor and a newcomer to Clemson University, she used her technical writing class to learn about the community. Her students developed a manual for college-age tutors working with local elementary students in the local America Reads program. The students covered content development, editing, page formatting, usability testing, and packaging of the manual. The project lasted two semesters and, according to students' reflections on the experience, represented a unique experience for personal and intellectual growth during their college careers.

Evelyn Beck's chapter recounts how students at a junior college researched, developed, and produced a manual for graduates of the college's office systems technology (OST) program. Frustrated and bored with teaching grammar and style through skill and drill, Evelyn decided her students would learn these necessary skills through a writing for the community project. Students went into the community to identify potential employers of the OST program's graduates, interviewed representatives of the employers, researched employee prerequisites and other conditions for employment, and published their findings in a manual that was printed and distributed by the junior college to students in the OST program. Evelyn's chapter details the trials and triumphs of real-world research and writing.

Chapters in Part II, "Writing for a Networked Electronic Community," describe students who participate online in virtual communities of learners to address issues of concern and to create change. Laura Schneider VanDerPloeg and Beth Steffen, teachers in Wisconsin, recount how they linked their middle school classrooms in Janesville and Beloit to analyze race relations in the two very different communities, one a racially homogeneous community and the other more diverse. Students formed an online community and engaged in discourse that led to a greater appreciation for tolerance and diversity. Their chapter shows how writing in a networked community online is made complex by issues of writers' anonymity and the escalation of rhetoric that is encouraged by online discourse.

In her chapter, Ketchikan teacher Rosie Roppel tells how her quiet rural island community was disturbed by the sudden appearance of gang behavior among youngsters. Rosie teamed online with colleagues in other rural places, where teachers had observed similar behavior among their students, to develop a writing curriculum that engaged students, parents, and school and community members in discourse about problems associated with gang behavior and possible solutions to them. Through relevant readings about gangs and reflective writing that was shared by the online community of learners, teachers and parents came up with information and ideas to fight the problem in their communities.

Students in Susan L. Miera's classroom in Pojoaque, New Mexico, run an editing and publishing service online for other students and teachers. Her students provide editing, layout, and proofreading services to students whose teachers are members of the Bread Loaf Teacher Network. Using a contract for services, Susan's students receive draft versions of other students' writing and respond as editors to help make the writing better and ready to publish. In other cases, students provide their expertise as layout specialists.

Janet Atkins, a teacher in South Carolina, tells how she linked her students in electronic discourse with a classroom on the Laguna Reservation in New Mexico to investigate the effects of the nuclear industry on people who live close to nuclear sites. Janet's students live near the Savannah River Site, one of the nation's few nuclear dumpsites and munitions plants. Her colleague in New Mexico, Phil Sittnick, taught at a Laguna Indian school near the Jackpile Mine, formerly the world's largest open-pit uranium mine. Both classes of students discovered that the nuclear industry had far-reaching effects on members of their community. Janet's students published several issues of *Devil's Food for Thought*, which documented through poems and essays their impressions of living close to this controversial industry.

Part III of this book, "Writing for Change," includes chapters describing students who engaged in writing projects that sought to make changes in the community where they lived. Jim Randels's students in the Students at the Center program, a cross-school program in New Orleans, did oral history research and combined that knowledge with their training in drama to write and produce a play, *Lower 9 Stories*, which addresses varied themes relevant to youth: teen pregnancy, sexually transmitted diseases, and the causes and effects of violence and poverty. Jim's students linked with several community agencies to accomplish this project, and his story gives a careful account of the complexity of creating such linkages for common good of a community.

The one interview in the book, with Rex Lee Jim, a poet and teacher, recalls his work on one of the first major writing for the community projects that we know of: *Between Sacred Mountains*, a compendium of information on lifestyles, folk knowledge, agricultural practices, animal husbandry, and history associated with Navajo culture. Rex began working on this book with others in the 1970s when he was in junior high school and finished it as a college student. His recollection of the work and of the people he met through it testifies to the profound dedication and interest that youngsters can discover in writing for the community.

Elizabeth Coykendall Rice worked with young mothers in Charleston, South Carolina, in a program called the Second Chance Club, designed to assist young mothers in establishing a network of support to help them finish high school and pursue other life goals. The young mothers wrote pamphlets to recruit other young mothers to their program. Moreover, Liz discovered the tremendous benefits of journal writing to the girls who were faced with the difficulties of being new mothers.

Alaska teacher Tom McKenna took a year off from teaching to research the best practices of successful teachers. His travels brought him to Janet Atkins's classroom in South Carolina, where he found students engaged in a variety of writing for the community projects. One in particular that Tom observed and writes about is the Water Ranger project, an investigation into the water quality of some sites in Hampton County, South Carolina. Tom's interviews with students show that dialogue and discourse of teachers and students are two important elements in writing for the community. Students used a variety of writing modes—from scientific journal techniques to poetry writing—to explore the watery world around them. When the local Westinghouse plant found out what the kids were doing, it invited them to test their waters and see how they measured up. The result: better relations between the school and the community.

Finally, the last chapter in the book is by J. Elspeth Stuckey. Elspeth's chapter supplies appropriate closure to the book because it is about the mostly untapped power of students to create changes in their lives and in their community. Elspeth recalls the years she served as director of the South Carolina Cross-Age Tutoring program (SCCAT) in the 1990s. This program paired at-risk youth of all ages as tutors for younger kids. The program was founded on the premise that the tutor learns as much as the "tutee" in any tutoring relationship. Tutors in the program were asked to write to Elspeth and other "correspondents" outside the school about their tutoring experience. Elspeth's hypothesis was that written reflection about teaching and learning would encourage intellectual growth among the tutors. She wasn't disappointed. To my knowledge, the SCCAT program remains one of the most efficient, sustainable, and successful programs associated with writing for the community. Elspeth's thoughts on how such programs can raise questions of inequity in schooling are an appropriate place to close this book. In fact, all chapters in this book raise controversial questions about the purpose of education and how writing for the community can shape students' and teachers' sense of themselves as active learners and community activists.

PART I

Writing for the Community

Chapter 2

OPENING THE DOOR BETWEEN THE WORKPLACE AND THE CLASSROOM

Marjorie Kleinneiur Morgan
and Lauren Kocks

In 1991 the Bread Loaf School of English offered secondary school teachers an opportunity to apply for grants to teach their students technical writing by designing or rewriting a document for a business, organization, or health-related group. I was studying at the Bread Loaf campus at Lincoln College, Oxford, when I received word that Middlebury College had offered me a grant for my ninth-grade students at Lake Highlands Junior High School in Dallas to tackle a writing for the community project. Enthusiastically, I envisioned my students having great opportunities because of the numerous businesses in the area. I teach in an urban community of Dallas, which is part of the Richardson Independent School District. Our community has a strong sense of pride, and our junior high has a culturally diverse enrollment.

LEARNING HOW TO TEACH TECHNICAL WRITING

My English classroom changed in 1987 when I read Nancie Atwell's *In the Middle* (1987). In the fall of 1991, I began my teaching of writing for the community to a mainstream ninth-grade class by assigning student "writing histories," which they shared, and "minilessons" on writ-

Writing to Make a Difference. Copyright © 2001 by Teachers College, Columbia University. All rights reserved. ISBN 0-8077-4186-8 (paper), 0-8077-4187-6 (cloth). Prior to photocopying items for classroom use, please contact the Copyright Clearance Center, Customer Service, 222 Rosewood Drive, Danvers, MA, 01923, USA, telephone (508) 750-8400.

ing skills with time for student and teacher writing and reflection in the classroom. Having read *The Foxfire Book* (Wigginton, 1972), I was aware of the positive effect of an outside audience on student writing. Our program required teaching a full English curriculum, so I had to incorporate their writing for the community project over many months to work it in with the other required work. Six weeks into the semester, after my students were getting to know each other, I asked both my students in class and their parents at a "Meet the Teacher Open House" to bring in ideas of outside groups they wanted to integrate into their writing for the community assignments. One of the parents was a lawyer who represented union members working for an insulation company. He suggested we rewrite the union bylaws and articles whose ambiguous language had caused considerable confusion and litigation.

That year the students and I learned more than technical writing. In March I took three of them to Clemson University to present the class project to students and teachers from other classrooms who were doing writing for the community projects in a number of states. In preparation, my three students had learned how to design technical documents and how to write fund-raising letters to Dallas and Richardson businesses for the $2,000 needed for the trip. I will never forget Ben, who asked if a student had to be passing to get the opportunity to go to Clemson. When I answered, "Definitely," he raised his grade to a B average, where it remained for the rest of the year. Students celebrated their success by writing a press release to invite local newspapers to come to hear student presentations about the project. The following year my students again raised the money to go back to Clemson to share their 1992–1993 writing for the community project with a Dallas business, Electronic Data Systems (EDS). This second conference at Clemson University was attended by students and teachers from across the country who had come to share information about their writing for the community projects. One of the other teachers, Margaret Cintorino of Fairhaven, Vermont, and I co-edited many of the presentation materials from this conference into a handbook for teachers and students.

Over the course of the next 6 years, I observed that my students valued the writing for the community projects not only for the technical writing skills they learned but also for the experience of writing for a large community audience. Working in project groups, leaders emerged as the students' confidence grew. I asked students to keep logs during the months when we worked 1 day a week on the project. At the end of the projects, they offered the following ideas on what they liked about their writing for the community work:

- Being in charge
- Making decisions
- Leading a group of my peers toward a goal
- Working seriously on a project
- Working collectively in a group
- Learning to edit peers' papers
- Getting work published
- Doing hands-on work
- Little talking and messing around
- Reading of my work by others besides the teacher
- Being motivated by high expectations
- Joining together and uniting as a class

As students wrote, they developed pride in the fact that their work went out to a greater audience. In 1993 Misty and Calli wrote that taking a field trip by bus to EDS was the highlight of the project because during their presentation of their work in a conference room to nine EDS employees they learned that the entire company worked in project groups much like my students were doing. The girls understood that they were learning job skills that would continue to be essential in and out of school. In addition, both girls wrote a newspaper article for the *Richardson News* about their six project teams' rewriting of seven pages each of the *EDS Benefits Handbook*. In subsequent years of working on writing for the community projects, my students moved from revising documents others had written to creating documents from their own research. For example, students obtained data from the American Cancer Society and wrote brochures directed against teen smoking. Other students researched juvenile diabetes and wrote and designed a brochure for teenagers with the disease who were entering Dallas Children's Medical Center.

Six weeks into the fall semester in 1995, I once again asked ninth-grade students to suggest businesses and organizations they'd like to work with on a new project. I began with an overview of projects other students in other parts of the country had done on writing for the community. We watched a video of a class from South Carolina making suggestions for revising a document on rabies. Former students of mine had also produced videos during presentations about their projects, and we watched them. The students looked at a variety of previous projects and read them carefully. After this overview, one of the students, James, suggested that we contact the Dallas Teenage Suicide Prevention Center; Lauren, a ninth-grader with scoliosis, asked that we work with

Children's Scottish Rite Hospital; and Jessica, working at the time for a veterinarian, wanted the class to contact the Society for the Prevention of Cruelty to Animals (SPCA). The SPCA excited the class more than the others, and the students all started to talk about the pets they owned. That afternoon I called each of the organizations and asked what we might do to assist them. That was the only teacher-directed work I did on the project, because I wanted to introduce myself and our mission to each group. The SPCA and Children's Scottish Rite Hospital responded enthusiastically.

At the end of September, the class overwhelmingly voted to create a summer "pet tip" newsletter for the SPCA. Ann Ramsbottom, educational director of the SPCA of Texas, agreed to come to our class in October, and she brought with her 50 or 60 radio spots she had delivered on local radio stations over several years. She talked to the students about balancing the number of articles on cats and dogs and health needs and pet interest articles. She repeated more than once that she wanted each student article to be no longer than it would take someone to read at a stoplight.

The next day in class I asked students interested in being project leaders to submit their name and the names of three students with whom they wished to work. I wanted some students in each of the six project groups to know each other, and I didn't want any leaders to pick teams in class. (This method of selecting teams has worked well. Often I have two project leaders in a group because I want to allow any student who wishes to become a project leader to do so.) I had learned the first year not to select project leaders because Nathan emerged as the best leader, and I had not chosen him. I went to the overhead projector, and the 30 students discussed which topics to choose. The logs that day contained the following information:

- Variety of topics
- Topics for each of the six project groups
- Five articles per group
- Co-authoring of longer topics

After the groups had divided up topics, members researched them. Jessica brought in many magazines and brochures from the vet's office, but Ms. Ramsbottom's radio broadcasts made up the greater bulk of the material. In October students made a project schedule:

- Research in November
- Prewriting and rough drafts in January

- Revising and layouts in PageMaker in February
- Artwork and field-testing in March
- Final revision and press release in April
- Celebration in May

We scheduled every Friday in November for research and in January for writing in class, with several days at the beginning of the month to discuss prewriting and conduct minilessons on document design. For 3 days at the end of January, students would go to the writing center to type in their drafts and do a mock-up of cut-and-paste columns and headlines on a manila folder.

In January the first step of the technical writing process included the prewriting stage, during which all students discussed our scope and purposes, our primary and secondary audiences, our tasks, and the constraints of time and budget. Then the writing began. Stephanie wrote in her log: "While working on the writing for the community project, I learned how to work with a group of people and how to get along with others to finish our articles. I also learned not to feel threatened by other people's comments on my writing. I tried to take everyone's ideas of what I should have and put them in my article."

At the beginning of each writing for the community session, I had goals for the groups. The project leader had the job of keeping each student on task, and students always had to be accountable for their work because I went from group to group and gave participation grades. Often I had students write a short log entry about what they had accomplished for the day. During the writing stage of the project, I posted the "Twelve Document Design Model Rules" in strategic spots in the classroom. These guidelines come from the *Guidelines for Document Designers* (Felker, Pickering, Charrow, Holland, & Redish, 1981) produced by the American Institutes for Research:

- Address the reader directly, by name or by using a pronoun.
- Write in the active voice.
- When you can, use action verbs rather than nouns made out of verbs.
- Choose your words with care. Avoid jargon. Define or explain technical terms that you cannot change.
- Don't rename for the sake of variety.
- Don't use extra words.
- Write short sentences.
- Put the parts of each sentence into logical order.
- Untangle convoluted sentences.

- Use lists when you have several items to discuss.
- Rewrite multiple negatives as positive sentences when you can.
- Avoid noun strings.

In February, after each of the teams had revised extensively, using the model suggested by the *Guidelines for Document Design,* Lauren and Jessica went to the writing center during their study hall to learn PageMaker. I assisted them with the basics, and Lauren did essential problem solving for tasks on the program I didn't understand. I learned that I do not need to have all the answers for the program because the students liked the challenge of reading the PageMaker manual. Furthermore, their parents have been a source for answering questions about the program. I have never let my unfamiliarity with a specific topic hold students back. Lauren wrote in her log: "Using PageMaker, I typed the newsletter. I learned how to use placement of information, different fonts, sizes, headlines, columns, page numbers, and editing within the newsletter. Learning PageMaker was a wonderful opportunity, and I'm sure I'll use it again."

As I pursue this method of teaching writing, I continue to be aware of how my role has changed. I don't have to be directing all the learning. Students direct most of the learning in these projects through deciding on goals, making timelines for work, dividing work fairly among themselves, and meeting deadlines. I am on call to bring in instruction related to writing in a just-in-time manner. When students need instruction with how to organize research, I am ready to help them; when they need instruction on fluent style, I'm ready with that particular lesson. This kind of project work has changed me as a teacher, but I also notice changes in my students, and I've asked Lauren Kocks to describe her experience directly in writing for the community. Her description follows.

LAUREN'S STORY

Since we had a diverse group of kids in our class, we did not know each other. The project helped us to get to know each other. I remember that we looked at the brochures for the American Cancer Society and for the teenagers with juvenile diabetes, and our teacher said we could make brochures if we wanted to. I was most excited about the fact that people in our community would read our work.

I remember that Ms. Ramsbottom suggested that we could write several newsletters or we could write one for summer. She also suggested that we could write the following brochures for the SPCA, specifically for young readers:

- Overpopulation of pets
- Spaying or neutering pets
- The humane killing of unwanted animals

We voted on a summer newsletter for kids because it would be distributed at pet adoptions at local malls in May, mailed out to pet owners, and offered at the SPCA office.

We liked the radio spots Ms. Ramsbottom brought to us. Also, Jessica brought in many brochures and pamphlets from the vet's office. In fact, I remember early in our research Lindsay wanted to ask Ms. Ramsbottom about some of the topics we found in those brochures. She asked what we should or should not do. After Lindsay faxed a business letter with questions, Ms. Ramsbottom sent us her answers and specific articles on diseases that cats and dogs get.

I asked to be a project leader, and at first I was scared because I was so shy. At the beginning my group did not get into the project because this was not the usual kind of writing. Students hesitated. But by the end of the writing, their work excited them. It helped that this was a topic we had picked so it was something we wanted to do. It also helped that our teacher gave a participation grade for our logs each time we worked in our groups.

Our group ended up with four articles because we collapsed two articles on house-sitting pets and taking pets to kennels into one article we called "Pet Sitter." Our class dropped several articles because they were too repetitive, and some students did not finish their articles.

When we started our research, we wrote phrases from the articles we had. Then before getting into our groups, individuals put the information into short paragraphs. In our group we passed the articles around for group editing. I remember that after our teacher did a mini-lesson on active and passive verbs, we went back and changed passive voice verbs into the active voice. We addressed the reader as *you*, and we worked on using bullets to make our ideas short and to the point. When we wrote about cat and dog diseases, we defined what the cause was and how owners could get treatment for their pets.

Some of the articles we wrote were informational to us. We had always heard that chocolate is bad for dogs and that cats like to put their smell on their owners, but we didn't know why until we did our research. Actually, we had arguments over who would write those articles that were answering our own questions.

We put our articles in columns in the writing center and pasted them onto the file folder, but the first time we had written in paragraphs without bullets. We revised again, and the project leaders helped everyone use bullets because the articles were easier to read. We had not used titles until then, and each project group wrote a title for its article that was short and creative. By this time we were into February, when we went back to the writing center to revise and to pass the articles to other groups to edit.

Since Jessica and I had seventh-period study hall, we volunteered to type the newsletter in PageMaker. First we read the PageMaker manual. That showed us the different page setups and functions. I remember that we put the newsletter in three columns. To have space in two columns, we boxed off the area for the drawing, typed around it, and then when we were done, we erased the box. When we did the mock-up on the folder, we had more variety of topics on the first page. On the second and third pages, we had both cat articles and dog articles. We knew our audience owned pets, and we knew the audience would be older than we were.

We had trouble with headlines. Our articles ran off the page, so I had to experiment with sizes and fonts. We had to select a font that our audience could read in a small size so that everything would fit on the page. We had *SPCA Newsletter* as our title. We showed our desktop publishing draft to the class. We had boxes around the articles that we had decided to take out. Ms. Ramsbottom asked us to use the title *SPCA "Pet Tip" Summer Newsletter* to differentiate it from other newsletters the SPCA sent out on a regular basis. She also told us to include the telephone number and the address of the SPCA so that readers could contact the organization.

By this time, James, Stephanie, and Catherine had worked on the artwork, and we had the pictures ready for Kinko's to scan into the program. We did our field-testing over spring break by asking our parents and one other person to read our document and make comments on our work. Many adults wrote on their copies that they were impressed with the work of ninth-graders. I know my mom couldn't believe we had done such a good job.

We faxed the newsletter to the SPCA for Ms. Ramsbottom to edit. She made a number of changes, including asking us to change the language in the article called "Finding a Home for Pets." She felt the language was too blunt for an audience of pet owners when we wrote about the death traps for abandoned pets. Until then, we really had not understood about the tone of our articles.

By May, I was no longer shy in front of the class, and I volunteered to write a press release telling about our newsletter and inviting the press to come to our presentation. Many students volunteered to write speeches about their work on the project. I wrote a speech about putting the document into PageMaker. We had to practice our speeches before the presentation, and we videotaped it the day we presented our work for Ms. Ramsbottom and our principal. Our picture appeared in the *Richardson News* and an SPCA newsletter. The benefits of this project included the following:

- Working with others
- Getting over my shyness (now I like to be in charge!)
- Knowing the basics of technical writing
- Using the writing process

I feel that I have accomplished something out in the community. We worked together to get it done. We were writing something for people with the need to know, and we wanted to make it the best we could.

WHY I WILL CONTINUE WITH WRITING FOR THE COMMUNITY

I think it's easy to see from Lauren's writing that she understood this project inside and out, and that she was aware of the many skills she learned and exercised while doing the project. One large benefit of writing for the community projects is that students get the big picture, sometimes for the first time. Writing is a process of gathering information, studying it, organizing and writing it, field-testing it, and revising it for a specific audience. Before I began doing such projects with my students, they might have seen these steps as disjointed. Knowing that a specific audience in a nearby community—such as young pet owners—is going to rely on their research and communication skills, my students now see the steps in the process as necessary. This is a skill that Lauren, now in the twelfth grade, has obviously carried with her.

Another benefit is that students learn the topics they study. The old saying still rings true: "If you want to truly know about something, write about it." By the time my students have finished their writing for the community project, they do know the seriousness of the topic they studied. Pet care is a serious topic, and so are teen smoking, juvenile diabetes, drug abuse, teen crime, and many other topics that my students and others in this book have written about. While students are informing a community about serious issues of concern to them, they are also informing themselves and making a difference in their own lives.

The third benefit I see in these projects is that students learn about the various communities in which they participate. It's very easy for a junior high child to feel isolated, not part of a community. Writing for the community projects show these children that there are multiple communities outside the school that care about what they think and that include adult mentors who are willing to guide them and praise them for their work, as Ms. Ramsbottom did. In the process, students become engaged with these communities or even become members of them. Leading students to community service that makes them feel good about themselves and about where they live is a life lesson that can't be taught out of context in a classroom; it can only be learned through experience and interaction.

REFERENCES

Atwell, N. (1987). *In the middle: Writing, reading, and learning with adolescents*. Upper Montclair, NJ: Boynton Cook.

Felker, D., Pickering, F., Charrow, V.R., Holland, V.M., & Redish, J.C. (1981). *Guidelines for document designers*. Washington, DC: American Institutes for Research.

Wigginton, E. (1972). *The foxfire book*. New York: Doubleday.

Chapter 3

GROWING THROUGH COMMUNITY

Opportunities for Ongoing Collaborations

Bernadette Longo

I am grateful that I had the opportunity to be a part of a team with Marla and Warren, and can honestly say that we did not have any major problems within our group. I am also glad that Dr. Longo assigned projects that were beneficial to the Clemson community. Community service projects are an excellent opportunity for college students to make a worthy contribution to society, and more instructors should try to incorporate activities outside of the classroom into their curriculum.

—NaTasha Edwards, university student

NaTasha Edwards wrote these comments to me in a post-project analysis of her work with America Reads in our Technical Writing class this semester. Her words struck me as a summary illustration of the idea and spirit I consider most important about growing as a community through classroom assignments: Students can learn to collaborate and to become contributing citizens while also learning writing and thinking skills through community service. I was glad NaTasha wrote these comments at the same time I was grappling with my own chapter for this volume. Her work made mine all the easier, which exemplifies the win–win nature of the most rewarding community service.

NaTasha's comments made me aware again of the impact that teachers can have on students. We can structure learning environments that reinforce the ethical and interpersonal lessons we try to build into

Writing to Make a Difference. Copyright © 2001 by Teachers College, Columbia University. All rights reserved. ISBN 0-8077-4186-8 (paper), 0-8077-4187-6 (cloth). Prior to photocopying items for classroom use, please contact the Copyright Clearance Center, Customer Service, 222 Rosewood Drive, Danvers, MA, 01923, USA, telephone (508) 750-8400.

our assignments. We can make opportunities for students to grow as participants in a group and as citizens of a community. We can help students see the impacts of their actions in contexts that extend far beyond our classrooms.

For me, the communities I want to work in as a teacher are based in personal knowledge, if not proximity. For example, I find that communities form when people interact with each other face to face. I know that there are many other ways to define community that would include interest groups that never meet as an entire group (such as teachers of technical writing or Corvair collectors) or online groups that meet virtually. But when considering community-based learning, I feel the most useful model of community is one that helps students acquire the knowledge and understanding that can only come when they look someone in the eye. There are lessons about consequences and responsibilities that students can learn most effectively when they are dealing with another human being in their community. In this sense, I use the term *community* to mean groups of people who either personally interact in the present or who have personally interacted in the past and somehow continue to share a connection despite the loss of proximity.

But before I say anymore about such generalizations, I would like to tell a story about how I came to Clemson and became part of a new community. My story will include comments from a friend who helped welcome me into my new community and with whom I have collaborated on many projects. Because I am a teacher, my story will also include stories from my students. This transition from newcomer to community participant is one that I shared with my students, many of whom were making similar transitions throughout their college years: moving to new parts of the state, country, or world; becoming adults and/or professionals; making decisions to move to other parts of the state, country, or world; becoming part of the Clemson community during their time at college. Throughout the last five semesters, I have grown into my new community in large part via the student collaborations I have supervised and the teaching I have done. One of these collaborations is the subject of my story.

"HOW DID YOU EVER END UP IN SOUTH CAROLINA?"

The question a newcomer hears most often is, "Where did you come here from?" I heard this question many times during my first year at Clemson University. When I answered, "I'm from California, but I spent the last 4 years in upstate New York," most people said something like, "How did you ever end up in South Carolina?" Now, I'm happy to be in South Carolina, and I'm not bashful about saying so. But I must admit that moving from California to New York to South Carolina in the span of 5 years—after living in California for 40 years—left me feeling displaced. When I started teaching at Clemson, I had just spent 4 years in near seclusion to finish my doctoral work. I had come out of that experience to move to the South, a region of the country I had never even visited, despite what I thought were my extensive travels in the United States. I was a full-time professor for the first time in my life. And I didn't know anyone within 500 miles. Of course, I met many friendly people soon after moving to Clemson. But I certainly didn't feel part of a community during the first year in my new home.

While I didn't yet feel a commitment to a community, I was committed to the students I was teaching, and our classrooms became small communities. In my first semester I asked my Technical Writing students to find projects they could complete as subjects for class assignments. Many of them chose work they were doing in their engineering or other classes, which made good content for their proposals, letters, and reports. I was pleased with their work but could see that the impact of the projects was confined to a classroom context, whether my classroom or that of another teacher. In my second semester, I had my Technical Editing class work on a simulated project provided by a large software company in the Northwest. While this project did provide a larger context than those of the previous semester, it presented other serious pedagogical problems with geography, scheduling, and technology requirements. I wasn't convinced that students learned the course content adequately.

Fortunately, during that first year I met Elizabeth Rice, who had been teaching writing and English for many years and had been at Clemson for decades. Liz was my introduction into this new community. She could tell me stories about the community and campus from her many years of experience. She was generous in introducing me to people outside the English Department. We talked about teaching and began to collaborate on assignments. I began to feel that I was making Clemson my home.

Toward the end of spring semester of my first year at Clemson, Liz was appointed the campus director of the federally mandated America Reads program to improve elementary school children's literacy skills. Liz was to train and oversee 15 college work–study students who would go into a local elementary school to tutor youngsters who needed extra help with reading. This program got under way in the fall, and Liz worked with a very limited budget for covering all the administrative necessities. Since I was teaching Advanced Technical Writing at the time, Liz and I saw an opportunity to get my students engaged in work that could help the America Reads program while also providing content for the course writing assignments.

STRIKING A BALANCE BETWEEN COURSE CONTENT AND CONTEXT

Liz and I wanted my Advanced Technical Writing students to develop a manual that Liz could use to train her tutors to work with the elementary school children. Early in the semester, I gave my students the option to work on this project or choose another project closer to their field. Almost half of my 24 students chose the America Reads project. One of these students, Amber Lofthouse, was completing this class as part of her master's degree in Professional Communication. She recalled how we started this project:

> The goal of English 490/690 [Advanced Technical Writing] was to develop a prototype training manual for the tutors involved in the America Reads program. The class divided into groups: content development, editing, page format, and cover and packaging. I was part of the content development group. Within our group, we split up and were each in charge of compiling different types of content: activities, book lists, the introduction, and vocabulary lists. I was responsible for gathering different activities that could be included for tutors to use with children.

Like the other students working on this project, Amber completed her individual tasks, worked with her group members to complete their group task, and collaborated with other groups to complete the prototype manual by the end of the semester. All the groups working on this project met with Liz in person and corresponded via e-mail. Liz provided them with samples of other literacy tutor manuals and sources of appropriate information. The students, however, needed to do much research on their own into the design and content of the training manual. As this work progressed, I was satisfied that students were learning course content (how to write professional proposals, reports, manuals, etc.) through this project. And Liz was satisfied that the manual was shaping up to be something she could use to train her tutors. We saw, though, that the manual would not be ready to use after only one semester's work. We needed another semester to complete the project.

I thought that if I could teach the next course in the sequence, Technical Editing, I could have my students continue working on the manual to completion. When I asked about my course schedule for spring, though, I found that another teacher was scheduled to teach Technical Editing. I asked this teacher if she would switch courses with me so my students could complete the America Reads manual, and she generously said she would. I had embarked on an ongoing collaboration with America Reads that has proven to be a source of deeper understanding and strengthened commitment to community for both me and my students.

A number of students from Advanced Technical Writing also enrolled in Technical Editing. Amber was one of these continuing students, and she described the second semester's work this way:

> My group's main project for the semester was editing the America Reads Tutor Training Manual that was developed in English 490/690. Although preliminary editing had been performed the previous semester, the editors did not have many of the skills that we developed in 495/695 [Technical Editing].
>
> The entire class was responsible for testing some aspect of the manual's usability before we divided into our group projects. The purpose of the usability testing was to provide the class members with testing experience, and also to acquire information about the manual regarding its usability. The testing proved very beneficial to my [page layout] group, because we were able to utilize the information to improve the manual significantly.

During this usability testing, each student in the Technical Editing class found a testing subject who was similar to the tutors in our target audience. For example, some testers found education majors to work with. Others found Clemson undergraduates who were eligible for the work–study program. Each Technical Editing student chose a portion of the draft manual to test with a subject. When we compiled all the test results, we had covered most of the manual and identified areas that worked well, in addition to areas that needed improvement.

By continuing this project through the second semester, students could gain more experience and knowledge about how writing and editing fit together in the development of a document for a specific audience. They could have the satisfaction of guiding a manual from its inception to completion. They could have a completed complex docu-

ment to show prospective employers. They could feel Liz Rice's gratitude when she worked with them to print the final manual to use the
next semester. They could see their work having an impact on others
in the community.

Amber realized her satisfaction at seeing a year-long project successfully completed, saying, "Being involved with the project from the
beginning, when it was just an idea, to the end, when the final copies
of the manual were printed, made me feel as though I had really accomplished something." Amber's experience proved beneficial to her when
she went into the job market a semester later. Just a few days ago, she
landed a good technical documentation job with a large manufacturing
firm in the Midwest. I was able to give her a knowledgeable and positive recommendation because I saw her work over the two semesters it
took us to develop the America Reads manual. The context for our
work grew well beyond our classroom while students learned technical
writing and editing skills.

OUR COMMUNITY GROWS

Other students from these two classes have their own stories to tell
about the impact of our collaboration with America Reads. For example, Patricia Drake, who was part of the page layout group in both
semesters, remembered her reaction to the project:

> All too often, the college experience becomes one big competi-
> tion—contention for the top grades, the highest rankings, the
> most honors, and, eventually, the best jobs. I don't doubt that all
> of these things were on my mind when I started my senior year of
> college at Clemson University. After all, I only had three literature
> courses left to complete my major and two writing courses for my
> minor. I expected my last two semesters to require very little ef-
> fort on my part. Little did I know that I would become involved
> in a class project that had less to do with my best interest than
> with the community's. And even less did I know that I would find
> this two-semester-long project to be fulfilling, stimulating, and ben-
> eficial for me.
>   Almost immediately, I found this assignment to be a refresh-
> ing change from all of those interesting, yet seemingly useless pa-
> pers required for literature courses. It held my interest not only be-
> cause it was a practical, hands-on experience but even more
> because we were working on something that had the potential of

becoming a powerful tool for educating the children of the community and possibly even the nation. And since I grew up in the Clemson community, I could understand the need for reading instruction and well-trained tutors. I spent much of my time in high school tutoring children in the area, and I always felt that the training material we were provided with did not effectively prepare us to instruct our students.

For Patricia, our collaboration with America Reads helped reinforce her existing commitment to her community, while also providing an opportunity to learn valuable writing and editing skills. Because this project was hands-on and directly relevant to a significant purpose, it held her interest and motivated her to succeed.

This year-long manual development, however, taught Patricia more than the prescribed course content of writing and editing skills. This is what she learned, in her own words:

> It was a scramble to the finish, but we were able to complete our project before one of our group members took off across the country to take a job in Seattle. While involved in the project, it became clear to me that it isn't always grades, or rankings, or honors that count the most. The skills (teamwork, layout, editing) I obtained from working on this manual were beneficial to me. But even more so, we completed something that could positively affect many people's lives, and this is where the true value of our project lies. This is what counts the most.

What teacher wouldn't be satisfied with these learning outcomes? Not only did Patricia improve her writing and editing skills; she also strengthened her commitment to community and collaboration. Now Patricia is retracing some of my path through life, having been accepted for master's work at the same school in upstate New York where I earned my Ph.D. I was happy to recommend her for this program because I had seen her work with her classmates on the manual. I am confident that she will excel in her graduate work and in her career. I am also confident that the extracurricular lessons she learned from our America Reads collaboration will stay with her for years to come and affect many more people. As I write this chapter, I think of Patricia working with some of the same people I worked with at our alma mater on the Hudson River. I begin to see how this kind of work can create overlapping communities.

MAKING CONNECTIONS

As our community grows in numbers, it also grows geographically and in spirit. In her comments here, Patricia mentioned a member of her team who took a job in Seattle near the end of the semester. This team member, Emma Nelson, found that her work on the America Reads manual had an immediate impact on her career choices:

> When the time came, I was impressed and proud that I could open my portfolio to prospective employers and talk about the America Reads challenge. My "passion" for such community-based work, I'm sure, helped secure me employment in one of America's leading software companies.

When Emma decided to take a job before the semester ended, we worked together not only to prepare her interview portfolio but also to make sure that she completed all her course requirements so she could get a grade in the Technical Editing class. During this process, I could see that Emma's coursework on the manual would be an important element to showcase for prospective employers. At the beginning of the year, I don't think either one of us could have foretold how important this project would be in Emma's immediate future. Looking back at this process, I can appreciate the many twists and turns our lives and expectations took during this year-long collaboration.

Emma herself expressed her sense of the unexpected when we started the year in the Advanced Technical Writing class:

> As a graduate student preoccupied with developing skills of my own, being able to help others in a meaningful, immediate way at that point in my life came as a big surprise. The America Reads program provided such an opportunity. As an Australian relatively unfamiliar with civil struggles over literacy, as one of the "Americans" to help out, developing training materials for reading tutors quickly became a mutually rewarding experience.
>
> Knowing that university professors were incorporating America Reads into their syllabus, thus ensuring that students equate higher education with a renewed sense of communal consciousness, sincerely spurred my efforts to deliver a usable training model for tutors. Usability testing and instructional design were the focal points of the four-person document development team—of which I was the leader—throughout the life of the project.

I share Emma's sense of surprise at the lessons we learned from this collaboration—lessons about communication in a broad sense, interdependency, conflict, compromise, support, frustration, understanding, cooperation, listening, and leadership. These are important elements of communication—and community. While we learned about communication through the act of making this manual, we also learned about community and ourselves. I question how often we teachers and our students avail ourselves of opportunities to learn about ourselves through making and sharing a community. How often do we have classroom environments in which we risk personal learning along with content coverage? My personal risk is often met by students' willingness also to risk something of themselves in our learning process. It is when we find this overlapping territory—where personal and academic needs coexist—that we can create community, explore the impacts of our actions on others, risk the consequences of sharing responsibility.

This overlapping territory between our academic and personal goals is an exciting area for teaching. Having found this zone really by accident during the course of this year-long project, I now try to map out similar terrain in all my communication classes. Emma captured the spirit of this overlap well in describing similarities between the project and community life:

> One essential task worth noting was to help volunteer tutors define themselves in a community. Fundamental usability questions included: What makes an effective tutor? What are the key characteristics? What qualities will reach in and touch a child, regardless of that child's aptitude for learning?
>
> Ironically, answers to such questions were simple and included concepts such as encouragement, understanding, planning, and creativity. In many ways, and so similar to the personal individual challenge, community work is about taking the necessary time to reach an end-goal. Community work, however, has the potential to do a whole lot more: It tests hearts, tries the patience, and provides a barometer to measure our ability to give, or ability to take, whichever way you prefer it.
>
> Perhaps now, through my educational experiences with working to help an important part of our community, I can bring back degrees of sensitivity sometimes lost in the free economy I'm now in.

As our community grows from the classroom to span the country, I am impressed with the rich learning that we gained in our America Reads project—a kind of learning that we continue to appreciate in our daily lives. Later this afternoon, Emma is going to visit me at my home. She is back in Clemson for the Thanksgiving holiday, and I'm looking forward to seeing her. We will undoubtedly discuss people we know in common through our master's program, such as one graduating student who may very well take a job at the same company where Emma works. She had impressed her co-workers so favorably that they are now actively recruiting Clemson students. In other words, our writing for the community project is now creating ripples in other, more distant, communities, and the boundaries that separate one community from another become blurred.

The current fall semester is now coming to a close, and some of my Honors Technical Writing undergraduate students have finished their America Reads projects for this term. NaTasha Edwards, whose words began this chapter, worked with two other students to develop a Web site for the Clemson America Reads program. NaTasha, who is a sophomore chemistry major, put her work into a wide community context in her post-project evaluation:

> In addition to generating publicity and knowledge for a government initiative on a college campus, our project raises various issues about education that, in fact, influenced the creation of America Reads. Fact: The United States is not within the international top 10 countries for education. From a more localized perspective, South Carolina is ranked 49th out of the 50 states. These statistics send an alarming message that America needs to invest more time in helping its students refine and strengthen their academic skills, particularly literary, thus helping them to become stronger and more competitive students.

I look back on my first semester at Clemson and the student projects that were helpful for teaching course content but did not provide a context for the work outside the classroom. I compare that to the simulated industry project in my second semester, which provided a context outside the classroom, but at the expense of our ability to cover course content. In my fifth semester at Clemson, I am pleased to see NaTasha expressing her understanding of how her classroom work fits into a national and international context of interdependent issues. I feel we have found a good balance between practical workplace experiences and academic rigor through our ongoing collaboration with Elizabeth Rice, director of the America Reads program at Clemson.

From the client side of this collaboration, Liz has found that her work with my students is both helpful and sometimes frustrating. But overall, the benefits for student learning outweigh the drawbacks of too little time and differing expectations:

> This is my second year running the America Reads program at Clemson University, and I am understaffed and underfunded. Any and all help I receive from business and technical writing students is much appreciated. Working with and on America Reads projects allows students to have firsthand experiences with community issues/problems. In the bigger picture, I think it gives students the chance to see how many nonprofit groups and agencies like America Reads are grossly understaffed and underfunded and how much help they could use from the "community" for brochure design, Web site creation, PR plans, strategic plan development, fund-raising ideas, and so on.
>
> Often faculty want to include writing for the community projects in their curricula but find that issues of transportation, scheduling, and so on hold them back. The "beauty" of looking for "extension" or "service" projects already existing on the college campus is that the "client" is more accessible, transportation isn't a problem, and the "client" is probably a faculty member who may be able to work more easily with students and with the concept of a project within the confines of a class/semester. In addition, e-mail, which is accessible to both faculty and students, is a wonderful vehicle for communication to and from "client" and students.
>
> Over the last year and a half, there have been several projects for America Reads. Probably the most useful, and the greatest undertaking, was the development of the tutor training manual. I met with Dr. Longo's students many times last fall to share with them the needs and wants of the manual. I asked for their input for design, materials to include, and so forth, but I shared my needs and input as well as my tutors' wishes. Over the course of two semesters, the tutor manual was written, edited, field-tested with the America Reads tutors, and finally published. The manual is now in its first year of use; the current tutors are monitoring what they find useful and what part(s) of the manual need more work or development.
>
> Having Dr. Longo's students develop a tutoring manual for the America Reads program was a godsend; I didn't have the time or the staff to work on a manual even though I knew it was an essential part of the America Reads program. We have shared the manual with other America Reads programs in the southeast at

the University of South Carolina and at Kennesaw State in Georgia. The directors of these programs agree that the manual is well done and has a wealth of materials in it.

By working with Liz Rice, who is a professor as well as the America Reads director, students could have firsthand experience with a real client in their community who had real needs and limitations. From knowing Liz as a flesh-and-blood person, students had the opportunity to learn how to formulate relevant questions, interview, analyze information, and shape persuasive communications, as well as to learn the standard course content of writing and editing. From Liz's point of view, this collaboration helped her accomplish goals with her America Reads program that she otherwise would not have had the resources to complete.

While this collaboration has been beneficial for all parties in the big picture, there are recurring issues that continue to frustrate all of us. Liz summed them up in these two points:

1. Students "expect" me to supply all of the information. I feel that they are capable of making many more design and content decisions than they feel they can make. Is this a lack of confidence in their abilities? Laziness? Newness of working with a "real" client?
2. Time constraints: There is never enough time in a semester to really feel "completion" in a project. In two semesters, the manual was finished satisfactorily. Another month for revisions may be needed this spring. More time is needed for community-based projects.

These issues that Liz raises are not unique to our America Reads collaboration. I see them in most of the projects my writing students undertake with real clients. Encouraging students to be more self-confident or mature in their dealings with people in authority is one learning goal I have for my students. But since it is a learning goal, not all students will achieve this confidence, and almost none of them will have confidence at the beginning of the project. And as for changing the length of the semester, I don't see any way around that except for using sequential classes, as in the America Reads manual example. But the reality of writing for the community calls into question a lot of the standard operating procedures of high schools and universities, including scheduling, course design, curriculum content, and assessment.

We hear more calls for making education "relevant" or "engaged" or somehow more interactive. Yet academic structures have not yet transformed from semester-based models with a narrow disciplinary focus into more flexible systems that can accommodate the diverse teaching approaches implied in interactive teaching that involves varied stakeholders in a community. The objective of teaching students to acquire skills that are developed over longer periods—such as confidence and maturity—continues to be thwarted when assignments can span only 10 to 13 weeks. Often, this time is not sufficient for students to become thoroughly familiar with the project requirements and constraints. Having opportunities to continue projects in two-semester blocks of time can deepen students' understanding of the projects and allow teachers to design assignments that help students reflect on and articulate that deepened understanding.

Writing for the community projects also allow teachers and students more thoroughly to explore ethical issues inherent in interactive work including varied stakeholders. Too often these issues cannot be adequately identified and explored in 13 weeks. For example, when students are working with a community organization, the students need time to get to know the people and culture of that organization. Then they need time to understand the scope of their project and how their work impacts internal and external audiences. In this process of coming to understand the impact of their work, students need to consider which groups of people have a stake in the project on which they're working. Only after identifying the stakeholders and analyzing their work situation can students begin to understand the ethical implications of their contribution to the project. It takes many weeks to come to this understanding, which is only the starting point for discussing ethical issues involved in a project. Too often this starting point is reached at the end of one semester, which means that ethical discussions get truncated in favor of final grading. Having the flexibility to create two-semester courses would allow for more relevant and engaged discussions of complex issues raised when students work in their communities.

WHAT HAVE I LEARNED?

When I arrived at Clemson, I was a newcomer in unfamiliar territory. Five semesters later, I feel that Clemson is my home and that I am becoming part of a community here. I don't get asked "Where did you come here from" as often these days. I recently returned to San Francisco for 3 weeks and realized that although I will always have a visceral connection to the land, the ocean, and the air there, I will never live in northern California again. I have come to anticipate azalea season in the upstate of South Carolina and am planting them in my garden next year. I have made some good friends in the upstate and even felt deeply at home here for the first time a few months ago.

Because I'm a teacher, though, my community is both permanent and transitory: Many co-workers, friends, and neighbors will be in our community for the long term, but most students will be part of our community for a few years and move on. This dual nature of a teacher's community means that the contexts for our work are ever growing as our students mature and take the lessons of our classes into wider contexts.

Placing coursework in a wide context doesn't necessarily mean that students need to work with a distant client, though. Within any campus community or even in a small town, you can find programs, offices, or individuals that can use student help for writing projects. For example, your campus might have a band that could use donations for new uniforms or instruments. Perhaps one of your classes could research and write a grant proposal to a philanthropic organization. Or you might have America Reads tutors at your school or in your community. Does their program need a newsletter that your students could produce? Is someone in your town in need of help due to an illness in the family? Maybe your students could organize this help by working with a community service organization. These types of projects bring local issues into a national context that helps lend significance to students' classroom work.

I have learned that my students have greater self-motivation to work when they see that their actions have a genuine impact on other people. For me, this is the best way to teach ethics and community participation, while also practicing these concepts to the best of my ability as a model for my students. At the same time, this community work has helped me explore my new home, get to know people, and create a place for myself in their midst. This process of placing myself in my new home has had a positive impact on others, because the work my students and I are doing is intended to help people who might not have had the resources to get work done another way. For my students and me, community-based writing projects have provided situations in which we can all win: My students become engaged in a community group and learn course content while they work with others; I have become part of my new community in a positive way by offering to help others; community groups have benefited from students working with them to complete projects they might not have been able to do without their help. We are growing our community.

Chapter 4

CREATING A WRITING COMMUNITY THROUGH DRAMA

Carol Collins

"But what happened to the snake?"

Emily's question was urgent and concerned. She and her fifth-grade classmates had just seen Vince and his group act out their idea for an original mythical story, "Why Snakes Don't Have Legs." Her question sparked loads of ideas for editing.

"Maybe he had to live out his life in the dungeon of the castle," Carla suggested.

"No, no," Will disagreed, "I don't like that. It wasn't his fault the villager whacked him on the head."

The class began to have fun, sharing suggestions for this group of authors. Vince, who had narrated the story for his group, looked at Emily. Her question intrigued him, but he didn't know how to answer. Then he looked at me, puzzled, eyebrows scrunched. So many suggestions. It was time to focus the ideas and questions.

This was great. Here was a group of very lively fifth-graders who had not especially wanted to write. (I was known at Ravenel Elementary as the visiting "drama lady." What was all this stuff about writing?) Some had shown enthusiasm. Most hadn't. They all, however, had leaned forward eagerly when I told them we were going to first act out our story ideas. Now everyone was animated, not realizing they were assisting the editing process. Just glad to be sharing ideas. And I saw they were gathering fuel, asking pertinent questions, pondering possibilities. Opening up the writing process through performance.

Writing to Make a Difference. Copyright © 2001 by Teachers College, Columbia University. All rights reserved. ISBN 0-8077-4186-8 (paper), 0-8077-4187-6 (cloth). Prior to photocopying items for classroom use, please contact the Copyright Clearance Center, Customer Service, 222 Rosewood Drive, Danvers, MA, 01923, USA, telephone (508) 750-8400.

In the past, I had enjoyed working with teachers and students with many themes across the curriculum, using drama as a tool to motivate, to excite, to strengthen learning skills, and to illustrate and underscore specific topics of study. As an outreach artist-in-residence from Clemson University's Theatre Department, in association with the Writing and Performing Across Communities (WAPAC) project, I had to make time count. I would visit individual classrooms only four or five times at most, so we had to devise easy-to-use but effective methods that would have "sticking power."

Over the years, the WAPAC project had collaborated with many teachers throughout the United States and had documented successful drama strategies for the classroom. We knew that using creative drama produced significant results—healthier teamwork, more solid understanding of specific curriculum content, livelier classroom environment, stronger verbal and thinking skills, even higher test scores! Now we were working with editing. Our WAPAC colleagues had proven that editing through improvisation and performance was vastly successful with middle and high school students. Would it also work with elementary students? Would the same sense of excitement in collaborating as writers and editors emerge? Would elementary students create a refreshing and safe community to test ideas and develop further writing drafts? These were my questions.

It turned out to be very simple. We had first acted out a myth from an American Indian tale that explained why bears hibernate. After performing, we discussed all the characters and actions and explanations. Then we brainstormed possible theme titles, using "why" as our lead— why rainbows have colors, wolves howl, stars twinkle. The class was divided into groups that would merely outline characters and actions to answer the "why" question. When they had an outline, they would get to perform a first draft. Groups huddled at their desks, excited to get down on paper the outline to their own story/performance. Taking turns, they shared their ideas by performing them.

Vince had narrated the outline of why snakes don't have legs, with the rest of his group performing the actions:

> Long ago there was a snake. Every day he chased the villagers. He had legs and made him fast. The villagers would run from the snake. The villagers got together and called out to the great god. He told them he would talk to the snake.
>
> The next day, a villager passed by the snake and hit him on the head. The snake got mad and chased the villager. The great god saw

this and took away the snake's legs. The mean villager then chased the snake into the palace and he was never seen again.

After the writers/actors received their supportive and earned applause, they stayed at the front of the classroom while we asked questions and gave suggestions. This was an essential part of the process. This was where we began to make important connections to writing and editing. This was where one simple, spontaneous question—"But what happened to the snake?"—could lead the class toward a whirlwind of ideas and could lead writers to understand concepts such as audience, consistency, cause and effect, closure. This is where students truly begin to think of themselves as writers, editors, collaborators.

Now Vince was puzzled. Where do we go from here? Everyone in the class seemed ready to make suggestions. How were we to pull out the most important points and questions? How were we going to help the writers get to their next step?

Simple again. I asked the class to confirm the most important points to the story and the most important questions. I told them to think of how they would describe the main points and characters. We confirmed:

Snake—fast legs, always chasing
Tired villagers
Punishing god
One mean villager

And we asked:

Where was this? What happened to the snake?
Why did the villager hit the snake?
Why didn't the god punish the mean villager?
What happened to the villagers?

Now Vince was smiling. He had clear points and questions to guide him. It was a good time for the actors/writers to respond to the class.

Mandy said, "I like being the villager." I asked why.

"That snake got me so mad! I didn't want him to just get away with all he did!" So now we were touching on character motivation.

Sarah wasn't quite sure. She asked, "But I don't want the snake to just live in the dungeon. That doesn't seem fair."

Marquitta agreed, "Yeah, something else has to happen."

"Maybe he could promise to do better," Vince suggested.

Of course, no one had yet brought up the topic of dialogue, which I've learned is not surprising. So we talked about how dialogue helps us understand what the character is thinking and feeling. I asked where we could use dialogue to help us tell the story. Class suggestions included: with villagers and god, with snake and mean villager, with snake and god. We then improvised a quick scene with the snake and the great god:

"Snake, you don't use your legs properly. I gave them to you so you could get away from the other animals."

"Please give me another chance."

"OK. I will give you another chance."

Now we had some movement toward dialogue to work with. The next step was for the groups to edit their first drafts, using the suggestions and important points we had discussed. All of this had taken only one class period. At our next session the following week, groups would share their revised stories, then individuals would write their own version of any of the stories presented. I left the class, seeing groups huddled again, adding notes to their first drafts.

While visiting other classes the next day, my good friend and teacher's aide, Nita, came scurrying up to me in the hall, waving a piece of paper. Excited, she shoved the paper toward me and said, "Look at this!" It was Vince's second draft:

> Long ago, in a town in China, there was a snake. And every day he would chase a villager. One day the great god came and said, "Snake, you don't use your legs properly. I gave them to you so you could get away from the animals that hunt you."
>
> The snake said to the god, "Please give me another chance." Then the god said, "Very well. I will give you another chance."
>
> One villager had overheard them talking. She didn't want the snake to go unpunished for all the trouble he had made before. So the next day, the villager picked up a stick and whacked the snake on the back of the head. The snake started to chase the villager.
>
> That night, the god came and said, "You have disobeyed me again. I am taking away your legs."
>
> The next day, the villager chased the snake into his palace, and he never came out again.

I said, "Hey, great. He has a setting, dialogue, has answered some questions." Nita interrupted, "You don't understand, Carol. Vince has never written this much before."

"Huh?"

This confused me. I knew Vince as a very intelligent person with a large vocabulary for his age and with strong problem-solving skills. Nita explained that, for some reason, Vince had always been frustrated with writing, never quite getting his ideas from his head, through the arm, into the pencil, onto the paper. She was overjoyed, I could see that.

"He did this yesterday," Nita continued with her enthusiasm. "He was so excited with acting out the story, that he got right to work, as soon as you left the classroom!"

I was really impressed. And touched.

The next week in his classroom, Vince and his group shared his own, second draft. Emily still didn't like the ending. After seeing all second drafts performed, we used creative drama scenes and improvisations to work on adding dialogue to our stories and on adding descriptive detail. This was my last day with this class. I left the class energized, feeling that using creative drama and improvisation could truly make a significant mark on elementary students and how they envisioned writing. I also left a little sadly, because I wouldn't know how the stories ended up in their final versions.

But I was wrong.

Nita called me at home. "You've got to see this. I have Vince's story."

"Uh-huh."

"No, Carol, you have to come read it." I drove over.

Stunned is one of the words I've used to describe my reaction. Nita told me that Vince had really wanted to work on his story. He had wanted to use more dialogue, to make sense to the villager's meanness. He had worked hard. He still had the snake disappearing into the palace. I asked Nita to tell him to give me a happy ending, with a good moral, and that my acting company, Celebration! Ensemble, would use it in our spring production. He did.

"Why Snakes Don't Have Legs," by Vince, has been on tour for two seasons as part of our outreach into the schools, where the ensemble performs original poems and stories by K–12 students. It was also selected for publication in *Carolina Writes*, a South Carolina annual anthology of student writing.

Touring the ensemble and experimenting with drama/writing workshops in the schools has broadened that sense of community that first appears in a single classroom. We become partners with the teachers and students. We know we are experimenting. We're not sure what is going to happen, what will work. But we are celebrating our ideas and our partnership in an important, meaningful way by exploring the possibilities through drama and improvisation.

Using improvisation helps students share observations and opinions openly; they see and hear what the characters are doing and saying and feeling. That simple process enlarges the possibilities for response, for questions, and for alterations or clarifications needed. By testing out ideas through performance, the students get a bit of distance from the "p-a-g-e" and can begin to understand, in a new way, things such as consistency, and character motivation, or even simple ideas such as setting, character, main idea, problem, and solution. And this way of sharing and responding is the key element that motivates students to appreciate and even want feedback; they get a unique and fun taste of what so-called literary "criticism" is really about. They begin to actually relish the editing process. They become a community of writers, working together to solve a common, creative goal—finishing the story with zest and polish.

Of course, "Snakes" is only one story. The Writing and Performing Across Communities project has been using creative drama and improvisation to strengthen students' reading, writing and learning skills for 10 years now. We celebrate many teachers and student writers for their work and have hundreds of writing samples in our files. It has been a great adventure, testing various improvisational techniques, from kindergarten through college, to enliven classroom learning.

And the most rewarding part of the process involves extending that sense of community by touring performances of the original work in the schools. This is where the writing truly touches other, larger audiences, from elementary to college students. What a great feeling to see the authors in the audience, watching their works performed. Often, these authors will later tell me, "I was surprised I wrote that!" Their friends will also feel special, explaining to younger students, "I helped him with the dialogue" or "We improvised that scene in class." One of my favorite quotes is from an elementary teacher who told one of our actors, "After you left, my third-graders couldn't wait to get back to the classroom! Here it is, the end of school, and they wanted to sit down and write!"

It is fortunate that our project is housed at Clemson University, funded through grants from Write to Change. This offers great flexibility in outreach, allowing us the time to create and conduct workshops, and to use university students as helpers, actors, and project assistants. We even designed and instituted two special credit classes for preservice and inservice teachers. This partnership among a university, public schools, and a community service agency has created a valuable model for the future. It has allowed us to test, explore, and risk. And it has resulted in a valuable premise for collaborative designs within the community: Young voices can be celebrated with little time or expense, with a huge impact on larger audiences.

Through it all, we've learned that performing does make a difference. Whether you have 10 minutes to show adverbs through action, or 5 minutes to act out why the main character in a story is sad, or 15 minutes to create scenes that illustrate main idea and sequencing, or a class period to improvise ideas for editing—even the simplest ideas can reap huge benefits. As learners, as collaborators, as explorers in the classroom, we develop a sense of ownership of our language and our creative ideas.

The story of Vince remains one of my favorites.

WHY SNAKES DON'T HAVE LEGS
BY VINCE REYNOLDS
FIFTH GRADE, RAVENEL ELEMENTARY, 1996

Long ago, in a town in China, there was a snake. And everyday he would chase the villagers. At that time, snakes had legs, and they were very, very fast!

"Keep away from me, snake!" all the villagers would cry.

But the snake would not listen. And all the villagers were very tired, always running from the snake.

"I can't do all my work because I'm always running from that old snake!"

"We have to do something!"

Everyone agreed something had to be done. But they did not know what to do.

One day the great god came to the village and he approached the snake.

"Snake, you don't use your legs properly. I gave them to you so you could get away from the animals that hunt you."

"Please give me another chance," the snake cried. "I'll be good."

Then the great god said, "Very well. I will give you another chance."

The villagers had overheard them talking. They were very happy that the snake would no longer chase them.

"Now we can do our work!"

"We don't have to worry about wasting all that time running away from the snake!"

But one villager was not so nice. He wanted to get back at the snake. So the next day, when he passed by the snake, the villager picked up a stick and whacked the snake on the back of the head.

"Ow, what did you do that for?"

The villager said, "That's for all the trouble you've caused us."

The snake was so mad, he forgot himself and started to chase the villager. That night, the great god came and said to the snake, "You have disobeyed me again. I am taking away your legs."

The snake was very sad, because he knew he should not have chased the villager, even though the villager had provoked him.

The great god called the villagers together.

"From now on, the snake cannot chase you. But because of your misconduct, I will give the snake something much more powerful to protect him. You must always respect the snake, and all the animals of the world."

The snake told the villagers, "I am sorry for the trouble I have caused. I will stay in the forest and not chase you any more."

And the villagers said, "We have learned a valuable lesson, too. We will never harm others because of silly things they have done."

From then on, the snake had powerful jaws and venom to protect himself. And the villagers learned to respect and revere the snake. And that is why, in China, snakes have ever since been a sign of wisdom.

NOTE

The first public performance of "Why Snakes Don't Have Legs," by the Writing and Performing Across Communities and Celebration! Ensemble, was performed at the Brooks Center for the Performing Arts, Clemson, South Carolina, May 1996. "Why Snakes Don't Have Legs" is reprinted with permission from *Carolina Writes*, 1996, Clemson University.

Chapter 5

WRITING FOR THEIR FUTURE

Students Research the Job Market

Evelyn Beck

Spring—when dogwood trees burst into bloom, when blackbirds congregate noisily in my front yard, when the sun brightens my pale complexion. All these miraculous seasonal changes I welcome. But for years, spring also loomed as the time of year when I had to teach a course I dreaded more than my annual encounter with the gynecologist: English 175, Proofreading and Editing. All instructors have courses they prefer and other courses that they teach dutifully, if unenthusiastically. But in our department in a small technical community college in South Carolina, English 175 was an unwanted orphan, abandoned by one instructor after another, teachers so frustrated that they seemed ready to echo the newsman at the end of his rope in *Network* as he opened a window and shouted, "I'm mad as hell and I'm not going to take it anymore!" As one of the newer faculty members, I inherited the course in turn; as I recall, I even volunteered to take it on. That is to say, I took up the burden as my lot. I did not look forward to it.

What's so horrid about this course? one might ask. It has to do not only with the arid landscape of grammar study but also with the student makeup. English 175 is a required course offered annually for office systems technology (OST) majors at Piedmont Technical College in Greenwood, South Carolina. It is the only course in the OST curriculum taught not by OST faculty but by English instructors. Facing a class of students working their way together through a curriculum—a tight-knit community I wasn't a part of—made me feel like the odd man out.

Writing to Make a Difference. Copyright © 2001 by Teachers College, Columbia University. All rights reserved. ISBN 0-8077-4186-8 (paper), 0-8077-4187-6 (cloth). Prior to photocopying items for classroom use, please contact the Copyright Clearance Center, Customer Service, 222 Rosewood Drive, Danvers, MA, 01923, USA, telephone (508) 750-8400.

Additionally, and more significantly, all OST majors are female. A classroom without men, I've discovered, leads to a loss of restraint. Women seem more willing to reveal both their strengths and weaknesses when they needn't consider how men view their behavior. This loss of inhibition, while empowering, ultimately led to a lack of civility amid mounting anxiety as the semester marched on and the project deadline neared.

Traditionally, this course has focused on grammar, leading students through workbook exercises, classroom activities, and tests to learn about everything from sentence fragments to dangling modifiers. Students yawn as English teachers plod on valiantly through the endless grammar drills and class lectures about the mysteries of the comma. Anyone who's ever taught grammar knows how deadening it can be. And helping students retain and apply such lessons to writing tasks, as much research of the last three decades shows, presents a formidable challenge. In English 175, cumulative tests consistently revealed that rules discussed earlier had faded from most memories.

Despite my notable lack of enthusiasm from the outset, I attempted to enliven class sessions by modifying my approaches. To teach verb conjugation, I passed out index cards to each student. Each card had an answer and a question, such as, "The answer is *began*. What is the past participle of *bite*?" The answer and question on each card are unrelated, requiring the player/student with the correct answer to speak up and answer, then ask a question. Each student read her card aloud, with the trick being that if everyone answered correctly, the person who started the game would be the one to finish it. In another activity, students made posters illustrating common grammatical errors in speech. (One I saved shows a cartoon bear, his mouth taped, admonishing, "Don't say: Maybe I should have *went* to class more often. Do say: Maybe I should have *gone* to class more often.") Another time, to illustrate how length was not the culprit in run-on sentences, I wrote three words on the board (such as "Once there was") and had each student in turn add three words until everyone had done so; the goal was to add words that made sense and that continued a single sentence without creating a run-on or comma splice. For spelling, I asked them to apply a list of spelling rules from the planet Quibble (for example, an apostrophe always separates any letter and a following *q*) to a list of made-up words, a prelude to discussing real spelling rules. They also had to come up with silly ways to remember words they commonly misspelled. (My example: Roseanne *Barr* exposed her *ass* in public. How em*barrass*ing!) These games, which often proved fun, not only elicited some laughter but forced dozing students into consciousness. Beyond that goal and with few exceptions, they were just games—and most failed to teach. I was not convinced that they helped students learn grammar any better than the dreaded, dull worksheets relied on in the past.

The biggest change was a plan for me to team-teach the class with one of our part-time instructors, Mary Dailey, during an upcoming spring semester. I had never shared a course with another teacher, and Mary was a stranger. Because I had taught the course before and because I had already planned a special group project, I actually crafted the assignments and schedule by myself, but Mary and I split the classes, with each of us taking responsibility for presenting the material equally across all the class meetings, usually by alternating. The prospect of teaching just half the time was a relief, though I wondered how students would receive the two of us. Would a pair of teachers be able to manage this rowdy bunch more effectively, or would chaos result?

The grammar games and the team approach provided some new possibilities for the course, but something else was still needed—a way to connect the isolated workbook exercises to a meaningful "real-world" project. A frame for doing this had presented itself at a Writing for the Community conference at Clemson University that I had attended a year earlier. At the conference, the fascinating, sometimes amusing, often deeply moving presentations described students who created meaningful writing in real-world contexts: a brochure for the American Cancer Society to discourage teen smoking; a children's activity booklet to explain Penn Farm, a historical center about life on Texas prairies; self-reflective journals from the Second Chance Club, a group of teen parents mentoring each other; an informative pamphlet on how to improve landlord–tenant relations; an exchange of autobiographical narratives between American and Japanese schools. All these efforts emphasized the principles of writing for the community: literacy, action research, and "real-world" writing and publishing. Across disciplines, these teachers had sought to motivate students and improve their communication skills by directing their writing toward projects that benefited their communities. The speakers at the conference included students as well, and I remember a group of teens from an area high school who spoke so proudly about what they had done for their town by writing and securing a $250,000 grant to construct a community center.

After the conference, my enthusiasm tempered by the wisdom that a small project would be more practical, I applied for and received a minigrant from Write to Change, a nonprofit organization that assists teachers in designing curriculum that includes writing and community action, to cover publication costs for a booklet about area job opportunities for my college's OST graduates. I wanted to draw my students into using their written and oral communication skills in a project that would benefit themselves and other students. I wanted to get them involved in the subject matter in a more meaningful way. I was hoping that learning about real jobs for which they might be applying at the end of the semester would inject some immediacy and interest into the work of the course. Gathering the required information would require oral and organizational abilities. And actually putting the booklet together would demand application of all their skills in writing and editing.

The project became the focus for two sections of English 175 during the spring semester. Thirty-two adult female students participated. These women, with an average age of 25 but ranging from brand-new adults to middle-aged displaced workers or returning homemakers, were mostly high school graduates, with perhaps 15% having received their GEDs. About a third were married, but most (perhaps 80%) were parents, meaning that many were single mothers. Perhaps most significant for this class, their oral and written language skill levels were often low, with class discussions frequently punctuated by such comments as "That ain't fair!" or "She don't even try." Not surprisingly, since office jobs are low-paying, students attracted to the OST major at our college are among our weakest students. They often lack academic skills but perceive an administrative assistant job as more professional and thus more appealing than working in a mill or a fast-food restaurant. Like most of the student body at Piedmont Technical College, which serves a growing but still rural seven-county service area in the upstate of South Carolina, students in my OST class live in small communities where they expect to remain after graduation. Most want secure jobs with little responsibility, and they expect to find such positions in local public agencies and private firms after minimal effort. Once employed, they usually prefer to blend in, to get through each day without too many demands. Judging by many of these students' school habits—late arrivals, late and incomplete work, lack of enthusiasm—the work ethics of the majority are often poor.

I described the project for the students in each of the two classes at the first meeting in January. Counting as 20% of their grade, it was described this way on the syllabus:

> GROUP PROJECT: As a class, you will be creating a publication for the Office Systems Technology faculty and students. The publication will include information about companies that hire Piedmont Tech's OST graduates and about the jobs themselves, such as du-

ties and salary ranges. The information to be included and the format of the publication will be decided on by the class.

You are expected to share in the task of creating this publication. Duties will include brainstorming, gathering information through telephone and personal interviews, checking the accuracy of your writing by sending it back to your interviewee for approval, and typing the final manuscript. Each student will receive two grades for this project:

INDIVIDUAL PORTFOLIO: You should keep a journal of everything you do toward this project, in class and out of class. You should also keep all drafts and copies of drafts, interview notes, and letters sent and received. You will turn this portfolio in with your business letter, which will formally describe your efforts. The portfolio will be awarded a maximum of 100 points.

GROUP PUBLICATION: Each group will receive a group grade for the finished project. The publication will be awarded a maximum of 100 points, with each member of the group receiving the same total.

The business letter related to this project counted as an additional 10% of the grade and was described separately:

BUSINESS LETTER AND ENVELOPE: You will write a business letter to me about your contributions to the group project. This letter must be typed, folded, and placed in an envelope addressed to me. The letter and envelope will be awarded a maximum of 100 points.

The rest of the course requirements included four noncumulative editing and dictation tests, a cumulative final exam, and a daily grade—similar to the previous year's requirements for the class. I had struggled as I prepared the syllabus, wondering if the project would fly and worrying that these extra demands would become a source of conflict and tension. In a 2-year college, so many students squeeze classes into days already packed with work and home responsibilities that they balk at outside assignments. I regularly inform students to plan on spending 2 hours outside of class for every hour in class, but they don't. And extra work that also required phone calls and travel and interviews—well, let's just say that simply presenting these requirements on the first day of class left my stomach in knots and my hair slightly grayer.

As expected, some students groaned at the prospect of extra work, mumbling that this was supposed to be an editing class, that nobody told them they had to publish some booklet. And what were they supposed to do if they didn't have a car? A few students, however, expressed enthusiasm at learning about job specifics prior to graduating; these were the women whom I identified immediately as high achievers interested in building skills and contacts before job hunting. They were headed ultimately to jobs as office managers or assistants to executives at law firms, hospitals, and industrial plants. Most of the students sat silently, withholding judgment, wondering exactly what their contribution would be.

The first step was obtaining a list of area companies that have employed Piedmont Tech's OST graduates as interns or regular employees. The list, provided by the OST department head, included 28 firms in our college's seven-county service area. Some were county agencies such as health departments and school districts, while others were private employers such as attorneys and family physicians. The businesses ranged from small, partner-owned firms such as Welch & Crain, Attorneys, to large retail stores such as Wal-Mart. Nearly half of the employers (13 of 28) were in the medical field. The next largest number (7) were legal or financial institutions. The remainder were in education, manufacturing, engineering, retail sales, and public service. (Piedmont Tech's OST degree offers students a choice of three areas of emphasis: accounting, legal, and medical.) Most of the firms (such as the Salvation Army) had hired only one Piedmont Tech graduate in the previous year or in some cases had worked with a Piedmont Tech intern. Some (such as Self Memorial Hospital) hired significant numbers of our students annually. This list of 28 employers was divided by county. While Saluda County had only 1 listing, Greenwood County (where our college is located) boasted 16 entries. We also secured prospective employers' telephone numbers from the OST department head.

Many students in my class knew each other from previous classes, since they were all in the same curriculum and since our college is somewhat small (3,000 students). So they decided on their own which other three or four students they wanted to work with as a team. As usual with team projects, highly motivated, high-achieving students sought each other out, while less academically talented students also tended to cluster together. Each group elected a leader. Though some instructors prefer to balance class teams by putting students of varying abilities together, I have found that students in self-selected groups are more effective at nagging one another toward project completion and less prone to blame the teacher when one or more group members disappoint them. A great disadvantage, though, is that the weaker groups tend to founder.

Once teams were formed, students received the list of employers. For smaller firms, one student was assigned to gather the necessary information. For larger businesses, two students from the same team worked together, dividing tasks as they saw fit. A total of 24 of the 28 firms on the list were selected by students, who tried to choose companies in their own counties, though this did not always work out. A few chose firms for which they now (or in the past had) worked. Each student or pair had to choose a different employer, and choices were honored on a first-come, first-served basis and tracked on a master list kept attached to my grade book. One firm not on the original list, a medical center, was added at the request of a student, bringing to 25 the number of businesses to be included in our booklet.

Once the project was organized and under way, we brainstormed as a class for questions to be included on the questionnaire that each student would seek to have completed by a company representative in person, over the phone, or in writing. This was perhaps the high point of student participation in class: Because they knew they might someday be employed by the organizations on our list, students were keenly interested in raising questions about such things as salaries, wages, and benefits. We finally decided on these topics about the company's hiring process:

Promotion opportunities
Shifts/hours
Dress code
Probation period
Company's mission
Company's future possibilities
Job application process

Students created their own questionnaires from these suggestions; their questionnaires had to be typed and were not to exceed one page in most cases. When asking the questions or delivering the questionnaire, students were also encouraged to ask for company literature that they could review on their own for additional insights.

We then spent a class period discussing the proper, professional way to approach a firm when seeking information. The preferred approach was a phone call identifying oneself as a Piedmont Tech student looking for information about that company for a class project and seeking a 30-minute personal interview. When interviews were not possible, students mailed a letter and questionnaire. Then the questionnaire was mailed back by the date requested or picked up in person by the student. Sometimes one or two reminder phone calls had to be made. For interviews, we reminded students to dress professionally, be on time, and look the person in the eye. We suggested that they go with questions written out and that they write down the employer's responses even if they were also using a tape recorder. We also required all students to send a thank-you note following completion of the interview (whether in person or over the phone) or following receipt of a completed questionnaire or company literature.

This part of the project proved the most challenging. Simply reaching the right person—usually the personnel director, but not always—was often frustrating, especially for students who did not have telephones, let alone answering machines, or for those worried about long-distance charges. One student called the number she had been given, but it led to the wrong county health department. In her journal entry for January 31, she recorded that she did not have a phone and that she had wasted her money making the long-distance phone call. She did not get the correct phone number until April 14. Once she placed the call, she was referred to someone in another county. She finally conducted the interview on April 19, shortly before the project's May 2 due date.

Many of our students attend school and also work, so they're not easily accessible, and some of the business contacts either failed to return calls or could not reach the students. The journal of student Melinda Moss records repeated attempts to reach her contact:

Called Sheree 3 times. She is not in and has not returned my phone call.

Another student, Emily Herron, recounted these frustrated efforts:

April 18: Called CLTC [Community Long Term Care]—spoke w/Nancy (intake person) & was told I needed to talk to Dick Copeland.
April 19: Called CLTC—Dick not there—will call back tomorrow.
April 20: Called CLTC—Dick C. gone to lunch.

Other students experienced frustration in making contact with professionals in their fields who were too busy to make time to talk with or meet students. Students found themselves calling several times before anyone would speak to them, and this difficulty caused students to feel they were pestering their contacts.

These were not happy students, and I'm afraid that they sometimes unintentionally expressed their frustration with the employers, a situation that is good neither for the students nor for our college. I only hope that the irritations felt by a few students went unnoticed by their community contacts. And while I do know that students were miffed when their inquiries did not receive immediate responses, I know that, in retrospect, they glimpsed the challenges of workplace communication. Perhaps this project also forced area employers into unfamiliar contact with students and provided a learning experience for them as well.

Once interviews were arranged, another problem was students who did not have free time during standard office hours and students without transportation. Student Lisa Wood noted in her journal:

> I had typed my questionnaire and was going to the bank [County Bank], but my car broke down. Then on top of that, I lost my driver's license.

And sometimes students appeared for an interview, but the company representative did not. Once students received the information, they sometimes discovered that all the necessary questions had not been answered. However, only the most ambitious, organized students made additional calls for extra information. The weaker students procrastinated, throwing something together as the semester ended, leaving no time for additions.

Students were given occasional class time in the computer lab to type up their information, though each group was limited to a single computer. All students were required to send a copy to the firm for approval. Then, if needed, corrections and additions could be made. As individual projects progressed, the overall class effort took shape. Each group selected a type style and format for their information, then printed out a copy. These copies were examined in class and a style chosen by class vote. Because students were so busy with individual work, this part of the project distracted them, using up time that most of them still needed to compile the information about their company. Since we ended up using the computer's default style, we might as well have just skipped this step or allowed our student coordinator to make the decision on her own. However, students did become familiar with all the steps involved in putting together a publication, so it did have some value.

In return for extra credit, one student volunteered to act as the project coordinator—collecting all information on disks, printing out copies, placing the information in alphabetical order according to company, writing an introduction and table of contents, and designing a cover. She also worked with the campus print shop to decide on the paper and to order 500 copies.

The spring sections of English 175 met for the final class on May 4. All inside pages for the booklet were turned in, along with journals noting individual and group progress and a formal letter to the instructors about each student's individual contribution to her group's project.

The booklets were printed just after the semester ended. The finished product is attractive and user-friendly. It includes the names of all the students who participated. And the entries on each business are very informative. OST students can learn much from this booklet as they begin the job hunt: the variety of firms seeking their services, the varying probationary periods after being hired (from none to 1 year), the range of entry-level pay scales (from minimum wage to $23,424 per year).

For all the students, the project made them more aware of the challenges of teamwork and the importance of deadlines. Sometimes that realization came in negative ways, as student Lisa Wood described in her journal:

> I really didn't do much on this project, and I know it wasn't very responsible of me. I let myself, my group, and my teachers down. It wasn't that I didn't want to do the project; it was just that I have had a lot of complications right now, and this project just wasn't my first priority.

The realization also came in positive ways, evident in this comment from student Melinda Moss's final letter:

> I feel this project has given me the opportunity to make new friends and see what the business world has to offer when the time comes for me to enter that world.

For most of the students, the project allowed them a closer look at the job market and the chance to make contacts that may have helped them as they looked for jobs after graduation. Even the parts of the project they found frustrating—the busy or uncooperative contacts, the lazy group members—tested the students' abilities to communicate professionally. And they also took with them the satisfaction of having created something that was helpful to new students in the office systems technology curriculum at Piedmont Technical College. Our admissions office quite happily accepted several hundred copies for distribution to students expressing an interest in the OST program. The OST department head, Susan Timmons, remembers handing the booklets out during several orientation sessions for new students. The college's job placement counselor, David Rosenbaum, distributed the booklets to new and prospective students for 3 years, until the supply ran out. "I think it was very helpful," he said, "because the students had a chance to see the types of jobs that are out there in their field, and it gave them some ideas about the places that they might go and search for a job. And I think that it was definitely helpful to the students who put it together because it gave them a project that they could work on that would make them use some of the skills they were learning not only in their English class but in their entire OST program." (See Figures 5.1 and 5.2 for two sample entries from the booklet.)

Whether this project improved students' grammar is debatable. It didn't necessarily sharpen particular skills, but it did make students more conscious of the impression that their writing makes on others. When they completed their pages and submitted them for approval to the people they had interviewed, most students wanted very much to present polished pieces of writing, so they solicited and relied heavily on peer and teacher suggestions. Writing for a real audience made the writing matter to students in a way that doing an assignment for a teacher could not match. How students were perceived by others clearly meant more than grades, and that did seem to translate into a new care for grammar, spelling, and punctuation that never manifested itself in traditional class exercises and worksheets.

The project also cemented our school's ties to businesses in seven counties, reminding employers of their workers who had graduated from Piedmont Tech and alerting them to potential employees preparing to graduate. It is hoped that our students' overall professionalism (despite a few lapses) made a positive impression as well. And these 25 employers also received a copy of the finished product, another sign of our students' professionalism and a suggestion of the breadth of our graduates' placement in their communities.

As a teacher, I stretched. The team-teaching experience was enriching in unexpected ways. I got to know one of our part-time teachers professionally as we plotted strategy outside of class, as I observed her at the chalkboard, and as we struggled together against resistant students. Mary and I became friends over lunches as we discussed her recent divorce and exchanged advice about disciplining our children. Watching someone else teach and interact with students helped me pinpoint strengths and weaknesses in my own presentations. From the stu-

FIGURE 5.1. Excerpts from "Beyond Piedmont Technical College: Job Opportunities for Office Systems Technology Graduates" (Beck et al., 1995).

COMMUNITY LONG TERM CARE
617 South Main Street
Greenwood, SC 29646
(803) 223-8622

CONTACT PERSON: Dick Copeland.

SALARY RANGE: $15,310 TO $23,424.

BENEFITS: Health, dental, paid sick leave, paid vacations (maximum of 30 days per year).

EDUCATION: High school diploma with three years of experience or a college degree.

EXPERIENCE: None necessary. Will train.

JOB DESCRIPTION: One of three available positions is an Executive Support Specialist: Office Manager for the area office and liaison between area office and central office; monitors and maintains office equipment and internal office communications to ensure efficient office operation; serves as a liaison for WordPerfect activities and is responsible for serving as a resource and trainer for WordPerfect applications; assists with initial processing of referrals in area office by gathering and preparing information during the intake process; prepares correspondence and reports for professional staff; researches and compiles information in support of material to be prepared; provides secretarial support in development and maintenance of area office filing system; and performs other duties as required.

SHIFTS: Flex work week (every other week you get four days off).

DRESS CODE: Dress pants and dresses; casual on Fridays.

PROBATION PERIOD: Six months.

COMPANY'S MISSION: The company was founded in 1983 and has 16 employees.

FIGURE 5.2. Excerpts from "Beyond Piedmont Technical College: Job Opportunities for Office Systems Technology Graduates" (Beck et al., 1995).

GREENWOOD COUNTY TREASURER'S OFFICE
600 Monument Street, Box P-103
Greenwood, SC 29646

CONTACT PERSON: Elizabeth Lowe, Treasurer.

SALARY RANGE: Pay rates are based on county pay grade schedule for each job classification. Pay rates vary depending on education and prior work experience.

BENEFITS: Dental insurance, health insurance, S.C. retirement, optional deferred compensation plan, life insurance, optional dependent life insurance, cafeteria plan for medical and dependent care expenses, optional membership to YMCA or credit union.

EDUCATION: Accounting experience or education preferred for data entry clerk, purchasing, and accounts payable/accounts receivable clerk. Accounting background required for deputy treasurer. Four-year accounting degree and public accountant certification required for treasurer.

JOB TRAINING REQUIREMENTS: Training depends on the job. The treasurer/certified public accountant position requires continuing education in excess of 40 hours per year. All other job training is on-the-job experience.

JOB DESCRIPTION: Treasurer, purchasing, deputy treasurer, data entry clerk, accounts payable/accounts receivable clerk.

SHIFTS: 8:30 a.m. to 5:00 p.m., with one hour for lunch.

DRESS CODE: No formal dress code. Slacks, dresses, or business suits are appropriate.

JOB APPLICATION PROCESS: Submit an application, which will be reviewed after the closing date. County employees are considered first. If no county employee is qualified, the remaining applications are reviewed. The job is filled based on qualifications. If you do not apply for a specific job, your application remains active for six months. If a position becomes available, the applications are reviewed for qualified applicants.

COMPANY MISSION: The county was founded in 1897 and employs approximately 340 people. The county manager is appointed by the county council, which is composed of seven council members elected for two-year terms from seven single-member districts. The county manager is responsible for all county departments and reports on the operation of the county directly to the county council.

A degree from Piedmont Tech could favorably influence the employment decision.

dents' perspective, having two instructors proved a bit confusing at first as they tried to decide who to question about a problem, but once we settled into a routine, such puzzles worked themselves out.

Though I no longer teach this particular course, I try to include projects with practical applications in every course whenever possible. And having withstood the criticisms of students unwillingly dragged into such efforts, I'm braver at insisting on their participation. Recently, I've required students to use e-mail and an electronic bulletin board. While this requirement is neither original nor excessively demanding, it has forced students out of the classroom to grapple with real-world technology on their own. Many of them protest. Some of them even drop out. But most of them stick with it, all the while cursing the computers and leaving me notes dripping with frustration. But they learn. Moving beyond the classroom continues to present enormous challenges, but the rewards do keep me pushing toward new kinds of educational awakenings.

REFERENCE

Beck, E., et al. (1995). *Beyond Piedmont Technical College: Job opportunities for office systems technology graduates*. Greenwood, SC: Piedmont Technical College.

Chapter 6

INQUIRY-BASED LEARNING

A Collaborative Model

Scott Christian

It is the last day before Christmas vacation. The large room is decorated with Christmas lights; a table is full of cookies, treats, and juice. Christmas carols are playing. There is a festive mood and an electric buzz passing through the line of eighth-graders outside the door. We are celebrating with an Authors' Tea, their first opportunity to see the publication *Away from Almost Everything Else: An Interdisciplinary Study of Nikiski* since the books arrived from the printer. Our guests include several community members who were interviewed for the oral histories, a local newspaper reporter, the curriculum director from the district office, the principal, and a few parents. As soon as the books are distributed, I experience my favorite moment as a writing teacher. The kids quickly glance at the table of contents and flip furiously back to the page where they see their names in print. Happy, proud, and giddy with the kind of excitement known only to adolescents, they scamper about the room signing each other's copies and talking about the book, the vacation, the weekend, and all of the other important things in their lives. It is a celebration of our community of Nikiski; it is also a celebration of our community of learners and writers—and, of course, the last day before vacation.

Nikiski is a small rural community on the Kenai Peninsula in Alaska. In many respects the spruce cabins next to the small lakes and streams, with the Alaska Range in view, evoke that stereotypical Alaskan home-

Writing to Make a Difference. Copyright © 2001 by Teachers College, Columbia University. All rights reserved. ISBN 0-8077-4186-8 (paper), 0-8077-4187-6 (cloth). Prior to photocopying items for classroom use, please contact the Copyright Clearance Center, Customer Service, 222 Rosewood Drive, Danvers, MA, 01923, USA, telephone (508) 750-8400.

stead that many people envision when they think of Alaska. But instead of making a living from a dog team or a trap line, the majority of people in our community are employed in the petroleum, commercial fishing, or tourism industries. In one way or another, just about everyone in our community makes a living that is dependent on the natural resources that surround us. Despite our healthy economy, we are still a small rural community, about 200 miles from the nearest major city, which is Anchorage to the north.

We have two populations in our school: those students who have been together since kindergarten, who are often related to the original homesteaders in the area, and a large transitory population consisting of families that move frequently as employment dictates in the resource industries. Our school, like several across the district, recently converted from a traditional junior high system to become a middle school. Last year, I was the team leader for an interdisciplinary team of four teachers. For our first interdisciplinary effort of the year, we selected our community as the subject of inquiry because we felt it a worthy subject for the students who have lived here a long time. They would get to know their roots and gain a better understanding of the rapid change that has occurred in our community. And for the newcomers (including new faculty), a community inquiry would help them become better acquainted with this unique town. Also, since one of our ongoing goals is to establish a community of learners, we needed a tangible example of a community to use as a basis for our discussion. As we had done previously, we used the interdisciplinary "wheel" model for planning (see Figure 6.1). We put the title of the unit, *Community*, in the center of the wheel and created spokes for the different disciplines, adding activities into each pie section as we brainstormed. Heidi Hayes Jacobs, in *Interdisciplinary Curriculum: Design and Implementation* (1989), calls this process the "interdisciplinary concept model."

This wheel was forefront in our minds and gave us a clear idea of the essential intellectual skills and factual content in each of our content areas, and as we selected activities, we strove to make the sequence rigorous but reasonable.

Our interdisciplinary team selected our community as a topic for a collaborative study involving math, science, social studies, and language arts. The result was a 70-page publication that featured oral histories from social studies, poetry from language arts, field reports and research papers from science, and statistical projects from math. The project in each class was an attempt to see our community through the lens of the different disciplines. Our students acted as historians, scientists, statisticians, and writers.

FIGURE 6.1. The Community of Nikiski.

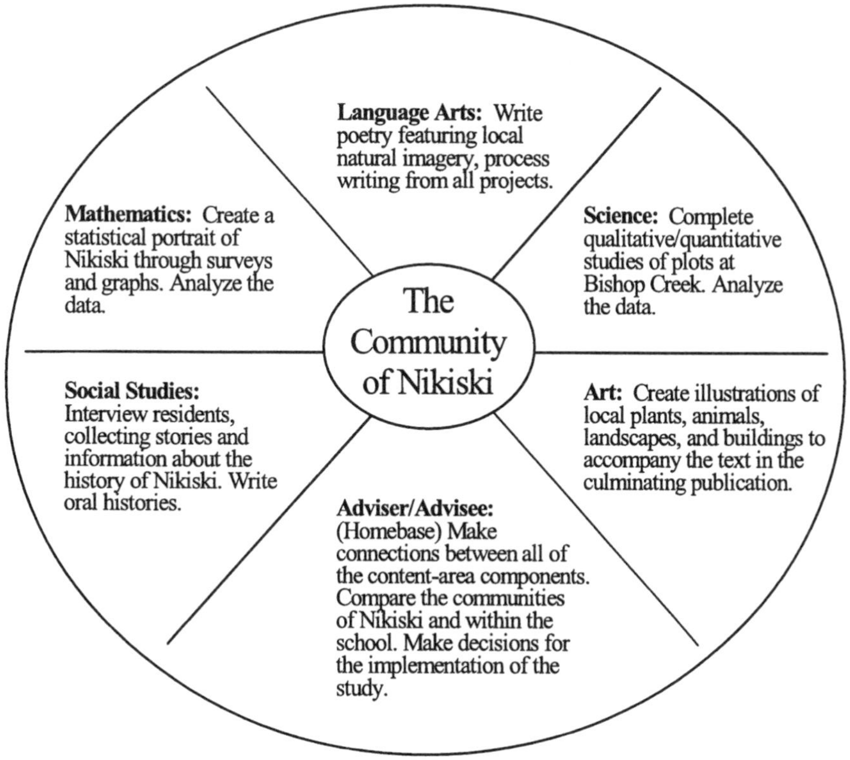

We felt that for our first attempt, the project was successful. The students came out of the study with a better understanding of our community and the surrounding area. In the following year, however, we wanted to take the project several steps further, to create a better publication, to go into further depth in the different areas as we collected data, and to encourage students to do a more thorough analysis of the data.

We began by asking the students to critique the work done the previous year. What was good about the book? The students liked the poetry and oral histories, especially those about people they knew. They liked seeing work by students they knew through church, sports, and the neighborhood. They were also very critical. They pointed out that there were too many errors in the book. They didn't like the cover or the way the book opened horizontally, like a calendar. They thought the oral histories were too short and that the publication should have included more stories. One of the most common criticisms was of the book's lack of visual appeal. They wanted more things to look at: pictures, drawings, graphs, and so on. I conducted the class like a town meeting, and we came to agreement on what the new edition of such a book would look like; what our criteria and system for selecting writing to be published would be; and the ways and means for the layout of the book, the cost of the book, and the color of the cover. The students felt that everyone who finished their work should be able to select at least one piece of writing to be published. They agreed that there would be a contributor's discount of $3, but otherwise the books would sell for $5. The most exciting suggestion was that we run a full-block schedule (160-minute periods, one each day) for a week, so that each class could have an entire morning to complete the layout of their section (math, science, social studies, etc.) without being interrupted by the regular bell schedule. It was also a time for culminating activities in the other subject areas. This was a bit scary for the teachers because it meant we would be teaching the same class for 3½ hours, leaving the comfort of our forty-two–minute periods. We had previously experimented with a double block, but this was a bold move. But, after all was said and done, teachers and students alike felt that the alternative schedule was worthwhile and a nice change of pace.

Between the "town meeting" and the final draft of the publication, the students worked hard in a variety of tasks—mainly but not exclusively related to our inquiry. In addition to the content-area classes, we also had an adviser/advisee class, called Homebase, which met for 20 minutes each morning. During this time much important work happened for the project. We distributed and collected surveys and handouts during this period. We engaged in frequent discussions in which comparisons were drawn between the community of Nikiski and our emerging community of learners. We took polls relating to the planning of the unit and brainstormed ideas for activities and schedules. In Homebase, we also brought together the different disciplinary perspectives to talk about community in the larger picture. There, we managed the portfolio assessment, as students brought finished work, reflective writing, and evaluations from all of their classes to include in their ring binders. And since we were experimenting with different uses of the block schedule, it provided an opportunity to carefully explain "who went where when" and what they needed to bring. Homebase was like a pregame warm-up to the daily scope of the study.

Now that you have a skeleton view of how the unit was planned—our goals and system for putting it together—I'd like to present the process for creating each component of the inquiry, a brief analysis of that work, and a discussion of the integration of technology in the study.

ORAL HISTORIES FROM NIKISKI RESIDENTS— SOCIAL STUDIES

The following paragraphs were written by students Carrie Pattison and Matt Kester, describing the process for writing the oral histories. This description begins the section of oral histories in the publication:

When we began learning about the process of the oral histories we read examples done by previous students so we would know just what we were really doing. We found somebody to interview. The requirements were that the person had to have lived in Nikiski for at least five years. The more years the better. Then we established a time and place to interview them. The next step was to create twenty questions to ask them. We were strongly encouraged to tape record the interview. We then proceeded to interview the source. While the interview was in process we were creating follow up questions to gain more information on the interviewee's answers.

After the interview came the task of taking the notes and turning them into a five to seven page, double spaced report, or oral history. We were strongly encouraged to write the oral history right after the interview. The oral history was to include three parts, an introduction with a description of the person, a question and answer section, and a conclusion summarizing comments about this person and their contribution to our community. We turned our first draft in and received it back revised. The next step was to respond in a group to each other's writings and help with content and wording. We then spent a few class periods in the Macintosh Computer Lab to type our second draft and turn it in. Then we received the second draft back. In order to have enough time to revise and correct our writings for the final draft, our core classes were run in what is known as a double block schedule for four days. All that happened was that first hour lasted until the end of second hour and third hour lasted to the end of fourth hour, thus having two core classes a day. When this was over we had our final draft to turn in.

A few comments about the students' perceptions of what was happening are in order. First of all, I love how they said they were "strongly encouraged." The social studies teacher and I both felt that the task would be more successful if students tape-recorded the interviews, but we couldn't make it a requirement. Not all the students might have access to a tape recorder, and some of the interviewees might be hesitant to have themselves recorded. Still, we managed to list the benefits often enough that the students felt "strongly encouraged."

I also had to chuckle when they wrote that they had received their drafts back "revised." Instead, that was wishful thinking. The students met in response groups after their first drafts. After the second revision, I wrote comments on the papers and individual notes to the writers and returned them for revision. Some students completed as many as seven drafts of their histories, while others were "finished" after two. We took each piece as far as the writer was willing to go. The only requirement was that the piece had to be revised at least twice, proofread, spell-checked, and edited for correctness before it was submitted for publication. The histories turned out to be lively, engaging, and very illuminating pieces about the history of our community. Here is an excerpt from Mario Bird's interview of Donnis Thomson:

> Homesteaders had to clear out their land (that was one of the law's requirements) and use the spruce trees for building, which meant cutting them the right size, shaving off the bark, and mantling them together. One other vital factor, besides building, was the fact that you had to live and eat. It's all very well to say you can raise potatoes and cabbage, and maybe you can get a moose, but think of the things we use in daily life: orange juice, soap, cereal, bread. You had to have heat. . . . It was very, very difficult.

This quote, and others like it, helped dismantle the romantic vision of homesteading that many of us still like to imagine. Sure, there was a great deal of freedom, excitement, and adventure on the frontier, but the common theme among the original homesteaders was that life was hard and the hours long. Other topics included the devastating earthquake of 1964, the evolution of the commercial fishing industry, education, religion, and employment. There was also a great deal of talk about regarding how things had changed from "the good old days." Residents talked about the day the post office opened, the first grocery store, the great blizzards, and years of drought. Several residents mentioned the excitement of receiving electricity, telephone service, and eventually television. There were also several interviews with younger residents and relatives of the students; these often included stories about leaving the lower 48 for jobs or love or adventure.

We were all impressed by the students' desire not only to bring these interviews to school but to get them right. The students and residents weren't talking just about Nikiski and Alaska; they were talking about themselves and what was important to them. An important by-product of these interviews was the generational interaction that cannot be achieved by field trips to the senior citizens' center for Christmas carols. Here, the young and the old were working together, creating something real and important.

Students also interviewed their parents, their neighbors, their former teachers. Time after time the interviewees expressed how delightful it was to sit down and have a meaningful discussion with a teenager. Despite all of the recent bad press about Generation X, teens today are capable of complex, sophisticated work of high quality. We can help them achieve this by making emerging technologies available and by making the most of best practices in teaching, such as cooperative learning, authentic assessment, integrated technology, and interdisciplinary teaching.

POETRY FROM BISHOP CREEK—LANGUAGE ARTS

The following paragraph was written by students Alden Ford, Casey Heath, and James Broussard, describing the process for writing the poetry:

This is a collection of poetry written by our very own Class of 2000. Our process was quite complicated, but it was definitely worth the effort. We think we can speak for all of us by saying that we really enjoyed working with the elements, atmosphere, surroundings, and inspiration of Bishop Creek. To start out the process, we read several selections of poetry including Robert Frost, e. e. cummings, and many poems by the class of '99 from last year. We then took a day long field trip to Bishop Creek, wrote a few very rough drafts of our poetry, and returned to the school to start a month-long process of editing, reading, editing, revising, reading, responding, editing, typing, and finally submitting our polished poetry to this wonderful, polished book! (Whew!) We all hope you enjoy this collection of poetry. Happy reading!

One of the things I like best about writing projects like this is the student voice and vitality that emerge when they are given choices in a process that involves a *real* purpose and audience. This writing—and the poetry, the oral histories, and the introductions to all of the sections—does not sound like "My Summer Vacation" or "The Discoveries of Magellan" or other perfunctory, teacher-driven pseudowriting that often happens in schools. I think the students did an adequate job in describing the process. I would like to add that in reading the poetry, and discussing their poetry, we continually talked about ways to use natural imagery as metaphors in our writing. The poetry writing was happening at the same time as the oral histories, so students could move back and forth from one project to the other during language arts, or they could finish one before moving on to the other. This flexibility was critical, as some students needed a great deal more time to revise a seven-line poem than others did with a seven-page oral history. A critical aspect of this component of the study was the sharing of my own poetry from Bishop Creek. I modeled my step-by-step process for revision. In a teacher research project the previous year, the six students whom I interviewed indicated that it was very helpful to see different ways of revising a poem. Nothing is more motivating for a 13-year-old than to criticize the poetry written by the English teacher. The following poems reflect very different writing processes. Michelle went through at least eight revisions of her poem, while Jason's was basically written, except for some minor tinkering, while he was on the beach.

AWAY FROM ALMOST EVERYTHING ELSE
MICHELLE ALDRIDGE

I look through a windy breeze
with waves pushing, shoving to their destination.
With endless mountains just barely there.
Sometimes you can only see the mountain tops.
As if they have flown away.
White tips in a gray sky.
I see not a bird, but a plane.
With a steady hhhuuum sound.

Birds feel so free here,
not scared to fly over an endless bay.
A feeling that can not be described,
too powerful to think of.
Away mostly by yourself,

away from almost everything else.
Because. . . .

No one can disturb the sea,
no one can make it move,
no one can touch it: like God.
So beautiful everyone ooos and aaahs.

EROSION
JASON GOFF

Walking down the beach, I realize,
As the trees pulled out from the hills,
Erosion has conquered them flawlessly,
Their roots hang out tightly, yet limp,
Grasping for life, wishing to be on the rich soil,
We slowly move closer and closer to death,
And those who grow on the edge,
Will fall early.

STARDUST VINES
SARAH SUPERMAN

It's nice to get out and away,
where the ocean is gray,
and the seagulls stay,

until they die.

Home of swallows in the bluff
chirping like we're intruding,
nice to get out and away
where I gather the past and future,

enjoy myself today
I know it's not the beginning
but from where I'm sitting

the earth is not disturbed.

Like a lot of English teachers, I used to be reluctant to write and to
ask students to write poetry because I didn't feel qualified. But after
giving students experiences in which they can gather sensory observa-

tions to use as metaphors for their poetry, I can see the power this genre unleashes. Also, I understand now that poetry is a critical aspect of this study, presenting the natural, spiritual, and physical essence of the area in a way that purely expository writing can't match. It is also a genre that is particularly suited to emotional, experimental adolescents, who are still willing to take risks with language and are thinking seriously about their relationship with each other, their community, and the world around them.

FIELD STUDIES FROM BISHOP CREEK—SCIENCE

This introduction was written by students Rachel Nightengale and Sandra Porter, describing the process for writing the field studies from Bishop Creek:

> The eighth grade class of 1995 was studying the plants and animals of Nikiski. We studied them to prepare for a trip to Bishop Creek. When we got to Bishop Creek, Mr. Morin separated the class into groups of four. We were then assigned an area of two square feet. In this area we were to record and count every sample of plant we found. Mr. Morin also taught us some plants' uses for survival. We found out that a lot of the plants here that we take for granted have some pretty serious value. Another thing Mr. Morin taught us was what an estuary is. An estuary is where fresh-water interacts with salt-water. Bishop Creek is a good example of an estuary. When we returned we classified our plants and reported on them for science class. TA-DA!!

I hope that this activity had some "pretty serious value." Phil Morin was the "gifted and talented" teacher, a phrase that applies equally to his teaching ability and to the students in his classes. Prior to the field trip, the students studied plants indigenous to our area through samples brought into the classroom, a visit by a local naturalist, a chance to play labeling games, and time to create illustrations. We were fortunate that Mr. Morin was available, because he is a very respected local naturalist in his own right. He could identify most of the plants in the plots selected by the students from memory. In my mind, the picture of a group of students kneeling on the ground next to an estuary, carefully sampling the plants and speculating on their scientific names and possible uses, is the essence of scientific discovery by doing. In this excerpt, the abstract from Valerie Hicks's piece "A Quantitative/Qualitative Study of the Plants on the Right Bank of Bishop Creek in South Central Alaska," you can get a sense of the type of scientific rigor that students applied to the study. This study included a map, illustrations of the plants, and graphs indicating the quantity of each plant found.

I. ABSTRACT

The eighth grade class went on a field trip on Wednesday September 13, 1995 to Bishop Creek in order to gain experience in a commonly used field biologist study technique. The secondary reason for this field trip was to obtain an analysis of the flora along the right bank of Bishop Creek. All of the students looked for different plants inside their two-by-two-foot plot areas. Then we recorded a description of what each different plant looked like and gathered samples for future reference and study. My group found four different plant samples: four *Lathyrus maritimus*, common name: beach peas; three *Claytonia sibirica*, common name: Alaska spring beauty; seven *Honkenya Peploides*, common name: seabeach sandwort; and five *stellaria*, common name: chickweed. I learned a lot from this trip. I learned how to be more observant of my surroundings, how to write down everything I did step-by-step, and, most of all, how hard a field biologists work is.

What does this kind of study mean to our understanding of community? Aside from seeing that there are other living creatures as a part of our area and community, it presents a different way of thinking about Nikiski and the beaches of Cook Inlet. Many students talked about how they had been to Bishop Creek on family picnics, to go "bluff jumping," to float the creek in an inner tube, to fish for salmon. And they described how the place looked so different to them after the field trip—after looking closely at a section of the estuary and sitting silently for 30 minutes, simply observing and recording their observations. Our community has an intimate connection with the outdoors. Families spend a great deal of time riding snowmobiles and three-wheelers, skiing, hiking, hunting, camping, and fishing. Many of us came to Alaska for these kinds of pursuits. And we've learned a lot about the weather, the seasons, and certain characteristics of certain species. But few of us have taken the time to look very closely at the outdoors, to gather data, and to speculate on how this information relates to our notions of community. Rural people have a unique relationship with the land. By making the community our classroom, we begin to articulate the complex relationship between members of a community and each other, as well as the place we inhabit.

STATISTICAL PORTRAITS OF NIKISKI—MATHEMATICS

The following introduction was written by students Jessica Stillman, Nick Lindeman, and Jenny Hilleary, describing the process for creating the statistical portraits of Nikiski:

> First we went on a field trip to Kenai. On the way back we made a list of businesses in our community. After that, the algebra class built a survey from input from core teachers and also brainstormed themselves. The surveys were made and sent out to all of the 7th and 8th grade Homebase classes. Then the kids took them home and filled them out. There were eleven questions on the survey. They were:
>
> 1. How many books are in the household?
> 2. How many magazines does your household subscribe to?
> 3. Does your household receive a daily newspaper?
> 4. Is there a computer in your house?
> 5. Are you connected to the Internet?
> 6. What type of work does your father do?
> 7. What type of work does your mother do?
> 8. How many generations has your family lived in Alaska?
> 9. How many years have your parents lived in Alaska?
> 10. How many times have you traveled out of state since you have lived here?
> 11. How many vehicles does your family own?
>
> We had a very good return on this survey. We sent out 168 copies, and received 126 copies back. Students then worked in pairs, during math class. Each pair was given a survey and they tallied the results. After that the groups got together and made graphs of the results.
> Now that you know this information we can tell you how this section of the story was written. In Language Arts class we loaded the graphs from the Stat Explorer program to Claris Works for desktop publishing. We wrote an introduction and a table of con-

tents. Here are the names of the people who put this section together: Sherri Bennet, Gerrad Bowlin, Anita Carter, John Covich, Rachel Day, Peter Dirks, Frank Gonzalez, Jenny Hilleary, Nick Linderman, Tommy Mitchell, Brandon Moore, Dayna Pritchard, Chris Ross, Mack Smitham, Jessica Stillman, Randee Wilson and Nick Wirz. We hope you enjoy this section.

We discovered that more than 70% of the respondents had computers in their homes. This survey also confirmed the results of previous questionnaires, indicating that more than 75% of the mothers worked outside the home. We learned that more than 40% of the fathers were employed in the petroleum industry, both on the local platforms and the North Slope (Prudhoe Bay). We discovered that over half of the respondents indicated that their families had lived in Nikiski more than 15 years. We had to keep in mind that all the respondents were adults who had children attending Nikiski Middle/Senior High. This assignment motivated students. From the development of the questionnaire to the tabulation of the statistics and creation of the graphs, they were very interested in looking at their community this way.

As students enter high school, they typically study algebra, geometry, trigonometry, and calculus in sequence. Some students in our community complete algebra in the eighth grade, and there is pressure from the administration for the students to have certain skills and knowledge before entering the ninth grade. We need to think about ways to teach these necessary skills, while integrating the curriculum. Fortunately, graphing is a basic skill that students need as a foundation for higher math and problem solving, so we could incorporate this activity into the unit. Most important, the students began to see our community through mathematical eyes, in a way that broadened our understanding of Nikiski.

TECHNOLOGY AS A TOOL FOR COLLABORATING AND FOR CELEBRATING AND SYNTHESIZING LEARNING

To this point, I've intentionally avoided discussing the technology integration in the project, because it was not central to our planning or implementing the project. We thought about what we wanted to do; *then* we considered how the technology fit. However, I will share our use of technology here.

Throughout this 12-week unit, we had regular access to a small computer lab in my classroom. This lab, known as Frankenlab because it came to life as a product of parts from many other entities, consisted of 10 Macintosh computers, 1 black-and-white flatbed scanner, and a printer. These were networked together with Appletalk. We also had limited access to the schoolwide computer lab, with a similar setup and 20 computers. Throughout all of the writing, the poetry, the oral histories, and the field studies, the students saved their work on floppy disks and printed and revised until they were ready to publish. As mentioned in the math section, the students used Stat Explorer to create their graphs. Then, once all of the work was ready to be published and we had selected the work that would appear in the book, we decided on the format and the process for putting the book together.

The desktop publishing process involved eight stages.

1. Students transferred their files from the floppy disks to folders on the server labeled for each content area. A helpful hint: The individual hard drives were all named "Don't Save Here!" so that when students went to transfer their files, they would go to the right place.
2. In pairs during the full-block schedule, students loaded these text files into the large book files (one for each section).
3. Two students worked continuously to scan photos and artwork. I had no idea how to operate the scanner, so the students taught me as they learned themselves.
4. Students printed all the scanned images and put them in a notebook, so that each group could select the images they wanted and insert them into their sections of the book. (The images were saved in one folder on the server.)
5. After the text and images were inserted, they went back, added borders, standardized the titles and bylines for each piece, and added page numbers.
6. A group of students created section dividers, while others read the different sections and collaborated on the introductions. As this was happening, we were continually printing and spell-checking to try to catch last-minute errors. As anyone who has done something like this will attest, the "correction" of one error often results in the creation of one or more new errors.
7. Two students worked together on the table of contents, and we printed our semifinal draft of the book.
8. The final step was to have the book read by two outside readers

for correctness only and to edit according to their proofreading. Then it was off to the printer!

What would I do differently in terms of the technology? First, I would completely avoid floppy disks. I had decided to use them because of an inherent fear of networks crashing and because of the portability of floppies. In retrospect, it would have been much easier for the students to simply save on the network from the first drafts. Second, I would have selected another software program for the math section, one that was more compatible with the desktop publishing program. As it stood, we could not edit the graphs once they were inserted. Third, I would have borrowed a digital camera to take pictures of the kids throughout the process to include in the book. Last, I would ask a group of students to convert excerpts of the book into a home page to hang on the Internet and into a multimedia presentation that featured not only the final work but also the entire learning process. All in all, though, considering the complexity of the task, it went very well. There are other changes I would make in the project that do not involve technology, which I'll discuss later.

Another critical component of this study was the constant collaboration between the participating teachers. We continually had to discuss logistics. When would the oral histories move from social studies to language arts? How would we divide the time on the field trip between field studies and poetry writing? How would we assess the students and when? Although we had 45 minutes each day for collaboration, our school e-mail system also turned out to be a critical tool. As the team leader, I would often start the day by posting a note to all the teachers (with a copy to the secretary and the principal) about what was happening during the day, from the use of the block schedule to discussion about events planned for the day. The more teachers work together to integrate the curriculum, the more time and communication are needed to make things go smoothly. Using school e-mail, we could check for notes when we arrived in the morning and respond if we had questions and comments. This avoided the need to spend the first hour of the day playing phone tag. It also gave us a record of the planning, which we sent to the entire staff so everyone would know where the students were supposed to be.

Another tangible product of this kind of continuous collaboration was the assignment sheet for the interviews. The following list of guidelines was passed back and forth between the social studies teacher and me as we discussed how the interviews should be structured. We designed it based on our experience from the previous year, the students' comments about what the oral histories should look like, and our time frame.

STEPS TO A SUCCESSFUL INTERVIEW
AUTOBIOGRAPHY PROJECT
SECTION ONE
DUE: SEPTEMBER 17TH

1. Decide who you would like to interview. Make sure that it is someone you have access to, someone who is readily available. The person should be older than you, and hopefully someone who likes to tell stories.
2. Brainstorm a list of questions. These questions should focus on the past. Questions about family, work, travel, and hobbies are all fine. You should also ask your interviewee to tell a couple of their favorite stories.
3. Meet with your teacher to review your questions. After they are approved, write them, or type them with a lot of open space after each one, so you can record the responses.
4. Make an appointment, and be there early. Have your pencil ready, and record a few observations before you begin. What does the person look like? Where are you doing the interview?
5. During the interview, be sure to look at the person while they are talking. Try to take only enough notes to help you to write the story later. If you think this will be hard, you can, with permission, record the interview also. But, for a short story like this, I suggest that you take good, legible, brief notes even as you record. If you are having a hard time keeping up, it is okay to ask the interviewee to slow down.
6. *Right after* the interview is over, start writing while everything is fresh in your mind. If you wait a few days, you will have a hard time remembering the details about what was said. Your notes will be much easier to understand right after the interview.
7. When you write it up, please do so in paragraph form. Avoid the question/answer format. Here is a good example.

My grandmother is almost ninety years old. It surprises me that she has as much energy as she does. She still loves to walk on the beach, to do her shopping, and to make fun of my grandpa every chance she gets. When I asked her about her favorite thing to do, she laughed and said, "I'm doing it right now! There's nothing I'd rather do than spend time with my grandchildren."

Here is a not-so-good example:

"How old are you?" I asked.
"Ninety," she said.
"What do you like to do?" I asked.
"I like to talk to my grandchildren," she said. (and so on)

Remember: It is very kind of the residents to donate their time to this project. Be prompt, patient, and respectful. And, as always, do your best work!

Likewise, the assessment for each piece evolved through conversations between us, and that all students completed a final checklist/evaluation before turning in their final work (see Figures 6.2 & 6.3). Students also received a copy of this assessment tool *before* they began work. I should point out that each item was discussed with the students when the assignment was made, throughout the process as needed, and before the students completed the forms. The key for an assessment to be authentic is for students to clearly understand what is expected of them. I've found that the vast majority of students grade themselves within a half grade of where I would place them. If anything, students tend to be harder on themselves than necessary. In my Language Arts classroom, no work was turned in until the students had evaluated it first. Students also wrote reflectively about the process for each component after completing the assignment and again at the end of the quarter as part of the interdisciplinary portfolio assessment.

In short, the technology was a means for the teachers to collaborate on the project—for planning, scheduling, reflecting, and assessment. And for the students, it provided a professional product to celebrate the learning. And as the students did the final revision and compilation of the book, it provided a means to synthesize the different disciplines according to which they had studied Nikiski. Frankly, without the carrot at the end of the stick—the opportunity for the class, as a community of learners, to create a quality publication to share with the community—I doubt that we would have seen the quality of writing and the perseverance to see the project through. Also, it is in the later stages of the writing process that students learn correctness, a critical stage that is often neglected in a desire to "cover" more of the curriculum.

FIGURE 6.2. Final Draft Checklist/Self-Evaluation: Oral Histories.

(Give yourself a score of 1–5 on each of these categories, with 5 representing excellence)

	Student Score	Teacher Score
1. Quality of Work	_____	_____
2. Introduction	_____	_____
3. Interview Text	_____	_____
4. Narrative (story)	_____	_____
5. Conclusion	_____	_____
6. Length (5–7 pages)	_____	_____
7. Typed (Mac Disk)	_____	_____
8. Editing/ Proofreading	_____	_____
9. Process (drafts completed)	_____	_____
Total	_____	_____

Comments: Please include your comments on the back of this sheet.

WHAT DOES THIS PROJECT MEAN FOR OUR STUDENTS, OUR PARENTS, AND OUR COMMUNITY?

First and foremost, this sort of collaborative project is a wonderful way to begin the process of bringing a group of students together and forming a community of learners. With a real, meaningful, and complex task before them, they were forced to compromise, to negotiate, to find consensus in order to get the job done. Also, this project successfully integrates a wide array of performance standards for the Alaskan Standards for mathematics, science, English/language arts, and social studies. More important, it encourages many of the skills, attitudes, and

FIGURE 6.3. Bishop Creek Writing: Self-Evaluation: Final Draft.

1. Is the final draft edited, proofread, and correct?

    2 4 6 8 10   _____

2. Will the writing have an effect on the reader?

    Is the meaning clear and presented in an interesting way?

    2 4 6 8 10   _____

3. Did you revise this writing fully? Did you put the time and effort in to

    make this the best piece of writing you can do?

    2 4 6 8 10   _____

Student Self Score

_____ X 3 = _____ (30 points possible)

Teacher Score

_____ X 3 = _____ (30 points possible)

habits of thinking that we'd like to see from our eighth-graders as they exit our program to the high school. For parents, it provides a tangible product through which they can discuss learning with their children and become involved in the learning process by chaperoning field trips, participating in interviews and questionnaires, responding to student writing, and celebrating the final product at the Authors' Tea.

WHAT COULD WE HAVE DONE BETTER?

If we were to begin the planning for this unit again, we would start with an essential question to guide the inquiry. Although we teachers had an implicit question, we would have helped ourselves much by articulating a driving question and continually referring to it throughout the study. Also, I think we should have dedicated a full week after the publication had been printed to return to the study and to synthesize the learning. We set aside a full quarter, about 10 weeks, for study. But we were rushed at the end to complete the work so that we could move on to the second quarter. Although we nearly doubled the amount of class time spent on the unit from the first year to the second, it still wasn't enough. I would have liked for the students to return to the study a few weeks later, to look at all of their work, to discuss in depth their new understanding of the community, and to write a formal personal essay about the experience.

Also, although we sent our planning e-mail and copies of meeting agendas to the administration, I don't think they had a clear idea of what was happening in the project. As a good friend of mine used to do, sometimes it's necessary to go to the office, take the principal by the hand, and lead him or her to the classroom to *see* what is happening. When push comes to shove in budget and scheduling discussions, it's important that administrators have firsthand knowledge of good work.

Finally, there were seven students who were not represented in the publication. Although it is true that regardless of the program there will be students who choose not to participate fully, I think I could have done more to bring these students into the process. They were intimidated from the outset about having their writing in the publication. By choosing not to have their efforts published, which was an option for everyone, they could also opt not to do the work. I think I was so focused on the big picture, and the immense volume of writing that was happening, that I didn't take the time to sit down with this group to offer alternatives, encouragement, and additional support. A tension exists in every classroom between working with students who are productive and recognizing the need to help those who are disengaged. The more I teach, the more I find myself investing my energy where the students are investing theirs. As Heidi Hayes Jacobs (1989) argues, interdisciplinary curriculum is by nature more accessible and interesting for students:

> Interdisciplinary curriculum experiences provide an opportunity for a more relevant, less fragmented, and stimulating experience for students. When properly designed and when criteria for excellence are met, then students break with the traditional view of knowledge and begin to actively foster a range of perspectives that will serve them in the larger world. (p. 10)

I think the vast majority of teachers, students, parents, and members of the community who were involved in the project would agree that the study of Nikiski was a project that created for most students the opportunity described by Jacobs.

This publication is a powerful statement to our community about the work we are doing, as well as a celebration of our evolving understanding of this small Alaskan town on the Kenai Peninsula. When you consider the media-induced stereotype of today's adolescents—that they are drug-crazed, violent, promiscuous, and lacking motivation and responsibility for their actions—it is critical that schools provide a more realistic picture. A quick scan of recent headlines features "epidemics" in youth drug use, teen pregnancy, smoking, and crime. Not only are most of these behaviors the direct result of adults and parents who participate in, condone, or ignore the behaviors, but the statistics are often skewed to meet short-sighted political goals. In Mike A. Males's *The Scapegoat Generation: America's War on Adolescents* (1996), he describes one example of this distortion:

> Myriad government and private youth-management interests assert that they are simply responding to the unprecedented malaise of today's "generation at risk." Examination shows the real issue is whether these interests are abysmally ineffective or actually contribute to youth problems. Consider first what might be called the "pre-crisis" period, 1970 to around 1983. The trends in youth behaviors are opposite of the impression given the public at the time of a building teenage catastrophe.
>
> From the early 1970's (when today's 40 year-olds were adolescents) to the early 1980's decreases ranging from 5 percent to 80 percent were recorded in adolescent murders, violent crime rates, venereal disease, smoking, traffic deaths, and drug deaths. Only unwed birth rates showed an increase, as they did for adults. (p. 29)

In other words, the statistics that indicate that youths today are actually in better shape regarding many critical issues in their lives, as compared to youths of two decades ago, are inconvenient to policy makers and the media, who are bent on using today's youth as an example of what's wrong with society. Yes, students are often less supervised at home because of changing economic conditions, and sometimes this increased freedom and lack of parenting results in poor choices. But in our community—and, arguably, elsewhere, because we are not that different from rural communities across the country—the vast majority of students have a clear sense of right and wrong, a desire to have a productive future, and the abilities and attitudes to be successful in school and work. Complex, collaborative work of a high quality that is shared in a public context is one way to suggest that young people are capable of a great deal more than causing problems for the adult world. And, as they passed their books around for signing at the Authors' Tea, ate Christmas cookies, visited with members of the community and each other, empowered by a real sense of accomplishment and the acquisition of "adult" skills, it was obvious that they were feeling pretty good about themselves and their community.

REFERENCES

Jacobs, H.H. (1989). *Interdisciplinary curriculum: Design and implementation.* Alexandria, VA: Association for Supervision and Curriculum.
Males, M. (1996). *The scapegoat generation: America's war on adolescents.* Monroe, ME: Common Courage Press.

PART II

Writing for a Networked Electronic Community

Chapter 7

WRITING FOR COMMUNITY AWARENESS AND CHANGE

Two Schools Talk About Race

Laura Schneider VanDerPloeg
and Beth Steffen

INTRODUCTION

I'd like to introduce a different topic: racism. I saw a video today, an old Geraldo episode. He was here in my town in 1992 to cover a white supremacist rally. There were people from the KKK, neo-Nazis, America First committee, and the White Knights. There was also a mob of people from Janesville, protesting. I have never seen so much hate in one place before. It terrified me. What makes people hate other races? Is it just a fear of differences? And where does racism come from? I am Native American and white. Watching these white men proclaim that their race was better than all others, and that everyone else was worthless, made me ashamed of the white part of me. I want to know what everyone else thinks about this.
— Jessie, eighth grade, Janesville, Wisconsin

By reaching out to other students online, Jessie opened the door for a powerful discussion between students from neighboring and widely different communities about race and culture. Her letter was posted to an online student listserv organized by Write for Your Life, a national student writing project concerned with adolescent health and well-

Writing to Make a Difference. Copyright © 2001 by Teachers College, Columbia University. All rights reserved. ISBN 0-8077-4186-8 (paper), 0-8077-4187-6 (cloth). Prior to photocopying items for classroom use, please contact the Copyright Clearance Center, Customer Service, 222 Rosewood Drive, Danvers, MA, 01923, USA, telephone (508) 750-8400.

being. In the dialogue that evolved, students from the cities of Janesville and Beloit, Wisconsin, reflected on their experiences with and ideas about race, challenging one another to think and rethink their assumptions, and ultimately writing for the benefit of their communities and lives.

READING THE SCENE: LAURA VANDERPLOEG'S EIGHTH-GRADE CLASSROOM, JANESVILLE, WISCONSIN

If you believe that you can't do anything, then you can't do anything. But I can.
                                              —Jessie, Janesville, Wisconsin

Every spring as an eighth-grade teacher in Wisconsin, I wondered what I could do. It was time in the year for the eighth-grade interdisciplinary unit on the Holocaust, when my students would learn the stories of Holocaust victims and survivors and try to understand not only the lessons of that tragedy but how those lessons applied to their teenage lives in a small midwestern city. While this is a challenge for teachers anywhere, the community where my students lived posed unique challenges.

Janesville, for its size, seems more a town than a city proper. Many of its residents were born and raised there, know their neighbors, and plan to raise their children safely there. Janesville prides itself on having fewer problems than neighboring communities such as Beloit and Madison, which are viewed as having economic difficulties, as well as social problems with crime, drugs, and juvenile delinquency. The city also distinguishes itself, notoriously, for its predominantly White population, a homogeneity that contributes to residents' sense of "safety," which has been "threatened" in recent years by a small but growing non-White population. The city is home to General Motors and Parker Pen, companies that have provided work for many of the city's residents and attracted outsiders to the area, causing suburban sprawl to increase. The growing economy has brought this and other changes that are often met with resistance and quiet mistrust. In spite of these threats to "security," Janesville struggles to maintain the image of a unified and idyllic front: it sees itself as the "City of Parks," a respectable middle-class family town that is safer and better than many other cities its size. The community sometimes tries to maintain this image at a high cost, ignoring the rise in juvenile crime and teen pregnancy among its own vaguely discontented youth, many of whom see their hometown as "boring." Life for my students in Janesville was comfortable, and this comfort was seldom challenged.

Except when the Ku Klux Klan held a meeting. Ken Petersen, a Grand Wizard of the Klan, was a longtime resident of Janesville and a figure who brought the city unwanted national attention. In 1992, the KKK and other White supremacist groups held a rally in Janesville, which drew the interest of Geraldo Rivera and his camera crew for their show, "Hate Summit in the Heartland." The city has a history of Klan activity and a reputation in neighboring communities for being racist. Because of this, many people showed up to protest the presence and message of the White supremacists, and Geraldo tried to interview both sides. While attempting to speak with Petersen and other KKK members, Geraldo became the target of a racial slur, and a fight broke out. Both a KKK member and Geraldo were taken to jail, adding fuel to the fire of national media attention and bringing an expanded sense of notoriety to the town.

In more recent years, Janesville's racist reputation has been kept alive through incidents that occurred between the city and its bigger, more ethnically diverse neighbors, Beloit and Madison. During the 4 years I taught there, from 1993 to 1997, there were several racial incidents at high school sporting events between Janesville and the other cities, in which Janesville students made racist comments to players from the other teams, drawing anger and criticism from whole communities. Even in the middle school where I taught, one year ended in anger and controversy because of the administration's failure to respond meaningfully to anti-Semitic written comments that eighth-graders made during a presentation by a Holocaust survivor.

And so I felt both fear and hope each year as I approached the task of teaching tolerance through the lessons of the Holocaust and applying them in some positive way to the community my students lived in. There was much at stake, and a conservative parent association and school board to answer to. I wanted my students, as much as possible, to have experiences that would awaken them to the reality of racial tensions already present in their community and engender a sense of social responsibility for solving those problems. In the spring of 1997, I began by showing them a videotape of the *Geraldo* incident 5 years earlier.

My second-period class, the first group to view the footage, watched in rapt attention and surprise, and afterward began to discuss what they had seen. One student mentioned that he had been present during the rally. When asked what he remembered, he said very little. The class pressed him further: "Whose side were you on?"

"I wasn't in the crowd," he said matter-of-factly. "I was watching from Ken Petersen's roof."

The whole room became quiet. Several students squirmed uncomfortably in their seats, stared at the floor, or looked at me with concern, wondering what I would say. But no one, least of all me, knew where to go from that point. How do you teach tolerance to the kid who's on Petersen's roof? And how do you teach respect for diversity in an overwhelmingly homogeneous community? I was a White teacher in a mostly White classroom: How could I challenge this lack of diversity? I knew that I needed to be able to respect those students who might be on the roof, who believed differently than I and who might even say things that would offend me. Such is the difficult lesson of free speech, and I knew that if we were going to get anywhere in a discussion about race, the invitation to talk had to be open and respect prerequisite.

In other classes, the video stirred students to a sense of community awareness that many had never felt before. Some could hardly believe that the events they saw on television had happened in their own hometown, and they were shocked to read the signs and hear the words of White supremacists voiced so openly and contemptuously. In a variety of uncomfortable and exhilarating ways, the video had done its job.

When I went home that night, I didn't have any answers to my own questions and very little idea of what I would do in class the next day. I ran straight to my computer, hooked up my e-mail, and retreated to the safety of my own community of teachers in the Write for Your Life project. My participation in the project over the past 3 years had brought me in contact with thoughtful and dynamic teachers around the country, who shared their ideas, frustrations, and inspiration online. Our listserv gave us the opportunity to work together and support each other as we struggled to make our teaching relevant to our students' lives. That night, I wrote the story of what happened in my class and of my struggle to know what to do. Over the next few weeks, my colleagues responded to my letter, which generated online discussion about issues of teaching surrounding race, tolerance, and respect.

The letters I exchanged with my peers also contained echoes of the letters that students began to exchange with one another over the Write for Your Life student listserv. While I struggled with my own challenges as a teacher, some of my students were wrestling with the sudden sense that racism and intolerance were present in the life of their community. They, too, began turning to each other, finding ways through dialogue to learn and grow. When Jessie posted her letter to the student listserv, she created a rare opportunity for students of diverse backgrounds to talk openly and intimately about race.

READING THE SCENE: BETH STEFFEN'S TENTH-GRADE CLASSROOM, BELOIT, WISCONSIN

Seventeen miles down Interstate 90 from Janesville, Beloit perches on Wisconsin's border with Illinois. Whereas Janesville's population and business community have grown dramatically over the past 10 years or so, Beloit seems to have frozen in size. Hemmed in by Illinois to the south and Janesville's sprawl to the north, many of the 35,000 residents of Beloit struggle economically as development and industry stagnate. About 50% of Beloit's elementary school children live in poverty.

Beloit is more ethnically diverse than Janesville, a community that some Beloiters find suspiciously homogeneous. The allegation in Beloit is that Janesville, through zoning and thinly veiled hostility, discourages minorities from settling there. In fact, one issue that seems to unite Beloit citizens is dislike for Janesville residents, whom many in Beloit perceive as bigoted. While the KKK rally in Janesville occurred several years ago, it is still legendary in Beloit and exists in many people's memory as a testimony to the racism present, even fostered, in Janesville. When Beloit was threatened recently with its own KKK rally, what happened in Janesville became the scenario to avoid at all costs. In the fall of 1997, the Wisconsin leader of the KKK announced plans for a December 6 rally in Beloit. Concerned community leaders actively sought to use the KKK's unwelcome presence as a catalyst for positive racial dialogue. Beloit's success in countering the potentially destructive influence of the KKK has become a model for other places in the country similarly threatened by hate groups' plans for public self-promotion.

The volatility of race as an issue for discussion complicates the successes Beloit has had in maintaining peace between racial groups. Many African American citizens of Beloit resent the racism they perceive in the city's police force; in the local media's coverage of a neighborhood that is populated largely by African Americans and stigmatized locally as "the hood"; and in the schools, where a disproportionate number of African American students drop out before graduating or are enrolled in nonaccelerated and special education classes. Many White citizens resent vocal complaints on the part of African Americans, whom they perceive to be carrying a grudge that dates back to the Civil War. While some Blacks and Whites regard each other with dislike or distrust, they often refrain from speaking their minds because conversations about race seem to lead nowhere and to end in mutual frustration. As an English teacher at Beloit Memorial High School, I have seen this dynamic play out again and again. Students express their disgruntlement with the status of race relations in our community in their journals, but in discussion they hold back from expressing what they feel because they know that others in the room will take offense. They sometimes privately express a need for self-censorship; their self-enforced silence leads to only partially articulated conversations about prejudice, social inequalities, affirmative action, and other racially infused issues. In turn, grudges result as students feel silenced, unable to say what they really feel.

Despite the messiness inherent in any dialogue about race, Beloit Memorial High School offers a rare setting to foster such conversation. Memorial is the only public high school in the city, and with an enrollment that hovers around 1,800 students, it is one of the largest high schools in the state. It is also one of the most integrated by virtue of the presence of nearly all the city's high school–aged children. Tensions in my classes have run high in the past. Convinced that an emotional conversation that acknowledges biases and fears is better than sugarcoated political correctness, I invite students to be as candid as possible, even as their candor leads to the risk of disagreement. If we can't talk civilly about race in school, especially in richly diverse classrooms where multiple viewpoints are present, then where in society can we talk about it?

In my Write for Your Life classroom, students are encouraged to mine their experiences, their concerns, and their issues for possible curricular connections. When Laura VanDerPloeg, a Write for Your Life colleague and teacher in the nearby Janesville Marshall Middle School, posted Jessie Boyer's message responding to the *Geraldo* episode about the Janesville KKK rally, I took it to my two sections of English 10 students and invited them to think about her question and to think about their own notions of race, hate, prejudice, and respect. The subsequent conversation, between our two schools, among students within my two classes, and among students across my two classes, opened up the issue of race for rational dialogue.

DESIGNING CONVERSATION: CONSIDERING WHAT WORKED

Several factors contributed to the success of the race dialogue. When people talk about race, often clichés or platitudes abound. In the ongoing discussion between Janesville and Beloit students, no one wanted to admit to problems with other races, even those who privately believed themselves to be racist. As the conversation developed, students pushed each other to clarify their assertions, to probe shallow claims of tolerance, and to define their assessments of the role of race in their own lives and communities. As students responded to each other, their thinking became more critical, their ideas more sophisticated, and their writing more sharp. The compelling demands of real readers for more explicit analysis of vague or trite terms and ideas led to powerful writing, thinking, and revision.

The conversation was complex as 45 Beloit students wrote at various times to 100 Janesville students. In each class, students read the letters aloud and discussed the issues they raised. In Janesville, students were asked to respond to any writer they chose, and they were given the option of posting this response online or keeping it in their reading journal. In part, their response was optional because of the logistical complexities of posting 100 responses each night; the option to respond in a reading journal gave some students a sense of safety, while still requiring them to think about what was being discussed in class and online. Beloit students could write to any writer they chose, if they chose—what they wrote was always designed to be e-mailed; it was never for their journal. Throughout the exchange, students were never forced to post their responses, although many chose to. As teachers, we felt it was important for students to generate and shape the exchange; our role was to support student talk in the classroom and online by giving students the tools needed to promote learning through honest and respectful communication. Once students saw that their letters would be read and responded to by other teenagers, they were eager to get involved. The idea of a real audience of their peers invited not only more responses, but genuine ones.

Since neither of the two schools had e-mail access, responses were typed by the teachers into their personal computers. This necessary step had the benefit of allowing teachers to screen students' letters before they were sent out. Given the sensitive nature of the conversation, we felt it was important to use this step to teach students how their language could affect others in ways they might not anticipate. Each teacher handled this situation slightly differently. In Janesville, letters that were unclear or that contained potentially inflammatory material created opportunities for conferences with the writers, giving students greater perspective on their work and the chance to revise. Students were asked to think carefully about what they wanted to say and how best to reach their audience. This does not mean that students' thoughts and feelings were censored, but that they were challenged to voice their ideas respectfully and constructively. In Beloit, students relied less on the teacher for this reflective role, and instead often wrote with a partner who helped determine if what was written reflected what was meant. Once students had revised and edited their letters to mutual satisfaction, the responses were put online as they were written, with only minor corrections of spelling and punctuation as needed.

In both classrooms, the letters were often read aloud as a text for class discussion. Students found their thoughts and ideas at the center of the classroom, which further motivated their writing and talk. The teachers acted as moderators, helping students learn how to listen and communicate respect.

RACE, RESPECT, REVISION

Looking back a year and a half later at the whole dialogue, we find that assertions, responses, and questions intertwine in a sophisticated tapestry of voices. The first thread of the conversation that we want to discuss here begins with Jessie Boyer's questions prompted by the *Geraldo* episode about the Janesville KKK rally: "I have never seen so much hate in one place before. It terrified me. What makes people hate other races? Is it just a fear of differences? And where does racism come from?" The response she received from a quiet, bright Beloit boy named Justin illuminated the touchy nature of a conversation laced with candor about racial views:

> Jessie, I don't know why the KKK and neo-Nazis hate other races. Every person probably hates them for a different reason. Maybe for some it is a fear of difference, but not very many. Racism comes from thousands of different reasons. I don't agree with the KKK, but I don't like niggers, but not all black people are and some white people are. Niggers are just the ones that cause violence, steal, and cause trouble.
> —Justin (Beloit)

His use of the word *niggers* alarmed, angered, and compelled many students to respond, both from Beloit and Janesville. However, because the conversation occurred in writing, across miles, between faceless strangers, the dialogue was permeated with civility and a noticeable desire to be understood and not misjudged. When the word *nigger* is spoken in class, the response is furious and emotional; students hearing that word react almost violently, and its introduction into a conversation shuts down any further discourse. When Justin introduced the word into the Beloit/Janesville dialogue, the responses he received challenged him to clarify his expression of ideas in active, heartfelt revision.

> Dear Justin: . . . We are both white females. Neither of us are racist and we think that even though you say you're not racist, that you might be. You don't like African Americans and you think that they cause all the crimes. We think that you should stop looking at the negatives and start looking at the positives. There are many African Americans who are not what you think. For example, Martin Luther King, Jr. and Rosa Parks. We think you should stop looking at skin color and start looking at personality.
> —Julia and Michelle (Janesville)

> Justin: . . . Black people are not the only people who steal, who are violent. . . . Just because some of the black people you know have been in trouble with the law, doesn't mean you should assume all black people have, at one point or another, been in trouble with the law. Don't you think that you should've actually thought about the black people you know and asked yourself, "Have they ever been in trouble with the law?" To call black people "niggers," just because of some of the people in Beloit, doesn't mean that all black people are troublemakers.
> —Ali (Janesville)

Justin took these comments seriously and answered each one. In so doing, he invoked narrative to illustrate his experiences and his beliefs. Often students in this conversation enriched their claims by detailed accounts of what helped or impeded them as they established their values surrounding tolerance. Stories became a means of expressing their ideas in more specific language.

> Michelle and Julia, I did not say I didn't like African Americans, and I didn't say they commit all crimes. A lot of black people cause crimes here, but not all. I am not looking at skin color, and I am looking at personality. There are a lot of blacks at this school, and I've met only a handful of them with good personalities. Most of them wouldn't talk to someone like me. I've been yelled at for doing nothing, stolen from in front of my face, slapped by someone I never met (the guy told his friends to beat me. When I asked why, he said, "Because I can."). My girlfriend's been raped by a black guy, my brother has been jumped for no

reason by black people. I could go on, but I don't want to bore you. But even after all this, I don't hate them all, just the ones that cause these troubles.
  —Justin

Justin's candor and the issues of language and experience that it raised were important in provoking spirited and meaningful dialogue. While many students were still critical of Justin's comments, he nevertheless challenged their comfortable sense of political correctness and invited a greater sense of honesty in the dialogue.

Beloit students were eager to find a Janesville student who would admit to being racist. Encountering explicitly defined racism from a Janesville student would confirm the Beloit students' stereotypes, but more important, students were impatient to get beyond what they perceived to be empty statements of tolerance. As the conversation continued, students from both cities began to share racially infused narratives from their own experiences—from having been exposed to racist attitudes at home to having witnessed public humiliations of people from different racial backgrounds. When those anecdotes entered the conversation, students seemed to take each other more seriously.

In the following response to Justin, Dana, a friendly and popular eighth-grader, challenged his use of the term *nigger*. Her attempt to understand Justin led to misunderstandings with Beloit students, who perceived her to be a racist labeling all Blacks as niggers.

> Dear Justin, What are you talking about? Are you trying to tell me that blacks and niggers are different? For some reason, I don't see the difference. One other thing is, how can you not agree with the KKK, but still tell everyone that you hate blacks? I am sorry, but I just don't get what you are trying to say.
>   —Dana (Janesville)

> Dana, Yes I did say blacks are different than niggers. Maybe not everybody feels that way, but I know a lot of people that do. A nigger is somebody that is a good-for-nothing, trouble-making, gang-banging, violent person. White people can be like this too. Most people call them wannabes. I don't agree with the KKK because they don't like all black people. I just don't like the trouble makers. I never said I hate blacks.
>   —Justin

The dialogue about race grew rich and complex as students from Janesville and Beloit read and responded to comments from both places, extending the dialogue in many directions at once. Some Beloit students, like Nicole, jumped into the conversation as critical readers, analyzing Justin's message and seeking better to understand Dana:

Dear Dana: I am a white female. I read the letter written by the Beloit student you were responding to. I also read the letter you responded with. By what you wrote, I am guessing you don't like blacks. Or maybe I misunderstood your comment. I was wondering if I could maybe clarify the letter written from Beloit because it was a little confusing. I think what he was saying was that he considers any person who does or commits an ignorant crime as a nigger. He doesn't think of niggers as only blacks as some people do when they hear the word. I believe also that not all niggers are black. Whenever I hear a person say, "I hate niggers," and I know they're talking about blacks, I will tell them that there is a difference between niggers and blacks. I don't like niggers, but I don't say that because most people's take on that phrase is different. Niggers to me are stupid people, not blacks. Seeing as how I'm not racist, I can pick out things about people I don't like instead of just picking out the race. I do not agree with the KKK and will never understand why a white man/woman can say that the world belongs to them when their race stole it away from the same race that they hate. America belongs to nobody, and if we could all understand that to be American is to be part of one big race of all colors, a lot of this racism would end.
—Nicole (Beloit)

Meanwhile, Dana herself was surprised and dismayed that her message had been interpreted as racist by the other students. She was bewildered to think her words had been misunderstood, providing an opportunity for a one-on-one conference and discussion. Like Justin, her desire for respect and understanding spurred her to explain herself and clarify her own thinking:

To anyone who responded to me: In my letter I may not have explained myself. I don't hate blacks. Some of my best friends are blacks. The thing is, is when most people hear the word "nigger" they usually mean black, or they mean it as a racial slur. In Justin's letter, I wasn't quite sure if he meant it racially or just as being another name. I hope this explains what I meant.
—Dana

From the very start of the conversation, students were driven to connect with each other, even when they disagreed. Their ability to respond to each other out of a sense of both respect and challenge demonstrates the power of audience, particularly a peer audience, on student writing. Rather than knee-jerk political correctness leading students to decry the use of the loaded label *nigger*, the dynamics of the conversation led students to analyze and explain their often strong feelings thoughtfully.

Myron, a shy young man, came to life and became intensely engaged during the race dialogue. In his first response to Jessie, he described his biracial status as the child of an African American mother and a Mexican father. Within his own family, racial tensions often erupted as some of his African American relatives urged him to avoid the company of "shady Mexicans" at all costs, while Mexican relatives spouted anti-Black sentiment. Myron's concerns about racism came from intense personal experiences, and he responded to the emerging conversation about the use of the word *nigger* from the heart:

> To anyone who uses the word nigger: Well I'm glad all white people don't hate blacks and Mexicans and other people of color. I don't think you should call anybody a nigger. I don't care if they're white or black or if they do something stupid. You shouldn't put a label on them that was at one time put on black people. Putting it on everybody it seems like an excuse to use the word. Why don't you just try to let that word die? I see where you are coming from, but when you see somebody doing something stupid, don't call them nigger, call them stupid. That's what I'm trying to say.
> —Myron (Beloit)

A desire for an authoritative solution to usage for the problematic *nigger* led Janesville's Christina to enter the conversation citing dictionary research:

> Hi! I am an 8th grader from Janesville. I've looked up the word "nigger" in a couple of different dictionaries. A few of them said, "A person with darker skin;" even more said, "an ignorant person." As you can see, the people who wrote the dictionaries didn't even know exactly what the word meant. On the same subject, but a little different, I was wondering if you have so-called "wiggers" at your school? Sometimes I hear people call themselves "wiggers," and they are proud of it. I really don't understand why they would be. The way I understand the word is that it means "white nigger." If that is true, why would they be proud if nigger

is supposedly such a bad word? Please write back with your opinion.
—Christina

The emotions surrounding the use of the label *wigger* unfold in a subsequent thread of our story, but ambivalence about the use of the word *nigger* and frustration about the focus of the dialogue surfaced in an impatient message from one Janesville student:

Dear Beloit Students: I know this might sound mean, but I don't really care right now because I don't personally know you, and right now, I don't care what you or your classmates will think of me. First of all, I am so sick of this black/white issue. But it all comes down to why *white* people are racist. Black people are too, you know, whether you want to believe it or not. If a white person calls a black person a nigger, even if they *do* have a reason for it, or even if the black person called them white trash first, they (the white person) would get in more trouble. And it's not fair. I just thought I'd tell you all how I feel.
—Autumn (Janesville)

In this letter, Autumn voices the sentiments of many White Janesville students who feel "put upon" by discussions of racism in which they perceive that they are made to feel guilty for being White. It is this attitude that fosters resistance in many White students, who feel that they will inevitably be made to look like the bad guys in any conversation on the subject. These students seldom see agency in their own attitudes or actions toward others and have difficulty extending their understanding of prejudice beyond a Black-versus-White perspective. They resent learning about or discussing racial issues in part because they feel that they are not allowed to voice their own views and frustrations.

Autumn's message evoked a strong response from Beloit's Ebony, and yet another call for revision and respect.

Dear Autumn, I am sick of the black/white issue too. But the way you came out and expressed yourself was too harsh. Yes some white and some black people are racist. But I am not racist. What you said in your letter I don't agree with. You said if a white person calls a black person a "nigger," even if they have a reason to, it's okay. There's no reason to be called a "nigger" period. That's just how I feel. And you said even if the black person called the white person "white trash," the whites would get in more trouble

for calling a black person a "nigger." Not necessarily, because some black people are stupid and get in trouble for their words. And some white people get in trouble for their words. The usage of the words nigger/wigger is wrong, point blank.
—Sincerely, Ebony
P.S. and I don't care what you think of me either. Not trying to be mean.

The spirited exchange between Autumn and Ebony concludes the first thread of our story, though it does not bring final closure to issues surrounding whether Blacks or Whites should have greater impunity in using controversial language. We were impressed by the level of engagement of our students in the race dialogue, not because they solved every issue raised, but because they honestly tried to explore their own values. In so doing they became critical writers and thinkers who questioned their own and others' assumptions and began to reflect about their own relationships to each other and to their communities.

THE SECOND STRAND:
WRITING ABOUT COMMUNITY CONFLICT

That the students involved in the exchange did not limit themselves to a Black/White discussion of racial prejudice is another credit to their accomplishment. In following a second, related thread that weaves through the conversation, we see students exploring the implications of intolerance in their own lives and communities. Students reflected on the issues that existed between them in more personal ways, one of the most immediate being that of the conflicts and tension that exist between the communities of Janesville and Beloit. Each community had strong ideas and feelings about the other. To many in Beloit, Janesville was a racist town, one where the residents believed themselves superior and were openly hostile toward outsiders. A common opinion in Janesville held that Beloit was a "troubled" town, economically struggling and socially volatile because of the higher minority population. In acknowledging the problems between their communities, students became aware that the problems of intolerance, mistrust, and stereotyping were no longer impersonal and that racism was not abstract; the "other" had a name and a face, and was talking to them. This issue emerged early on in the dialogue. In response to Jessie's initial letter, Jason H. wrote:

Dear Jessie, I think other people have an idea of what one race acts like and they think that everyone from that race acts that

same way. I feel this way of thinking is taught to them by someone such as their parents, and in Janesville it elevates the thoughts
about racism. From my experience, my uncle moved to Milton to
get away from other races. He always thinks he is better than everyone—even other people from our family. I hate the idea of having a preconceived idea about someone before you even get a
chance to meet them. Another reason for racism is trying to be
like everyone else. For example, there are so many racist people in
Janesville and people are scared of standing out so they learn to
be racist like everyone else.
　　—Jason (Beloit)

Dear Jason, I completely understand what you said about preconceived ideas, and I hate them as much as you do. I think you're
wrong, though, about everyone wanting to blend in, so they become racists. I think that if someone here in Janesville doesn't
want to stand out, they will keep their same beliefs, racist or not,
and not voice them or act on them. Not too many people change
their beliefs to be like everyone else, at least not beliefs about racism. They just keep their ideas to themselves.
　　—Jessie (Janesville)

As with other elements of the conversation, students used narrative
to discuss issues of community conflict in personal and specific terms.
In acknowledging the attitudes of both communities, students openly
expressed pain and frustration at the harm that stereotypes had caused
and realized among themselves that they were facing the human consequences of a prejudice that had previously been an abstraction.

Jason H.: I live in Janesville, and I'm white, but I was born in Beloit and most of my family lives there, including my father. So I
am in Beloit quite often. But I hate how a lot of people from Beloit assume I'm a snot, and that I'm stuck up because a lot of people from Janesville are. I know, too, that many people from Janesville think that people from Beloit are all bad and involved in
crime. I don't understand how two towns next to each other think
so badly of one another. I agree with a lot of what you are saying,
and thought I would share some of my thoughts with you. I
would enjoy hearing back from you.
　　—Jennifer (Janesville)

Jennifer: From my point of view, I don't know you enough to be
able to call you a snot. Some of my family lives in Janesville, and

I know that they sometimes think they are better than us. I've also heard that a school in Janesville didn't participate in Martin Luther King, Jr. day. Our school got a whole day off for Martin Luther King day. That tells me something about the people who run that school. I never said that everyone who lives in Janesville is the same. There are always exceptions wherever you go. Someone is always going to be different and have different morals. I always go back to preconceived ideas and generalizations of people which are what I feel are the reasons for the stereotypes between Janesville and Beloit.
—Jason (Beloit)

In many letters, we notice that students are eager to identify their racial background to the audience. In a medium that could potentially be colorblind, students made themselves as visible to each other as possible. In identifying themselves, students also revealed their membership in certain social groups or subcultures, as we see in Stephanie's response below to Luke and Marvin. First, the letter from the boys:

To Janesville Students: My name is Luke and my partner's name is Marvin. I'm a 16-year-old white male, and my partner is a 17-year-old mixed (black and white) male. We see racism all around. Don't think Beloit is perfect. There is still racism, it is just hushed as opposed to Janesville voicing their opinions. I went to a Janesville party one time, and because my pants were too baggy, the students there told us "niggers" to leave. I'm 100% white; why they called me a "nigger" I have no clue. We think racism here is lesser because we are exposed to such a diverse environment at a young age. We adapt to each other. In Janesville you can't make adaptation because the diversity is at a minimum. Please write back. We want your responses.
—Luke and Marvin (Beloit)

Dear Luke and Marvin: I do agree that there are racist people in Janesville. Just so you know, I'm mixed, white and black. My friend April is white. We get along fine, even though we are different. I think a reason Janesville is maybe more racist than Beloit is because barely any black people live in Janesville compared to Beloit. That's all I have to say for now. Thanks for listening.
—Stephanie (Janesville)

While several Janesville students openly discussed racism in their own community, Beloit students were eager to hear more prejudiced voices and were somewhat bewildered by the tolerant nature of many of the students' responses. This led one student, Clinton, to write a letter to the Janesville teacher, asking for responses from "racist people." While no one responded to this call, several Janesville students did acknowledge racist attitudes within their own families, taking a risk to share a less-than-flattering picture of life in their home and community.

> Clinton, My name is Jenny. I am going to answer the question that you asked in your letter you wrote to Ms. VanDerPloeg. I am going to tell you that yes, there are racist people here. I think that they may be embarrassed to write back. I don't know why they would be embarrassed to be racist, because that's what they believe in. I believe that all people are equal. I have many friends that are of different races. I have also gone out with guys that are of different races. My dad is racist. I don't know why. I really hate it, because he is always telling racist jokes and dissing blacks. He owns two businesses. He hardly ever hires people of different races. I am always yelling at him for being racist. I am tired of it. I know how you feel about racists. I will try to get *someone that is racist to write to you. Peace out*
> —Jenny (Janesville)

While no one answered Clinton's call to reveal their racist nature, students did begin to move beyond their stereotypes of one another and to look for the things they had in common. Beloit student Myron reveals that his encounters with prejudice aren't restricted to racial identity or to Janesville. Once again invoking narrative, he shares stories of bigotry, while looking beyond the initial, superficial intercommunity stereotypes.

> Dear Brandis, I'm glad you agree with me. I used to go to the Janesville Mall just to kick it, and as soon as I would walk in, it's like all eyes were on me just because everybody would look at me. It's like they never saw a mixed boy with braids and baggy clothes, but I just ignored it. I stopped going to Janesville period. Do you ever come to Beloit? I'm not going to brag about Beloit because Beloit has its stupid people and stupid cops. For instance, it was a Friday afternoon. I had just got home from school, and I was standing in front of my house, and I was talking to my friend, and for some reason this white police officer told me to go into my house and of course I didn't. I told him he better ride on.

It just goes to show you can't get away from it no matter where you go. I'm moving to Atlanta, and I hope they don't have a lot of stupidity.
—Myron (Beloit)

In Jessie's response, we see the end of this thread in the conversation: Although the discussion began out of community conflict, it ended with words and hands extended in the hope of friendship.

Dear Myron, Please, please don't judge people from Janesville by the few you saw at the mall. Of course, in every large group of people there are some that the rest are ashamed of. Sometime, come back to Janesville so you can meet the real people.
—Jessie (Janesville)

WRITING FOR SOCIAL CHANGE

A third strand of talk reveals an emerging sense of empowerment among students. As they saw the impact of their words, many became aware of the power that writing and speech have to change others and the world around them. The very act of participating in dialogue with one another was a form of social action that had the power to affect change in their communities. Students began to believe that their acts of literacy could make a difference, could react against the racism and tolerance they had discovered.

In response to Jessie's initial letter, Colin proposed action in response to the threat of the KKK. His ideas led other students to reflect on what, if anything, middle and high school students could do about racism:

Jessie, In response to your letter, I think you should get a petition and give it to the head of the Klan—I hear he lives in Janesville—because if all the racism keeps up, all there is going to be left is a race war. I am a 16-year-old black/white boy, so you can call it whatever you want to, but like you I am kind of stuck in the middle. I feel that there should not be such a thing as racism. I don't know. No man is pure because if he was, God would have made him something special, and ain't none of them racists something special.
—Colin (Beloit)

Colin, I don't think giving a petition to the KKK would solve anything. They already know that very many people oppose them,

and that has only made them fight more vigorously. I really like, though, that you are thinking of peaceful, effective solutions to this problem.
—Jessie (Janesville)

After Jessie rebuked his suggestion of a petition, Colin retrenched. His next message reveals the bitterness of a young man who feels powerless, trapped between two racial identities. In his response, we see that Colin recognizes his own need to be heard, a need that is met through his participation in dialogue and answered by Noreen. First Colin's letter:

Noreen: The letters that I wrote and Amber and the rest of the class wrote I really don't think are doing anything but wasting pen and pencil. There is nothing going to happen because we are little kids. We aren't going to make a difference until we put or show how we feel to a higher power that can get a hold of someone—or at least find someone that will at least listen, but I don't think anyone will listen to a black mixed or to all minorities.
—Colin (Beloit)

Colin: I don't exactly agree with you—just because we are still young, it doesn't mean that we can't make a difference. You could start off by doing little stuff around your school/neighborhood and work up to doing something that will really make a difference. So—just because we are young, it doesn't mean we can't do anything to make a difference.
—Noreen (Janesville)

For some other students, their weakened sense of agency stemmed from their belief that the conversation somehow did not apply to them. Kevin T. and Kevin B. expressed the feelings of several White students on both sides of the conversation when they wondered how they fit in:

Dear Jessie, We don't know what to say because we don't have that problem with the white supremacists. If we did, we shouldn't have a problem because we are white. If someone did call us something, it wouldn't bother us.
—Kevin T. and Kevin B. (Beloit)

The boys' complacency spurred other students to challenge them. As the dialogue progressed, students acquired a stronger sense of conviction that they had a place and a voice in their communities, and they sought to persuade each other of their potential for activism.

Dear Kevin T. & Kevin B., Are you saying that if there was a big problem with white supremacists where you live that you would agree with them and let them degrade your friends? In an integrated school, you must have at least a few friends of a different race. You also said that if someone called you something, it wouldn't bother you. Would it bother you if someone said something about your friends or family?
    —Jessie (Janesville)

Dear Kevin T. and Kevin B., Yes, you do have a problem with white supremacist groups. Just thinking you don't have to worry because you are white shows that you could easily be pulled into one of those groups. If you aren't picked on because of your race, you could get picked on because of your religion. Any way that you look at it, you are affected by discrimination. And it's people that don't care who keep these discriminating groups thriving. I hope you change your minds, because every little bit helps.
    —Tanya, a non-racist white girl (Janesville)

Dear Tanya: I realize that we do have a problem with racism, and no I could not be pulled into one of the groups because I wouldn't stoop that low to do it. Yes, everyone is affected by discrimination. I really don't know what to think about racism yet, but I probably will if it happens to me or any of my friends or family, and no, I'm not picked on because of my religion either, because I don't really have one—or, put it this way—I do, but I don't show it all the time. And yes, I agree. Every little bit helps.
    —Kevin T. (Beloit)

Ultimately, many students came to see their talk as a form of action:

. . . I feel good that my thoughts and feelings are affecting other people at different schools in a different city. I appreciate that someone else shares my feelings.
    —Adam (Beloit)

. . . What a person believes, thinks, feels, and their attitude is what makes a person who they are. I am 100% white. Living in Janesville is a disadvantage in the sense that I don't get to live with people of a different race or background. I have a few black friends, and that is it. I would love to live in a more diverse city, with people who are different than me. A lot of people think that

everyone who lives in Janesville is racist. I am not racist at all. I love people of all colors. I love talking to your peers and to you. I think that communicating like this might help solve the problem of racism.
—Sara (Janesville)

Sara's observation that "communicating like this might help solve the problem of racism" was taken to heart by students from both communities. In Beloit, students in one of the two sections involved in the exchange with Janesville decided that racism and prejudice were rooted in a lack of exposure to people of other races. As the conversation with Janesville was unfolding, students in the Beloit class had often worked in pairs or groups of three to respond to messages from Janesville students. One day, a Beloit student noticed that the groupings in their class were almost all heterogeneous—not by design, but because the class was so diverse, students often turned to whoever was sitting next to them and the resulting arrangements contained kids of different ethnic backgrounds. In the early days of the class, they had clung to members of their own racial backgrounds in group work, but as the conversation with Janesville called attention to race as a component of experience worth reflecting about and analyzing, students found themselves eager to compare stories with others who had different backgrounds.

Over time, participation in this exchange developed and strengthened students' voices, helping them negotiate their identities and experiences through the dynamic give-and-take of conversation. The exchange reached an exciting conclusion when Janesville students invited their Beloit friends to their Authors' Coffeehouse Celebration, an evening set aside for students to read and celebrate the publication of their eighth-grade book and culminating Write for Your Life project, *Opening the Door to Our Hearts.* Seven Beloit students accepted the invitation. Given that the visit was on a lovely June night right before finals and that the trip was purely voluntary, the fact that sophomores who had started the semester professing antipathy to all school-related functions chose to visit another school, to meet eighth-graders no less, was an exciting development.

The Janesville students received their Beloit visitors warmly and enthusiastically, taking them on a tour of the school and signing copies of their publication for their guests. On the way back to Beloit, the sophomores wrote their last messages to Janesville, thanking them for the memorable evening, which brought together people who had begun a relationship, skeptically, across the impersonal space of e-mail and the constraints of the written word.

Students can change the world, if we let them. If we let them talk and if we listen and get out of the way. If we make room in our classroom for the issues that are real, that matter, that make a difference in students' lives and communities. These are the big lessons, the ones that we as teachers have learned over and over.

In the schoolyear following the exchange, Beth was sitting in her room during a prep period, feeling drained by a new batch of sophomores whose hostility to school was enervating. Nicole, a former student, popped in to say hi, asking about Beth's new students. Beth admitted that they were resistant to school.

Nicole offered the best kind of help, the kind that teaches us as teachers: "Do you want me to come in and talk to them? To tell them what they can do? To tell them what we were able to do, talking to Janesville, because we cared?"

She couldn't have said it better.

Chapter 8

RURAL COMMUNITIES, GANGS, AND SCHOOL VIOLENCE

Writing for a Local and an Electronic Community

Rosie Roppel

There was yet another horrible shooting in Littleton, Colorado. Kids are killing kids, and again, the U.S. is trying to figure out why. I am thirteen years old [and] live in a small town, Ketchikan, Alaska. A small town just like the ones where these awful shootings always seem to take place. Every time those stories come on the television, I can't help but notice how easily it could be this town next. And I want to know why this is happening just as badly as any parent or police chief does. The thing is, I am right in the middle of it all. I am in the same age group as all of these kids.
—Jackie Jacobson, Schoenbar Middle School, Ketchikan, Alaska

One August afternoon, a white 875-foot Princess Line cruise ship floated into Ketchikan, the Salmon Capital of the World. A rare blue cloudless sky framed the towering snowcapped mountains behind Alaska's first city. Tourists lined the railings, some pointing cameras at a Tlingit totem while others exchanged waves with the handful of locals on the wooden docks. A few teenagers dressed in sagging pants draped themselves over their rusted BMX bikes, scowling with indifference. Longshoremen tossed large snakelike lines to secure the ship. This is

Writing to Make a Difference. Copyright © 2001 by Teachers College, Columbia University. All rights reserved. ISBN 0-8077-4186-8 (paper), 0-8077-4187-6 (cloth). Prior to photocopying items for classroom use, please contact the Copyright Clearance Center, Customer Service, 222 Rosewood Drive, Danvers, MA, 01923, USA, telephone (508) 750-8400.

quite a romantic welcome for foreigners visiting Alaska for the first time. One might think inhabitants isolated on an island 1,000 miles from any metropolitan area, approachable only by boat or airplane, would have escaped the violence and gang problems of urban life of the lower 48. Not so!

As the tourists scoured our town, I sat in the high school auditorium during our fall inservice listening to Dr. Jack Sasser from Dotham City Schools in Alabama impress the theme of "Necessary Reform in Our Educational Environment" upon the minds of my fellow teachers. A colorful graph presented evidence of declining student proficiency in math, science, reading, and writing. I thought about my eighth-grade middle school boys proudly parading around in their sagging pants and gang colors and sporting shaved heads and hats on backwards, while girls proudly expose the hickeys on their necks. I was wondering, "How can I apply Dr. Sasser's ideas to my classroom when social problems in our school take priority over reform?"

I thought back to my classroom of the previous year. Posters of Michael Jordan; a snowboarder, one of my students, getting *big air* off a natural pipe on top of Deer Mountain; Shakespeare's bust; the Bread Loaf School of English in Vermont; Oxford University; pictures of my family; and student writing adorned every inch of wall space. A decorated chart with everyone's birthday and upcoming student activities hung front and center. Students busily revised creative writing pieces as I cruised the class, offering pointers and encouraging those who looked stumped. A few students slumped at their computers and fidgeted with their gang colors as their classmates scrambled to finish second and third drafts on the word processors. One secretly composed an obscene message on the computer screen for the next class to read.

I recalled how many times a few of these 13- and 14-year-olds have been suspended from school for intimidating other students and teachers, stealing from the school and each other, smoking cigarettes, cutting classes, interrupting learning, drinking, and violating probation. Many times these students worked well one on one, but in groups they had even been intimidating, threatening, and, in some cases, dangerous: Some students had been sufficiently frightened to quit school, and their parents were home-schooling them. Graffiti blemished our school inside and out. A rash of vandalism and insubordination had put the school in total chaos. Even our 12-year-old female honor students brought a bottle of liquor to school and got intoxicated. Persistent tardiness, excessive absences, and continual disruptions had made learning very difficult. These problems seemed more serious than ever, and we began to see the influence of gang behavior, even some violence. A few were affecting a majority.

Dr. Sasser's lecture interrupted my drifting thoughts. "Necessary reform"? The reform in education Sasser was talking about could not happen until student behavior was reformed. The problems I mention here did not stop at the end of the schoolday either. This incipient gang behavior was a community problem. Students who wanted to be gang-stas in Ketchikan had stalked middle school and high school students after school and on the weekends. Some children had been beaten, and parents had pressed charges. The police had reported car-jackings and break-ins. Children had sneaked out of their houses at night and run away from home. One 16-year-old lunged at his mother with a knife, missed, and cut his younger sister.

"We have always had mischievous teenagers, but never teenagers so angry before," a parent said to me in the local grocery store, a very common place for a parent–teacher conference in a small town. "My child is afraid to go to school or walk home by herself anymore." Another mentioned the child in Oregon who killed his classmates and his parents. At that point, I thought about the high school boy who un-loaded rounds of ammunition into the school, killing students and a teacher in Bethel, Alaska, a much smaller village than Ketchikan. Violence was coming closer to Ketchikan. We, too, have had our own scares. Recently, a student broke into a local business, stole guns, then hid up on the roof of our middle school the day before our field day. Fortunately, he was found the following morning before daybreak. Students did not want to do schoolwork that day; they wanted to talk about it in the classroom but were afraid to speak about their fears for a number of reasons. Students needed a safe place to talk. Teachers, too, needed the sympathetic ear of someone who could offer help.

"What is happening to our children on our little island of 9,000 people?" I thought. Ketchikan was a thriving Tlingit fishing village centuries ago; now people in Ketchikan work at sport and commercial fishing, construction, tourism, timber, and the usual professional occupations. About 40% of our population is Tlingit, Haida, and Tschimpsian; there is a small Filipino community and a mix of "others" from all over the United States and the Pacific Rim. We all see each other regularly at grocery stores, movies, local plays and concerts. I wondered why and how violent behavior among our youth had come to our small island community.

CONFRONTING THE ISSUE OF GANG BEHAVIOR

Last year, recognizing the beginning of gang problems, the school district brought in "gang experts" from Portland, Oregon, to educate the faculty, community, and student body. These experts, tattooed ex–gang members and probation officers, spent time with our students and discovered that indeed we did have the beginnings of gangs; they called these kids "wanna-be gangstas" (WBG). The gang experts explained to the adults that WBGs were very dangerous because they would do anything to prove they are real gangstas and *not* wanna-bes. The ex–gang members suggested that the community tighten up and work together. The result was a unified front: The school board joined with parents, students, teachers, the administration—that is, the entire community—to create a strict discipline plan, which was put in place during the last month of the schoolyear. The leaders of the wanna-be gangsters were expelled immediately from the school system, leaving their followers with no leaders. Most of their followers were able to concentrate again on being successful in school, but it seemed there wasn't much discussion. We had attended to the symptom but not the cause. Students still needed opportunities to ask questions, reflect, complain, and take control of their lives. They needed guidance to understand the causes of this behavior in order to find ways to avoid it.

By the end of the schoolyear, because of the new no-tolerance discipline policy by which students were expelled from the school system for insubordination, threatening other students, refusing to obey the dress code, wearing backpacks into the classroom, or coming late to class, the school climate had become (in my opinion) superficially reformed. Students who refused to follow the rules were ejected from the system immediately; parents were relieved, and teachers and students relaxed. It was a good start but not the complete answer, because even though the gang disturbances decreased in number, I suspected we still had not addressed the cause of the behavior. Students still sat glassy-eyed and listless, drawing marijuana leaves and gang graffiti on their notebooks. Many of these youths were irritable, ready to explode in anger, brooding, and isolated from other students. The troubled students suppressed their outward anger just to stay in school but still had no opportunity to openly discuss their concerns and fears.

USING TECHNOLOGY TO CONNECT
AND CREATE COMMUNITIES

At the time of the flare-up of the gangtsa wanna-bes, I had been a member of the Bread Loaf Teacher Network (BLTN) for 2 years and had participated in many online writing and literary projects using BreadNet, an electronic computer network that connects rural teachers and students across the nation. One of the outstanding capacities of this system is its ability to create new communities of learners. At an annual meeting of the BLTN, I asked my colleagues about their experience with gangs in their communities, and many of us were shocked to learn that minor to serious gang activities existed in nearly all our rural communities, including areas in Alaska, Arizona, Mississippi, New Mexico, South Carolina, and Vermont. At the meeting, we discussed how we might use writing and literature as a springboard for a collaborative inquiry into gangs, school violence, and racism. Studying these topics collaboratively online, we hoped, might form a community in which students discovered ways to create understanding and change in behavior. We made a plan to use BreadNet's computer conferencing technology to facilitate this activity. Though the end of the schoolyear was nearing, we began the project, hoping to make a difference in our communities.

Three colleagues and I created what we called the "Gang Conference" on BreadNet and planned to do gang-related reading and writing activities via e-mail. Our project was based on the premise that intensive reading and writing about gang behavior would lead students to self-discoveries related to the topic. Once students began to understand how gang behavior affected their lives, we hoped, they would be able to discover reasons and methods to change their behavior. In the relatively anonymous writing context of computer conferences, local impediments to discussion—such as peer, gender, and racial intimidation—don't exist, and a listening ear is always present. In computer conferences when students write to a real audience of peers, they are consistently more serious about their writing than when they write only for their teacher or classmates. The instant feedback provided in a computer conference also offers some incentive.

Using BreadNet, we uploaded information about gang behavior, and the technology enabled us to create an archive of background information for all online participants. Through reading and writing together, we hoped to come to some conclusion about why isolated rural students form gangs of a violent nature. We also hoped to work collaboratively to develop ways to raise awareness of the problem in our home communities. We wanted a safe place for children to discuss serious issues. As an added resource, some teachers met with parent–teacher groups for support.

READING AND WRITING ABOUT GANGS

My online colleagues and I selected books, articles, and pamphlets about gang activity. We exchanged titles on BreadNet and discussed the benefits and problems in our classrooms, mailing stories and articles to one another online and through regular mail. We selected the following texts for our students to read, favoring autobiographical texts that included moral lessons:

* Excerpts from the novel *Always Running* by Luis J. Rodriguez (1994) (appropriate for ninth-graders and up). An ex–gang member who now counsels gang members in inner cities wrote this book. His son became a gang member.
* *The Chocolate War*, by Robert Cormier (1974).
* *Monster: The Autobiography of an L. A. Gang Member*, by Sanyika Shakur (1994), a.k.a. Kody Scott.

In preparation for our online discussions, my students discussed these readings in our classroom, citing interesting passages. Then students wrote responses to the readings and responses to writing prompts, which they shared with their online peers. Some of the prompts and what I learned from my students follow.

Prompt: Describe What You Know About Gang Behavior in the United States.

Many students knew about the Crips and the Bloods and many of the initiation procedures. Students had knowledge of gang attire, customs, lingo, and territories around California and Seattle. A few of the students even knew names of people who belonged to gangs, people they had known in other places where they had lived prior to coming to Ketchikan; they were experts on the subject. No one admitted, however, to participating in gang behavior. We discussed other communities in Alaska that might have gang problems. I asked how students find out about gang procedures. Students mentioned that some kids had moved to our island from Los Angeles and had imported some knowledge about gang behaviors. Others said they were learning about gangs from the news on television and from Web sites that provide information. I learned that youngsters can actually join gangs through the Net.

Prompt: Does Ketchikan Have Gangs?

In the responses to this prompt, I could not believe the diversity of opinion coming from students belonging to the same grade. We only have 98 students on our team and 400 in the whole school. I thought all students would know what was going on, but I was wrong. After my first writing assignment, I realized how important these issues were to discuss. What I called gang behavior, others called mischief. My students' responses to this prompt indicated that they need help identifying and examining vital issues that concern them, because left unexamined, unrealistic perceptions can lead students into bad behavior. Here are some responses to this prompt:

Ketchikan does not really have any gangs like the Royals. It has gangs, of course, but not ones that kill each other. . . . In Ketchikan kids only smoke, do drugs, and hang out. If the kids that are not in the gangs don't want to join or be associated with the gang, they usually try to avoid them as much as possible.
—Donald Sodorstrom

In Ketchikan, I think there are a lot of wanna-be's but not very many gangstas, if any. Most everybody stays out of their way unless they want to be in the gang and don't go near their "hangout places" like the trails and the mall where they smoke and drink.
—Angela Pfeifer

There are also problems of violence in the youth of Ketchikan. Though I have no personal experience in this area, I hear lots of stories. Most recently a friend of my sister was stabbed at a party and the person who did it was found beaten to death. There are a lot of people who use drugs. . . . There is vandalism too.
—Sarah Lamm

Gangs in Ketchikan may be linked to some of the juvenile crimes that have occurred here. They think they can gain respect by doing whatever their gang members want.
—Donald Alderman

The wanna-bes of this town dress, walk, and act like gang members from down south as much as they can.
—Amber Machado

Last year kids wore their colors to school. They had red bandannas for belts and wore their sagging pants. They wore their hats backwards so people would know who they were. Then we got the dress code. The kids would wear their colors so the kids could see it, but didn't think the teachers could.
—Melissa Leary

Prompt: Why Are Kids Involved with Gangs?

According to students, their peers got involved with gangs for a variety of reasons, which reflects the complexity of the problem and possible solutions. Students identified peer pressure and parental permissiveness as common reasons why kids turn to gang behavior.

> The kids stay out all night just to hang with their friends on the streets; even on the school nights they stay out all night. Their parents don't even care what their kids do. The parents don't even take care of their own lives as well.
> —Misty Frank

> Parents often get their kids started with drugs or gangs. Not always on purpose, but because their parents do bad things and kids just carry it on because that's what they've seen all their lives.
> —Molly Berntson

> In my eyes, those teenagers either have bad home environments or have been victims of peer pressure.
> —Chennelle Gamblin

> Some problems are that these kids have a strong need to belong, to be part of something they didn't have when they were growing up. Sometimes it gets too late for them to realize that it doesn't help them.
> —Sherrel Scudero

Prompt: Identify Alternative Activities That Might Deter Gang Behavior.

Students mentioned everything from initiating Big Brother/Big Sister programs, to enforcing a stronger discipline, to giving students free passes to the recreation center, to building a skateboard park, to punishing parents who let their kids run wild in the streets, to enforcing the town curfew. The responses to the prompts were encouraging because students were thinking and writing seriously about an issue of concern to them; however, not everyone was participating. Some of my at-risk students were reluctant to engage in the project.

RECEIVING E-MAIL RESPONSES TO WRITING

Students revised, edited, and sent essays and reflections to their peers in classrooms in Arizona. My students began to open up a little more, revealing some of the problems in our community. I decided that if I wanted students to open up, I was going to have to open up, too. I wasn't being completely honest with the students about my fears for them and for myself. So, the next morning I moved desks and chairs to the back of the room and asked my students to sit in a circle in the middle of the carpet. I sat with them and told them how much they meant to me and how scared I was that they might be involved in gang behavior. I asked them to talk about how they felt about this. Students opened up and talked sincerely about the problem. I asked them to talk with their parents, and I talked with my colleagues and professional staff to see what kind of strategies we could form to address the problem. The next day a student came in with a brochure for educators on "Student Violence." This was a beginning.

After we posted our essays about gang behavior online, we received the following response from a student in Arizona, a candid reflection on his involvement in gangs. His teacher received permission from her student (who wished to remain anonymous) to share this with us.

> My dad died when I was four years old. My mom is a very diffi-
> cult person to live with. When I was ten years old I always
> wanted someone to look up to, but my father died. I had nobody
> to turn to so I joined a gang in my school. I grew up with them.
> We became very close. And when I turned thirteen, I was ready to
> be loyal to my gang. I wanted love, attention, aud respect. So I
> got initiated. I was beaten bad! I was in pain for two days. I never
> came home, never went to school, and never had time for my fam-
> ily. Then I started selling drugs. I made about 300–400 dollars a
> week, even more. Now I wonder if the gang loved me, then why
> was I beaten. Gangs are not about honor or respect, it's about
> your life. Gangs is a one way track, there ain't no turning back.
> Think about it.

My students first wanted to know where this person lived; they couldn't believe they were writing to someone who actually had become involved in gangs and was still in school to write about it. Students then embarked on many days of classroom discussion about how this situation could be prevented in Ketchikan and what students, parents, and the school could do to help students faced with a similar situation.

My students put their responses online for the students in Arizona to read and respond to. These exchanges between students at Schoenbar Middle School and in Arizona empowered students to talk honestly about their concerns and needs. A few students in my class who were actually involved in local gangs finally opened up and told us about incidents such as car-jackings and gang initiations that had occurred on our island city.

While students discussed the issues in class and exchanged information in their online correspondence, my colleagues and I were carrying on our own separate discussion online. One of our concerns was the coarseness and vulgarity of the language in the books and materials on gang behavior that we had gathered for our students to read. We discussed censoring the material but thought it would turn students against the project. Other, more minor, problems of this project online were distributing large quantities of reading materials, establishing suitable timelines for varying teaching schedules, handling technical computer problems, and creating substantive contexts in which students could communicate online about the subject. These problems were solved by maintaining flexibility and keeping teacher communication ongoing throughout the project.

OBSERVATIONS OF CHANGES IN STUDENT ATTITUDE AND BEHAVIOR

After reading related texts, reflecting on them, and then writing essays for each other, students collaborated to write other essays to send online to participating schools. Many students formed new opinions and attitudes about gangs. Some wanna-bes and gang members understood better their own involvement. Many kids affected by the gangs articulated their feelings and opinions about gang behavior. I observed that some students were more candid in online discussion than they were in classroom discussion. What students could not express in class discussion sometimes came out as a piece of writing for our online audience of peers. For example, Jeff wrote this poem:

WHY?
JEFF WILLIAMS

"Why do these people stand on the corner smoking?
Why do these people do drugs? Why do they do this?" I ask
    myself.

The people fight for the fun of it.
It's like they like to hurt people.
These people hurt people for no reason.
When I look at them the wrong way they come to me wanting to
    know why.
I say, "I don't know."
So they hit me and hit me just for the wrong look.
These hateful people are just bad 'things.'
They are no human of my kind.
I would never hurt someone just for the wrong look.
I just ask myself,
"Why?"

After Jeff shared this poem with his peers online, I praised him for his candid, careful work. I asked if I could share it with the class. He let me read it and hang it on the wall with poems by other students. Before this project, Jeff did not hang any of his writing on the wall, and I believe the relative anonymity of the online conference helped him discover his thinking on this difficult subject and gain confidence to stand behind what he wrote, a development I noticed in other students as well. By discussing their problems in written form online, they learned to express these ideas in the classroom. Most students became more tolerant of each other, and some teachers became more sympathetic to student frustrations and problems. As a result, I observed that behavior in and out of the classroom improved and student attitudes became more positive.

I'd like to include in this chapter an essay by one student, Jamin Cook, a handsome, healthy, and intelligent eighth-grader. When he walked into my classroom he seemed a model student: always on time for class, diligent, and competent. I never could have guessed that he had doubts about his abilities or confusion about his identity. His writing reminds me that students do care about each other and value and desire personal self-esteem and acceptance.

ONLY IF WE COULD CARE
JAMIN COOK

Many people have told me that the real world is like a vicious dog going for the throat. What makes a dog vicious? Mistreatment, neglect, hunger, loss of care, and hate makes a vicious dog. We make the world that vicious dog when it could be a cute, faithful, loveable puppy.

As a teen, I have looked down the throat of the dog. I see teens like me doing drugs, breaking rules, demoralizing, harassing, and not giving a care for anything anywhere. The temptation to be like the rest of the world is great. Just to be accepted.

The reason we do things of violence is that we don't care. I have always been the one to care about my grades and my future, but there was a gap in my life when I didn't care. I was going through the motions of getting into a new school after moving away from all my friends. I did uncaring things people would never have guessed me to do.

My whole life people say I have been nice, considerate, and confident. Adults say that, not kids. Kids call me brown-noser for getting good grades and always doing what's right. People always said I'm smart, but I'm not, I just do my homework, study, and obey the teachers. One day I quit being a goody-goody because I was snubbed by my classmates and pulled the school fire alarm.

The alarm was rigged with an ink spray so I split knowing I totally messed up an assembly. It felt so good to do something bad after following the rules for so long.

From that day on I became a troublemaker and was accepted by my peers. I was a bully, I cursed, and skipped school. I kept a 4.0 in school, but don't ask me how I did that without caring. I lost all respect for myself and others, and I found I couldn't get along with the teachers very well. People that had trust in me and admired me did no longer. I stopped caring too because not caring was cool.

I started getting invited to a lot of parties by the popular people, girls took a great interest in me and, I got in fights. Life was wonderful without cares! My first drug was alcohol, a wine cooler. It tasted really good but I found out I got drunk very easily. My friend said I danced too close to the girls; I had never danced at all with a girl. My friend said I put on a show of drunken break dancing.

When I woke up with a horrible headache and a stomachache, I cried. What was I doing drunk? Why was I doing this to myself? I looked at myself and asked what good I would do the world drunk. If I wanted to make this world better, which has always been my goal, here I am making it worse. I had to change back to what I was.

From there on it was a fight. I went back to being a goody-goody. My only problem was that I had made many friends that were doing the wrong things. I almost became like them permanently. They kept asking me to try some Joe, which is Oregon slang for dope. To keep myself away from those temptations, I asked myself what good to the world would it be if I did that drug or got in that fight. . . .

I wish people would want this world to be a better place and always ask themselves, "What good will this do to make the world better?" If people cared; if they hoped. I have two sayings that I love. The first one is: "Damn the torpedoes. Full speed ahead." That was said by a captain of a destroyer in the Pacific while he was cornered by three enemy ships. He survived the fight by ramming one, while torpedoing the second, and shooting at the third. He used all three strategies simultaneously and won. We are like that ship surrounded by problems. Instead of only one third of us going for one problem and the other two-thirds doing nothing, we need to all work together to solve it.

My other saying is, "Always try. Always hope. Try to hope, and hope to try." I say this to encourage myself because I have never had anybody really encourage me. When I do good things, some people notice but most don't; they would notice if I didn't do good things because it would affect them for the worse. I try to encourage my friends and other teens but they don't take it.

I had no idea that Jamin had such thoughts until he opened up in this writing project and began to communicate with his peers. Other students, I found out, had doubts, too. For example, some students think picking on other students is not abusive because they have observed it so often in the school setting. After many discussions with my classes, students finally realized that incessant picking on students can amount to a kind of gang behavior. Students now have some "hope" to do something about it. It might not change situations radically or immediately, but it will change how the students feel about themselves and the people abusing them.

In their essays, students pointed out that violence sometimes results from students' losing their self-esteem and hope. For example, Chris Cumings wrote a paper that shows the concern of most of my students:

SCHOOL VIOLENCE
CHRIS CUMINGS

I think that we have a terrible problem on our hands. School violence has gotten out of control. It seems like every other day I turn on the news and another act of violence was committed at a school. I have a few ideas on why so many kids have turned to violence and few ways to prevent it.

Statistics show that the average child who watches two to three hours of television a day will see 6,000 murders and 20,000 acts of violence by the time they graduate from high school. That does not count violence in movies. Many computer games also have a lot of blood and killing. The solution to this is not to regulate television and computer games. That would be a violation of the First Amendment. Parents should take more interest in what their kids are watching and playing. In the most recent school tragedy, the killers looked up instructions and built pipe bombs in their very own home, and their parents say they didn't even know. This serious tragedy could have been prevented if parents had paid attention to what their children were doing.

The Internet is a great thing, but it is no help in the fight against school violence. Children have much more access to stuff that they never could have laid eyes on ten years ago. Once again simply sticking a chip in your computer will not prevent kids from accessing the information they want. Parents should closely monitor what their kids do on the computer.

Something needs to be done at the school level too. The reason for the Colorado shooting was that the suspects were made fun of. If school authorities would have stepped in sooner and found a solution to this problem, once again, a serious tragedy would have not happened. One solution would be for the government to allocate money for every school in the nation to install metal detectors. Those would take a lot of time and money, but it would be well worth it. That alone won't stop the problem, though. If someone wants to shoot everyone in school, a metal detector won't stop them. So, the problem must be stopped before it starts.

Everyday when I go to school I look for students who appear to be out to get someone or something. I see so many people who fit that description that it scares me. If someone would just take time to talk to these kids and find out what's wrong, a tragedy in waiting could be prevented.

REACHING ALL THE STUDENTS

Students like Jamin and Chris who had done well in school were more likely to open up and write about the topic than students who were at risk of being involved in violent or gang-related behavior. Steven Doran was a very bright student but had refused to work in school. He influenced other students in the class to heckle the teachers and refuse to work. Since I don't believe in suspension, I try to reason with each troubled student separately. I had discussed Steven's attitude with him and the need to change it. I talked with my team members in school about moving Steven into a group of successful students, thinking he would become positively influenced. It was a gamble that didn't pay off. He always sat in the back and rarely joined group work. He rarely spoke out in class. He avoided eye contact with me. His grades slipped lower and lower.

During the middle of our gang-violence study, something got to Steven; he seemed to want to say something—but no, he wasn't about to open up to his classmates. I told Steven I wanted to know what was going on, and I asked him to write. He wanted to know if he could use "real words" instead of "school words." I told him to use whatever words he needed. I told him I was the only person who would read it. (After I read his paper, I asked him if I could publish it, explaining that we would need a parental release. He agreed and had his parents sign the release.) The first paper he wrote shows his need to recognize that someone cares and then have that someone give him guidance in his actions. He comes off as tough, as though he doesn't care anymore, but the truth is that he does care and wants to change his life. This is the first paper he wrote for me:

> Parents don't realize how they are raising kids, letting them hang out, do drugs, run around, have no role models—as some people would say—being brought up in the 'hood,' or raised on the streets. Kids who don't have parents around some or all the time, get the wrong idea about things. When parents find out they need to get their kids under control, it's too late. Nothing will work!
>
> If kids grow up as fighters, they'll stay fighters. My friends and I don't care anymore if we get in an argument with someone, get in a fight, a brawl, do drugs, or even if we get arrested.
>
> I can think of examples of all of these things happening to me. But we were brought up in a way that I don't care! No one or nothing scares me. If someone bigger than me tries to jump me, at least I have friends that will help, and we'll go down fighting.
>
> We call each other hard ass when we win a fight or cuss all the time. But you know what? Our parents don't give a damn!
>
> A bunch of my friends and I were sitting at the bowling alley just talking about what we were going to do. Just about that time a

yellow truck pulled up and about 15 people jumped out of the back. One of them came up and pushed my friend and said, "Why have you been talkin' shit!" So they got in a fight and another guy from the truck pulled out a knife, so all of us jumped in.

There were people getting hit with sticks, getting stabbed, and some had their heads smashed on the pavement. All of us walked away thinking, Oh well, just another day.

Pulling knives on people, getting our heads bashed into pavement, getting stabbed in the back, 10 people on one, getting smacked over the head with a wooden dowel are situations that happen every week. I've done all of these or had them done to me. The violence in this town is getting worse. People just have to know where to look for the fight. I see two to four fights a week. I saw one person get stabbed in the eye. He almost died. We don't care what happens anymore. We do what we do even though our love is towards family and friends. Our parents see us bleeding all over from the head and first they ask if we were hurt. Most will say, "Hell No!" They don't care but we don't either. We stand up to an adult. We have friends that will help us out in a fight and we always help them.

I was stunned reading Steven's paper. I immediately sat down with him to discuss it. "Is this real?" I asked. It was hard for me to admit that my students could be involved in such things. I asked him if others at school knew about this, and he nodded his head. I asked Steven if he would share his essay with the class. No, he didn't think that a good idea. But in time he did share it. I then asked if he had ever talked with a counselor, and he said he was seeing one regularly. I asked him if we could put his essay online for our partners in Arizona to respond to. I told him I was writing a chapter on violence and gangs and asked if he would contribute his writing to it to help teachers understand where kids are coming from. He seemed excited about helping out. During his class period, various people shared their feelings about themselves. Steven had difficulty believing that these classmates, the popular students who were athletes or on the student council, could have low self-esteem as he did.

A week later, Steven ran into my room with another piece of writing. The following piece reveals that he really did care more than his tough exterior would allow. I believe the writing process led him to self-discovery, examination of his actions, and a willingness to inform the community of students at our school. He read this piece in class the next day.

I think anything could happen anywhere. A lot of teens and kids are capable of many different things. I think it just depends on what kind of family and friends they have and how they get treated. I feel really bad about what has happened in the past few years. It's a stupid way to express feelings. If they had really good friends they could talk problems out with someone.

I don't feel great about myself; I mean I want to live with my mom and brother in a cool house with no problems or conflicts. It would be better for me if I applied myself even a little more to school and get a graduation. My cousin Chris has been a big influence in my life. He was senior class president and a 4.0 student. In four weeks he's graduating as a film artist from college. He works for Ketchikan Daily News in the summer filming events around town. And my friends are always there for me when I need them to talk things out and solve things. Don't forget fun every now and then.

Talk things out. Don't get in trouble or hurt for something that isn't worth it. Resolve problems. Don't resort to violence or killing.

A couple of weeks later I heard a rumor at school that a knifing was planned behind the mall and that they were going after Steven. I ran to his locker and asked him what he was going to do about it. He said he would probably stay with his cousin on his boat for the night. "Why don't you go home?" I asked. No answer. "Do you realize what could happen if you go to that fight? People could get seriously hurt or killed. Do you want to be responsible for that? Think about the discussions we've had about choices. What are you going to do?" He promised me he would not go to the mall. I told him I was going to call the police and tell them what was going to happen. I told him to call me if he needed help.

The last day of school Steven slipped me a note and thanked me for helping and caring so much about what happened to him. He told me about his plans to get a job for the summer. He said he was looking forward to seeing me at Ketchikan High School next year, where I was transferring. I ran into him on the street a couple of weeks ago and he gave me the thumbs up when I asked him how things were going. However, Steven remains an ongoing concern of mine.

STUDENT SOLUTIONS TO GANG PROBLEMS

The most successful part of this project was the students' online collaboration, which often directed our classroom discussions. Students became familiar with their online audience by discussing a piece of literature based on gang behavior. Once trust was established, important changes took place. Superficial, sensationalized discussion evolved into careful consideration of real issues of vital concern to my students: peer intimidation, illegal behavior, the lure of gangs, alienation from family and friends, gang and date rape, and feelings of powerlessness. After students identified and articulated the problems, they began to look for solutions. Erin Beasley wrote the following:

> Some things that have happened to me that made me feel bad about myself are when I make fun of or pick on people. The way it used to be was that I felt better when I hurt other people, and I didn't realize it. When my peers started bringing it to my attention in this project, I thought about ways I could change, like complimenting people, smiling more, trying to look at the good side of things, and not judging people. I began thinking about how people determine who is "different." Maybe people I think are different, think I am different.

Students like Erin began spontaneously to monitor one another's speech, pointing out inappropriate and hateful language. They became advocates for maintaining a constructive, positive manner toward one another. Erin and many of her classmates at Schoenbar Middle School became convinced that our school community should do something about the habitual and cruel teasing of students that occurs in schools to prevent experiencing a tragedy such as happened in the communities of Bethel, Alaska, and Littleton, Colorado.

AT THE CENTER OF THE CURRICULUM: WRITING FOR THE COMMUNITY

Throughout the project, my colleagues online and I wondered what we were stirring up. Students confided illegal acts, rape, and theft. One of the teachers online received a student journal that indicated the student was involved in felonious gang behavior. She was desperate to know about her legal obligations. Initially, she did not feel comfortable going to her administrator about the problem, so she wrote to me online; I counseled her, and she decided to inform her principal about the student's journal. I, too, sought help from my colleagues online and from my school's counselor. At times, I was scared, frustrated, or confused about my role. This project opened up communication—among students, teachers, parents, police, and counselors—about topics of concern that had previously gone unexamined. Students now view me as a more sympathetic teacher, but my role and my relationship to them are more complex.

Now as I think about educational reform, I realize that I did what Jack Sasser had recommended in that first inservice that got me thinking about how to reform my classroom. At first, I didn't see how one could reform curriculum when social problems disrupt the classroom to the extent that students cannot learn. The success of this project was built on placing the social problems at the center of the curriculum. I altered my lesson plans to address problems troubling students, and in doing so we also addressed most of the Alaska State Standards because we engaged students' higher-level thinking skills for problem solving. We integrated technology. Most important, students wrote personally and persuasively for a community of peers in their school and online about issues of vital concern to all, and problems were identified, some of which were solved. A variety of communities participated and intersected through writing for the community: Students, teachers, parents, police officers, school administration, and an online community of students and teachers used communication to address the topics, and students discovered ways to improve our community.

REFERENCES

Cormier, R. (1974). *The chocolate war*. New York: Dell.
Rodriguez, L. J. (1994). *Always running: La vida loca, gang days in L. A.* New York: Simon & Schuster.
Shakur, S. (1994). *Monster: The autobiography of an L.A. gang member*. New York: Penguin.

Chapter 9

BEYOND E-MAIL

Writing and Publishing for the Cybernet Community—A Scenario

Susan L. Miera

Pojoaque High School, located in northern New Mexico, population 634, grades 9 through 12, is situated some 15 miles north of the state capital, Santa Fe, at a crossroads in an agricultural valley, one way leading to Los Alamos and the other to Española and Taos. The school's population represents the community at large: 60% Hispanic, 20% Anglo, 19% predominately Pueblo Indian, and 1% other. Like many rural communities, Pojoaque is a bedroom community from which its inhabitants drive the 15 to 20 miles each morning to work at Los Alamos National Laboratory, at state government jobs in Santa Fe, or at retail stores in Española. Many residents also drive to nearby destinations to work in the tourist industry, which continues to thrive in New Mexico. In recent years Indian gaming has also employed members of the community. For the most part, then, the daytime population of Pojoaque dwindles to students, school employees, and retirees.

Years ago, when students graduated from Pojoaque Valley schools, they could rely on finding jobs in Los Alamos or Santa Fe or depend on realistic prospects of inheriting land for their own homes in the valley. The current generation can no longer depend on an agricultural livelihood, however, because even the large tracts of family land have been subdivided to their limits. Los Alamos National Laboratory has drastically cut back on current personnel and on new hiring. Because

Writing to Make a Difference. Copyright © 2001 by Teachers College, Columbia University. All rights reserved. ISBN 0-8077-4186-8 (paper), 0-8077-4187-6 (cloth). Prior to photocopying items for classroom use, please contact the Copyright Clearance Center, Customer Service, 222 Rosewood Drive, Danvers, MA, 01923, USA, telephone (508) 750-8400.

New Mexico is one of the poorest states in the nation, state government jobs are not as readily available as they once were. The skyrocketing cost of living, limited good-paying jobs in the immediate vicinity, and continuous rises in the cost of property and property taxes have forced employees to stay in jobs longer than they have in recent decades. These perennial problems of making a living are common to many rural communities these days.

Like schools in many rural communities, those in Pojoaque Valley are the center of community activity, of progressive learning, and of sustained educational reform. Student friendships spawn family friendships and augment family bonds; sports activities and other extracurricular competitions draw members of the entire community to cheer on their nearest and dearest. It is in this atmosphere of warmth and friendship that the community of Pojoaque hopes to improve its educational and economic future.

The concept of writing for the community has usually referred to communication contexts in which writing serves a local physical community. Brochures, fliers, forms, and other kinds of written products (and oral forums) serve to inform local audiences of vital concerns, advertise local activities, advocate local change, or build local consensus through collaborative research. Typically, youngsters involved in such projects work face to face with each other and members of their community to research a community issue, organize the information, field-test the document, revise it, and report it. Usually these activities are done within the local community. But technology has effectively changed this local notion of writing for the community for me and my students at Pojoaque High School. Our recent writing for the community projects have begun to include cyberspace communities whose members may never physically meet.

In networked communities, communication sustains cohesion. This is also true in local geographic communities. In addition, geographic communities usually share cultural assumptions, language conventions, and sometimes even a common physical appearance, which engender familiarity and trust in the community. Networked communities of students, however, must create these qualities, and I have found that establishing nonthreatening personal dialogues among students in such communities helps them work together smoothly and efficiently. These dialogues work best, in my experience, if they are guided by teachers who have themselves developed a trusting relationship. As a member of the Bread Loaf Teacher Network (BLTN), I have many colleagues who teach English in far-flung places and who are willing to create communities of learners online. I know these teachers well; we have a common educational experience at the Bread Loaf School of English, and so we are able to model for our students how to communicate and collaborate online to get work done.

I teach one particular class, Telecommunications/Editing and Publishing, in which students have been very successful in creating networked communities of collaborators. When students at Pojoaque High School sign up for this class, the first thing I tell them is that it is not an Internet class.

"So what is it?" they ask.

I tell them the class provides a publishing service for clients (students and teachers) in classrooms across the country. Our focus on using language and publishing documents that serve real clients transforms my students from passive observers in the classroom to active collaborators, allowing them to create and participate in a working community as real contributors. Most important, it is a writing class with many authentic audiences.

The class usually fills up within the first half-hour of registration. I'd like to think that my reputation as an innovative, fun teacher attracts students in droves. But although I do have good rapport with students, their motivations for taking the class have much more to do with the opportunity students envision in working with other students.

When I began teaching this class 4 years ago, we had a shortage of technology and students had to share computers with other students, sometimes as many as four students per machine. Solving logistical problems like this often required some creative thinking and collaboration by me and my students, but the class was successful, even with its great limitations, and has remained successful as we have upgraded our technology. Currently, each student has access to a computer on a daily basis.

The allure of the words *computers* and *technology* draws students to the course. I have no scientific evidence to support this hunch, but I've often observed that students work harder and accomplish more when they have access to state-of-the-art technology. Some students who refuse to pick up a book will read screen after screen of illuminated 12-point font. Students will analyze with delight a piece of literature introduced online, yet I must beg those same students to read the same text in a paperback or an anthology.

I don't quite understand the seductive effect of computers, but I'm very grateful for it, because each year students seem eager to communicate using technology, and along the way, I have observed them become better writers in the service of our "clients," other students and teachers in the Bread Loaf Teacher Network.

KNOWING OUR LIMITATIONS AND BUILDING OUR SKILLS

Taking the Telecommunications/Editing and Publishing class earns juniors and seniors credit for English III, English IV, or Communications Skills in the class. District policy requires that students must pass English I before they are allowed to enroll in any higher-level English course. Other than those stipulations, there are no prerequisites for enrollment. Understandably, students who enroll bring various levels of skills, so each year begins with an assessment. To meet our three goals—telecommunicating, writing, and editing—we must ascertain our strengths and weaknesses.

Initially, assignments are threefold. Each part leads students through the process necessary to write and publish online with peer collaborators in remote schools:

1. Students Learn Writing and Editing Skills

Experience has taught me that grammar and usage skills are acquired and maintained through practice. For at least the first 9 weeks of class, students participate in an intensive writing workshop focusing on their own writing and correct usage and grammar. They learn first to see their own mistakes, to correct them in their own writing, and then to correct them in other people's writing. Weekly, I post these assignments online to my students; they download them, complete them, and return them to me electronically. Thus, in the process of improving the mechanics in their own writing, they also gain the rudiments of manipulating text online.

2. Students Learn to Access a Telecommunications Network

As associates of the BLTN, consisting of some 200 rural teachers affiliated with Bread Loaf School of English at Middlebury College, Vermont, my students and I use BreadNet, a computer conferencing network for Bread Loaf alumni, students, and faculty. With each assignment, students get practice in using the telecommunications network, learning the importance of meeting deadlines, and improving their writing skills. As part of this writing process, students also learn the protocol and etiquette for responding online to writing prompts, using critical thinking skills, collaborating with a cyberpal, and learning the writing process as they correspond with others.[1]

3. Students Learn Desktop Publishing Skills

To prepare students to design layouts for our online clients, I require students each week to place one of their own writing assignments into a desktop publishing application (Adobe PageMaker 6.5). Then they print out a hard copy that will be included in an anthology of their work. Moreover, when writing is workshopped in an electronic medium, it is usually framed by personal messages, so students also learn to edit out personal information and correspondence that should not appear in the hard-copy publication. This gives students practice in basic and advanced computer and publishing skills. They also learn basic elements of design and how to use graphics. This practice with their own writing familiarizes my students with the entire process of working with a client through all stages of writing: generating, revising, editing, designing, laying out, proofreading, and publishing.

PUTTING IT ALL TOGETHER

Once students learn the process, they are ready to "contract" with other classrooms in the network. Our "client/contractor" relationship is usually effective because I work in a small, closed community. Most of the teachers in the BLTN community share common learning experiences and beliefs based on our shared experience at Bread Loaf. My students and I are collaborating with people we know. Working with the students of teachers I know personally and with whom I share some pedagogical philosophy helps our students have a positive experience with a minimum of misunderstanding about expectations. I doubt the outcome would be as successful working with total strangers on the Internet, although a greater emphasis on building a trusting collaborative environment at the outset would help ensure success. The following steps lead to a successful online publication:

1. Send Out a Query

Students e-mail a letter to a general bulletin board in the BLTN community. In the letter, they announce the services they can offer. As a free service, they offer to act as student mentors in writing skills, to respond to creative writing pieces, to assist students in editing their writing for usage and grammar, and to publish literary anthologies of writing. In their letter of solicitation, students also inform anyone interested that jobs will be completed on a "first-come-first-served" basis and that because of financial constraints, only one photo-ready copy and one bound copy will be mailed to classrooms requesting the publication of anthologies. Students ask that responses to their query be done through e-mail so that a record of receipt can be accurately recorded.

2. Brainstorming and Estimating

I form three groups of students in my class. As replies to the query letter are received, we distribute them to groups on a rotating basis. When they receive a response to a query, members of each group look at the request, brainstorm about possible publication ideas, assess the amount of work required, and determine a reasonable timeline for completion of the project. With these ideas in mind, the group replies to the querying classroom and defines the parameters for the job. The partner classroom then has the option of accepting, rejecting, or negotiating the deadlines and details with the understanding that evaluations will be ongoing throughout the exchange and that adjustments can be made. The class quits accepting new client work 6 weeks before the end of our schoolyear to ensure that they can finish all the contracts.

3. Deadlines

Once client and contractors agree on parameters, we work to meet the deadlines. Students on both sides learn that if an emergency arises and a deadline cannot be met, then an explanation is required online at least 24 hours prior to the deadline. If this happens, we negotiate an alternative deadline, and it is posted with an explanation for the delay. Hardcopy anthologies are sent out in time for printing on the other end. Final deadlines are agreed upon before beginning a job.

A typical exchange from query to publication follows.

PLANNING AND PARTICIPATING IN AN E-MAIL EXCHANGE

To ensure a successful experience for   the client class, I usually do a lot of planning with t   \cher well in advance of the actual project. A typic.   ing poetry that focused on "sense of place/sense of self" wa   1 to us in the summer of 1998 by Renee Evans, a teacher at C   High School in Crownpoint, New Mexico. Renee's students ar\   .tly Navajo and their first language is Navajo, whereas Poj\   idents are predominantly Hispanic, with only 19% of the stu\   being Native American Pueblo. During the summer, Renee and I planned a computer conference writing project to involve her students and my Native American Literature class in Pojoaque. This project led to the writing of poetry. My Telecommunications/Editing and Publishing class was contracted to edit and publish the final anthology of our students' poems.

Because my Native American Literature class was a co-client with Renee Evans's class and my Telecommunications/Editing and Publishing class was the contractor, I had a dual role from the inception of the project. In a typical place-based physical community this relationship would be harder to duplicate, but online dialogue enables boundaries to be eliminated, and roles of contractor and client are often mixed in cyberspace communities.

What follows are Renee's initial planning ideas and a number of short correspondences that led to our common reading and our writing and publishing an anthology. (All planning was done via BreadNet, but it could have been done through other e-mail systems, such as Eudora.) It's difficult for two remote classrooms to begin working with each other unless the teachers have laid some of the necessary groundwork. Each of my projects online with other teachers and their students usually involves some logistical planning like this:

SUBJECT: EXCHANGE IDEAS

Susan: . . . How about a personal memoir exchange? Or sense of place poetry? That might work. Or a cultural exchange focusing on descriptive essays of fact rather than on storytelling. What makes one Navajo, Pueblo, Hispanic, etc.? How would you define yourself in your own place? I was thinking that since we are so close to each other, we should consider having our classes meet in Albuquerque or Farmington—something to think about. Okay, what now???
—Renee

SUBJECT: EXCHANGE?

Hi Susan: Sorry, I've been in the middle of finals, but I'm back. Did you find my note? It may have been sent to China as I understand is common:-)

Poetry of place sounds like a great start. Do you have some specific texts you have in mind? I will be on the lookout when I get home. And then will we have the students write their own poetry?

I look forward to hashing this out in more detail over the next couple of weeks. It is important to note that I won't be back on line until the 12th or 13th when I arrive home. If you need to reach me I'll be able to access hotmail.
—Renee

Subject: Finding Self

Susan: Here's a recap on our project ideas. We want our students to share their own culture as an avenue to finding themselves. We will start with basic introductions on email, which will be followed with responses, and students will move into an exchange of personal memoirs, "sense of place" poetry, or cultural, descriptive essays of fact. What makes one Navajo, Pueblo, Hispanic, etc.? Students will define themselves through studying concepts of place. Students will also study creation or emergence myths. Then we will look at Native American literature by Luci Tapahonso, and students will share their responses to the literature with each other.

I have a class called NMHSCE (pronounced nimskie). Basically, it is a class for students who have failed English or the New Mexico test. One thread that was consistent among them last year is that they all spoke fluent Navajo and are limited English proficiency. This leads me to believe that your students as an authentic audience would be very useful to them.

I plan to write letters to parents and administrators. I also plan to write a press release for the district newsletter and the local newspaper.
—Renee

I include Renee's planning messages to show the kind of attention to planning that is necessary for a successful online writing project involving remote classrooms. Putting students on the Internet doesn't free the teacher from planning. In fact, online collaboration probably increases the amount of planning a teacher must initially invest in classes. It also becomes necessary for teachers to establish a working relationship between themselves. In essence, when a colleague and I engage in such networked projects, I participate in his or her classroom and he or she participates in mine. Knowing one another's differences and similarities in teaching styles helps us establish and maintain understanding and trust between ourselves and among our students.

When students know they have a safe forum in which to post their writing and receive responses to it from peers, they can begin to take risks as writers, stretching their limits and forging a writing community online. The following examples illustrate the process.

The initial message is often introductory in nature. Embedded in the message is a creative piece of writing based on a predetermined theme, in this case "Finding Self." Valerie's poem included in her introductory note below to a Crownpoint student is modeled after N. Scott Momaday's poem "Delight Song."

> Dear Crownpoint Student,
>   Hi my name is Valerie Lujan. I'm 16 years old and I live in Pojoaque. My interests are drawing and I love just having fun. So what are your interests? Are you involved in any extra curricular activities? Our assignment for this week was to write our own delight song. Here's mine. Please respond.
>
> I am the sun in the bright sky
> I am the elk roaming across the land
> I am the rainbow that stretches across the earth
> I am the shadow that follows a child
> I am the eyes you feel watching you
> I am the first bright star in the sky
> I am one of a kind
>
> I am the thunder in the sky
> I am the smile on your face
> I am an eagle in the sky
> I am a world of different colors
> I am the peacefulness in the forest
> I am the love in his eyes
> I am the tenderness in his heart
> I am the whole dream of these things
>
> You see, I am alive
> I stand in good relation to the earth
> I stand in good relation to the gods
> I stand in good relation to all that is beautiful
> I stand in good relation to my friends and family
> You see, I am alive, I am alive

Although the initial messages may be a bit formal and staid, as student cyberpals get to know one another online and through their poetry, their writing becomes more articulate and their messages more speculative. The exchange between Crownpoint High School and Pojoaque High School on "Finding Self" had a rotation of four poems and messages. As just mentioned, the first poem was a "Delight Song" of introduction. This first round was followed by a hand poem, a childhood poem, and a connection poem. Some examples follow.

In the next example, one can see that the idea of community began to build after the initial introductory messages. Crownpoint student Shawn begins her exchange with Aldo in Pojoaque with personal correspondence. Her messages clearly indicate her understanding of the community's developing sense of shared concerns regarding the quality of the writing. Note the text that I've made italic here and in later examples:

> Hi there, Aldo. *I am new in this group. I was in another group, but the person I was writing to isn't in school anymore, so my teacher put me in this group.* Well first of all I would like to introduce myself and say a few things about myself. My name is Shawn Enrico (female), I am a freshmen only up to second semester and I am 16 years old. My hobbies are playing volleyball, reading books, or just listening to music.
>
> What nationality are you? Do you know where Crownpoint is? How big is your school? Where is your school at? We never heard of your school. Do you know how to speak Spanish? We're learning. Tell us more about yourself. *Well, here are our hand poems. Tell us what you think about them. We enjoyed your poem. We liked the way you used the words in your poem. Seems like you have done many things with your hands. It was a great poem.*

THESE HANDS
BY SHAWN ENRICO

With these hands I have held
 a dying, poor horse.
With these hands I have touched
 my nephews and nieces.
With these hands I have made
 a log cabin on the living earth.
With these hands I have worked
 a run down vehicle.
With these hands I have learned to kill
 an elk and a deer.
These hands are the strength of my spirit.
These hands are the warriors to my enemies.
These hands are the limitations of myself and everything.
These hands grow old, weak, and feel
 unfamiliar walls

As they try to reach out to find
the world I used to know and trust.

In the following two examples, the idea of writing for a community of writers is particularly evident. By this time students from Crownpoint and Pojoaque had become more open with one another, and the sense of community is so strong in these notes that a reader not knowing these students would never know that they were more than 200 miles apart and had never met except through online correspondence.

Because of her personal trust in her partner, Yolanda Charley from Crownpoint could speak honestly about herself in her poem "She Was a Little Girl." Likewise, her partner Sam Hena from Pojoaque could become introspective about his own personal connections to past, present, and future in his "connection poem." It is clear that writing in an online community gives students purpose in their writing. Again, note words I've placed in italics: First, I present Yolanda's note to Sam, written collaboratively with her classmate Orlanda.

November 12, 1998
Dear Sam:
   Hey, 's up? So how are you doing? We're doing fine as well. *We received your poem and we both thought it was cool. I, Yolanda, like the part where it says, "A little boy with two dirty hands and his hair full of sand coming home from the hills." I, Orlanda, like the part where it said, "Walking along dirt paths stomping on broken glass and splashing through the clear river water."*
   Wow! You're a SENIOR and all this time we were writing to you we thought you were a freshmen. It seems as if everyone wants to go into the military nowadays. You are right they do rule. Why is it that you're taking English 9 while you're a senior? Is it that you didn't pass that class?
   So, how do you like responding back to us? We like responding back to you a lot. We enjoy every bit of it. The only thing about it is that sometime we don't have enough news. Also, we get to know other students we have never heard of and get to know them.
   What events do you like in track? Our teacher, Ms. Evans, has not given us another poem to write about so our letter won't be long enough. I guess this is all the news we have for now. Until next time. *We both like to hear from you soon.* Laterz!

Orlanda Martin and Yolanda Charley

She Was a Little Girl

She was a little girl
with long tangled pony-tail
in a very joyful mood.
A lightning strike
as bright as her.
Shattered glasses, water puddles,
and leaves of all colors
to show that now it is fall.
Under the clear blue sky
there she lies
in the cornfield.
The night so clear that
it shines like a beam of light,
the stars glowing,
and the moon as bright as gold.
Shooting stars falling
and gliding away
into the clear blue sky.

Sam responded with this note:

Dear Yolanda and Orlanda,
    What's going on? I'm doing good. *I read both of your poems
and thought that they were awesome. I like the lines "The night
so clear that it shines like a beam of light, the stars glowing, and
the moon as bright as gold." That sounds cool and you get a cool
vision of what it looks like. I also like the line: " . . . as she crawls
desperately for the cookie jar she's as happy as a big clown in a
circus."* I'm not taking English 9. I'm taking English 4. It's my
last requirement. *This is cool, writing to people who we never
met, and getting to know them.* Do you have the Internet at
home? If you do, let me know and we can get to know each
others a little better.
    Here is my poem:

Connection Poem

My Saya was strong
She survived the great flu

She mourned the death of her loved ones
And moved on
And achieved many goals.

Grandmother,
Hands working magic
On the oak loom
Weaving a belt of life
And teaching me
About myself.

Birds chirping in the trees
Cool water splashing
Around my knees
Roar of thunder in the sky
Flash of lightning sparks my eye
Today is a good day to die.

They will always be with me
Watching over me
Laughing at me
And pitying me
Giving me the strength
to overcome.

The final student example of the "Finding Self" electronic exchange is a poem by Aldo from Pojoaque and a personal response from Kristen in Crownpoint to Aldo. Kristen's message speaks directly of the trust and sense of community they established online. Her writing and Aldo's flourished in this forum, drawing on the energy that this authentic audience provided. Here's Aldo's poem:

My father had courage
He was always there when we needed him
He would give us everything we wanted
He would keep us satisfied
He was my role model growing up
He made me what I am today.

My uncle is very important to me
He created something for the family
It would help us constantly

He sweat and sweat until he got tired
He had finished what he had worked hard for
He had built a garage

I am on the couch
Watching TV with my family
I get up cause I am tired
I enjoy being myself
Cause I am with the people I love
With the people I grew up with

Pieces of my family
We all finish what we start
My father my uncle and I are all of one people
If we don't finish what we start It will never get done
We are all important
Important in our own ways

And here is Kristin's response to Aldo:

Dear Aldo,
I'm glad you liked my poem. I hope that was your honest opinion. Just kidding. *I trust you. Your poem was pretty cool, it tells a lot about who you are. I liked the ending where you put everything together. Especially the line where you said, "We all finish what we start."*
Yeah, my dad is a loving father, he would do anything for his kids. Well, beside school, life here isn't good. There are no malls, no arcades, no cool places to hang out. I've been told I'm very artistic, but like my poems I don't believe so.
Anyway, yeah, I have worked with clay, it's fun.
So what are your plans for Christmas? Do you have family in Mexico? When did you come to America? All I want to do for Christmas is spend time with my boyfriend. Well, we will write again soon. Later!

Sincerely,
Kristin

At the end of the writing exchange between Crownpoint and Pojoaque, Renee and I wanted to bring the electronic exchange to a successful close. The following e-mail correspondence shows that collaboration in publishing the work of networked communities presents teachers and students with numerous daily decisions to make, just as real work does. When teachers expect students to produce real work for clients, it's important that both parties be in continual communication and agreement about the work being done. The following examples show that teachers continue to build their own sense of place in and around those of their students.

> Renee: I thought the last poem was supposed to be one of our own format. My students wrote connection poems modeled after Rex Jim's poem. I have two desktop publishing students beginning work on the anthology. I'll need your last poems by Monday or Tuesday following Thanksgiving along with your "About the Authors" pieces. We're shooting for a Dec. 10 deadline date for publication. We will send you one photo-ready copy and one bound copy at that time. I can't promise that any late poems will be included, but we'll do the best we can to accommodate those.
>   —Susan

> Dear Renee: I wasn't able to get on line today because of a major power outage at school. Consequently, my two DTP students couldn't get on line today, so I can't promise that you'll actually receive your anthology by Friday, but I really am trying to get it to you before break. If not, it will be sitting on your desk when you return after Christmas. When is your last day, anyway? Ours is the 18th. It's looking great, though. You'll be happy with it. Send me the address to the high school, okay? We need to revamp for January, too. I'm losing a lot of students! Let's talk. Hasta.
>   —Susan

> Dear Renee—
>   I sent the anthology out today. Sorry I never got around to calling you over the holidays. It turned into one of those vacations where I never found time for myself. I'll be in touch as soon as we return. Hope your vacation was more restful than mine. Hasta.
>   —Susan

All of the included messages are evidence that electronic exchanges do indeed bring validity to student writing. When students write to real audiences, they are more insightful about literature and take time to respond in articulate ways.

EVALUATION AND REFLECTION

In some writing for the community projects, a "final" copy would be field-tested and fine-tuned before distribution to the general public. In an electronic writing for the community project, however, the hard-copy publication is more likely to be the final copy, which is published only for participants as a culmination of the project. The reflective process enables members of the community to assess their skills, to assess the importance of writing for and within a community, and to set a foundation for future writing for the community exchanges.

Although reflections do not necessarily need to be exchanged, participating teachers and students might ask themselves the following questions so they can build on their experiences during future work online that links students in a writing community. What did each side learn from the experience? What could have been changed for the better? Students' answers to such questions inform how contributing to a community is a powerful experience in problem solving, learning about technology, developing a work ethic with communication skills, and learning about one's capabilities.

Upon completion of the exchange between Crownpoint and Pojoaque, Elena Talache, a senior, wrote:

> Helping to create this anthology helped me in many ways. When I was working on it, I was able to experiment with page layouts and text style to create something that I would like to read and, hopefully, other people would like to read also. Secondly, I was able to experiment with graphics and try to find the ones that were most appropriate for the page that it would appear on. Lastly, working under a deadline made me realize how much time and energy it takes to create something publishable.
>
> Overall, I enjoyed working on the anthology. When we had unforeseen problems occur, we had some stress, but that only helped to motivate us to finish our project. After this experience, I wouldn't mind working on another anthology.

Co-publisher Deann Martinez, also a senior at Pojoaque, was more practical in her assessment of the project. She wrote:

> My reflections on doing the anthology were a bit confusing at first. I mean, it was hard for me the first few times because I was new at using the procedures used for this project. But luckily, I had Elena next to me helping me out. That made me understand

more of what I was doing. During the whole project I enjoyed working on it and really liked getting to know what it is like to meet a deadline.

Although both girls were honest in their reflective assessments of the project as a whole, both reflections fall short of the overall message of the publication. In their introduction to the anthology, these students wrote:

> *Finding Self* is a compilation of poetry written by student authors to gain better understanding of themselves. The students from Crownpoint High School and Pojoaque High School wrote poetry spinning off the idea that one can understand themselves better through poetry. Through the poetry the students wrote, they gained a better understanding of themselves. In the "Little Boy/Little Girl" poetry, the authors reminisced about their times as young children and how they saw their world through young children's eyes. The "hands" poetry touched on the authors' influence from their physical surroundings, and in the poetry with the theme of delight, the authors found joy in their everyday environment. Finally, the poems with the "connections" theme tried to connect the ideas of the past, the present, and the future for each of the authors.

The opportunities for students in electronic writing communities are quickly opening up and evolving. Adolescent students are fascinated with the idea of making friends, learning from people who live in different places, establishing a working relationship based in the curriculum, and collaborating on texts. Adding the dimensions of analysis, reflection, and publication to networked communities of writers gives students a deeper view of who they are and how they can contribute to the increasingly more complex global community. They also become better writers, editors, and users of technology to produce professional documents of high quality for the community.

NOTE

1. Though BreadNet is our medium for communication, most schools do not have access to a conference-based network. The process can be somewhat duplicated using other conferencing-based systems.

Chapter 10

ASKING THE HARD QUESTIONS

Writing About Environmental Risks for Rural Communities

Janet Atkins

At a recent gathering of friends, I was accused of having the *Welcome Back, Kotter* syndrome because I had returned to my high school alma mater to teach. Like Mr. Kotter in the TV sitcom, I went off to college and, after marrying, returned to my hometown to teach secondary English. I remained in that position for 15 years, teaching in the same classroom that was once my tenth-grade homeroom. Unlike Mr. Kotter's community, however, my community was rural; nonetheless, I discovered that issues particular to both settings could have global implications. One such issue was how young people feel about their environment.

I remember now that as high school students each of my classmates and I received yearly questionnaires asking if our parents were employed by the Savannah River Plant, previously known by locals as the bomb plant, now known as the Savannah River Site (SRS). The questionnaire card was always rather mysterious, just like the site itself, which stationed guards at the entrance to its forested acres that no one but employees with badges could enter. Everyone knew that the SRS produced bombs that were used for mass destruction, even though we were told they were produced to protect our country from communist aggression. Because of the many jobs afforded by the site, public outcry was minimal; people just really didn't want to know what truly happened at the bomb plant.

Writing to Make a Difference. Copyright © 2001 by Teachers College, Columbia University. All rights reserved. ISBN 0-8077-4186-8 (paper), 0-8077-4187-6 (cloth). Prior to photocopying items for classroom use, please contact the Copyright Clearance Center, Customer Service, 222 Rosewood Drive, Danvers, MA, 01923, USA, telephone (508) 750-8400.

Today, a new generation of students attends Wade Hampton High School. More aware of environmental issues, these students feel less pressure from home to keep quiet in deference to job security. SRS is in a "cleanup mode," which means they are trying to eradicate traces of nuclear contamination from the site. That site includes more than 198,344 acres (310 square miles) populated by a wide variety of wildlife and made up of wetlands and forests. From time to time, rumors circulate about three-eyed frogs or other aberrations along with possible layoffs and plant closings. Geographically, we live in an area known for its "black waters" at the headwaters of three significant rivers in South Carolina: the Ashepoo, the Congaree, and the Edisto, otherwise referred to by locals as the ACE River Basin. A haven for hunters and other naturalists, the isolated, rural area endows the people who live here with a strong "sense of place." That very situation is what interested my group of writing students in doing research on water quality one year, with a project on the nuclear fuel cycle the following year. Their findings were reported to their fellow students as well as to parents and friends in their small town, 40 miles downstream of a major nuclear facility. We called our study the Nuke Sites research project.

The idea for the Nuke Sites research project was first broached in the driveway of the Bread Loaf School of English in Vermont, where I attended summer school. In a conversation with a fellow student, Phil Sittnick, I began to be aware of just how powerful an issue the nuclear fuel cycle was for our local environment in Hampton. I had already facilitated several projects with my students that centered on an action and advocacy theme, so my students were primed for something else to "stick their noses into." When my students participated in the online conference that looked at local watersheds, their reports showed that the water was generally polluted by fertilizer runoff from the local farms, many of them owned by families in the area. My students had wanted very badly to find something in the water from local industry, but they were unable to point the accusing finger. Ironically, it turned out we were looking for the wrong source of pollution, because a few weeks after we completed our study, one local industry was cited for being the fourth-worst air polluter in the state. Having taken on one industry, they were now ready to point the accusing finger and blow the whistle not only on a corporate giant but on the federal government.

Tip O'Neill once said, "All politics is local." I'd say the same about education. What really matters most to students is what's going on in their own backyards, around their own dining room tables, or in their own Friday night gathering places. In suggesting that my students and I research the impact of nuclear industry on our own environment, I was sure I'd be able to use the process of writing to inform not only my students but also the larger community. The students in this study were part of a class that published a quarterly writing magazine, and as we began our studies of nuclear issues, we knew we would dedicate the next issue to our findings.

My fellow Bread Loaf student Phil and I decided to work together with our respective classes on the issue of nuclear contamination. Phil teaches at Laguna Middle School on the Laguna Reservation in New Mexico. This school serves the Laguna tribe and sits close to the Jackpile Mine, which was the world's largest open-pit uranium mine for many years. Family members of many of Phil's students had worked in the mine, drawing out the uranium for a variety of uses. One of the most significant uses of the uranium was to build nuclear weapons at the SRS in South Carolina. Phil's students live in a place where the nuclear fuel cycle begins; mine live in a place where it ends, where toxic nuclear waste is now stored. Phil and I felt that the close proximity to these industries had a potentially pervasive effect on our students' respective environments and their lives.

Our basic plan was simple enough: Through reflective and creative writing, research, and discussion, students at both sites would work collaboratively to express their ideas and opinions. As we would find out, people in Laguna were affected by the existence of the Jackpile Mine in ways similar to how we were by the bomb plant. When I went to visit Laguna, Phil, his students, and I watched a slide show produced by NARMIC (National Action Research into the Military Industrial Complex). The show was slightly dated but gave a great deal of pertinent information about the two sites we would be studying: the Jackpile Mine and the Savannah River Site. Viewing the slides we learned that "because of the radioactivity in the ore, uranium mining was an unhealthy occupation. It was especially bad in the early days" (NARMIC, 1980, slide 20). One Navajo miner who was interviewed said, "We lost my dad to lung cancer, and I also had an uncle that we lost with lung cancer" (NARMIC, 1980, slide 21). Another miner said, "There weren't any safety precautions. The only time the ventilation worked was whenever an inspection team came around" (NARMIC, 1980, slide 21). Instances of a careless or callous attitude of the government toward its employees in the early days of the nuclear era were not unheard of. In South Carolina this attitude manifested in another way: Government officials gathered residents of Dunbarton and Ellenton, small communities of South Carolina, to tell them "why their property must be taken over" (NARMIC, 1980, slide 64). More than 250,000 acres were emptied. A sign outside of the towns read, "It is hard to understand why our town must be destroyed to make a bomb that will destroy someone else's town that they love as much as we love ours" (NARMIC, 1980, slide 65).

So the stage was set: Phil's students living in Laguna, a site associated with the beginning of the nuclear cycle, would engage in discussion via electronic communication with my students in Hampton, a site associated with end of the fuel cycle; the subject of their discussion would be the impact of the nuclear processing industry on their local environments. They would broach subjects such as environmental racism, community health, and nuclear proliferation.

My visit to Laguna Middle School was made possible in part by a minigrant from Write to Change, a nonprofit organization sponsoring writing projects that result in community action. I was given a week of professional leave by a very generous principal who believed that what I was doing would benefit my students. I visited Phil's classroom and school for 2 days. I talked to students and observed them working in their classrooms, and Phil told them a little about my work and my students. The opportunity to work with another teacher and visit his school, though a rare experience in a teacher's tight schedule of classes and preparation, is one of the best professional development opportunities I was ever afforded.

While at Laguna Middle School, I spoke with Nick Cheromiah, the principal, as well as Floyd Solomon, the cultural liaison for the school and the Laguna tribe. Floyd took me on a tour of the Jackpile Mine and gave me a great deal of historical information about the work that was done there—and is still being done in the reclamation process now that the mine is closed. We spent an hour together talking about the pros and cons of the mine and how the Laguna people benefited from both the mining itself and from the reclamation. I learned, however, that working in the mine conflicted with much of Laguna culture, language, and religion. I realized that as my students and I discussed the effects of the Savannah River Site on our lives, we certainly needed to consider how our environment could be reclaimed and what permanent losses we faced because a nuclear graveyard is in our backyard. I took a number of photographs, though my small snapshots can't do justice to the vastness of the mines. To understand the magnitude of the western landscape, I had my students think of going into a great cathedral and seeing what appear to be tiny stained glass windows near the top of a vaulted ceiling and then being told the windows are 20 feet tall. In the same way, it's difficult to perceive the depth of those holes in the earth; it's hard to imagine how the mesas on this site must have once looked.

While I was visiting with Phil, he and I took the opportunity to plan the online collaboration that would take place between our students in February. After we viewed the NARMIC slides, Phil and other faculty members at Laguna put together a study guide for his students based on a cross-curricular look at the issues of the nuclear fuel cycle. He gave me a copy of this study guide, which in the long run saved me a great deal of research time when I began teaching the same information to my own students. We would use it extensively to try to come to understand the implications of rads and rems, alpha and beta radiation, and other scientific terms that would come to be part of our everyday vocabulary in our struggle to come to terms with what had happened or could happen to our environment as a result of the nuclear "free-for-all" that occurred in our parents' and grandparents' lifetime.

Teaching material that I had had little exposure to since my own high school chemistry class was more than a little challenging. In what would become one of the most ironic moments of this project, I clearly remember the reaction of other teachers who would come by my class-room, which normally emanated discussions about Shakespeare or Donne, only to hear discussions of electrons, atomic numbers, and radiation. They would do a double-take and often stop at the open door to listen to how this discussion played out in the room of an English teacher. In our research, we used many sources in finding out what we needed to know, including our new classroom Internet access. On the Savannah River Site's Web site (Savannah River Operations, 1996), we found the following: "The SRS is a key U.S. Department of Energy (DOE) facility, focusing on national security work, environmental cleanup and waste management, and economic development and technology transfer initiatives." If the experimentation with and development of nuclear devices had caused no harm to our environment, we wondered, why did the facility now have to operate in a cleanup mode? My students were particularly interested in finding an answer to this question when they toured the facility, but they were not given any information other than that there was a significant amount of mechanical pollution (oil and detergent); no admission of radioactive pollution was given, even though we were told that highly dangerous items were sealed in concrete bunkers and that robotic arms were used to handle fuel rods in F Canyon. These buildings were huge, restricted areas where the spent fuel rods are cased in glass that would later be put in stainless steel casing and eventually stored in underground vaults.

In other words, we all knew that the deadliest of toxins existed near where we stood, but no one acknowledged the truth that we had a potentially hazardous site in the southwestern corner of our state. As

long as it was contained, and in the process of being cleaned up, everything was as good as could be expected. Or was it?

This information fueled the thinking and speech of my students.
Their reactions ranged from cautious distaste at what had happened to
open rage. As we discussed the issues in class, I could see the wheels of
thought begin to turn as they faced the implications of looking at this
issue. They were forcing themselves to look at things differently from
the way their parents and other older members of our community had
looked at them. What my parents' generation had considered a national
security issue and what my own generation perhaps considered a necessary evil, these students were now considering a mistake. Plain and simple. And to express that realization, they had to find their own words.
They had asked the hard questions. More questions would follow, but
how could they talk about this information they had gathered that was
so important to them and those with whom they shared this small rural
community? I found that as these students learned more and more of
the truth about nuclear experimentation, the more they wanted to
know. If, as Harvard educator Courtney Cazden (1987) says, the goal
of education is "intra-individual change and student learning," then our
students were certainly heading in that direction with their sustained
inquiry and collaboration (p. 99).

My class of students in South Carolina had already had a good bit
of experience using telecommunications as a medium of communication, and they were becoming better users of the Internet as well. To
connect Phil's students and mine for electronic discussion, we used
BreadNet, the communications system of students, alumni, and staff
and faculty of the Bread Loaf School of English. Much has been said in
articles by other teachers who have used telecommunications in their
writing instruction, and I agree with the general observation that the
writing is much more authentic and varied. Sometimes online student
writing is even more carefully crafted than the papers I receive as finished essays. The daunting task of writing for an audience of one's peers
seems to encourage care in the craft that we teachers don't normally
see when we alone are the audience. What my students needed was an
opportunity to share their discoveries and engage others in asking the
same hard questions that they had been asking.

The writing assignments began with a descriptive piece of their particular site, which we followed up with a well-documented opinion essay on whether or not the use of nuclear energy was/is an acceptable
risk. In his essay, Lee Norment, a senior at the time of this project,
wrote the following in *Devil's Food for Thought*, Wade Hampton High
School's collection of poetry and prose:

APR 2 1 2009

GAYLORD

PRINTED IN U.S.A.

While the [SRS] site may not be technically in our backyards, it is close enough to affect the people of Hampton. It largely affects the economy of our area. The SRS currently employs 14,000 workers. That number is down from 25,000 at the plant's peak during the Cold War. The plant also has a negative affect. On several occasions in the past, nuclear waste has been shipped through our town. The waste was sent by railroad, and the rails run right through the middle of our downtown area. It is difficult to weigh the economic rewards with the nuclear hazard. It is hard to overlook the $85 million in goods and services purchased in South Carolina. However, where does money supersede health?

Lee's essay does not denigrate the economic benefits of the nuclear site, but he does not blindly elevate them over other considerations either. He, along with a number of his classmates, actually witnessed one of the "nuke trains" on its run through town. It was escorted by police cars and was undoubtedly of great concern to officials. In the same publication, René Payne Moore, another senior, took a more emotional route in exploring the question of acceptable use:

Is nuclear power essential? Is life as we know it essential? The uranium that is essential in nuclear power has been extracted from open pits and underground mines; pits and mines that had to be worked by someone. . . . The greed of man and the quest for power has caused a serious disruption in our environment. As a result of this Earth-murder, the people of the Laguna, Acoma and other Indian nations will never be the same. Just as important our Mother will never be the same.

My students built on their understanding of the issues by viewing the slide show I had watched with Phil and his students. My students were deeply moved by the information about the elimination of Ellenton and Dunbarton. The residents of these "disappeared" towns were forced to relocate to "New Ellenton," a community created just for them. Our students also looked at a reproduction of *We're Making a New World*, a painting that depicts a barren, postapocalyptic landscape with a weak, white sun rising over the naked tree tops. I asked the students to discuss the painting in class and to write a response in poetic format. These writings were uploaded on BreadNet and sent to Phil's students in Laguna, who also shared similar writing with us. The conversations between my students and Phil's, along with the discussions we had in class, gave my students a chance to connect to the past, reflect on the present, and speculate about the future. A poem by one of my students drew these responses from Phil's class:

> The questions that you asked [in your poem cause me to] believe in the new world. Who wouldn't, I mean? It has already happened to us like in World War II. Is the transformation that you describe irreversible? Well, I think that would be up to the reader to decide what would happen next or what [the new world] would look like.
> —Rebecca

Obviously, the poem affected Rebecca's thinking about a major apocalyptic event. The imagery caused her to make connections between a past event such as World War II and a possible coming event that might actually be so devastating that the results would be irreversible. Writing about these issues in a literate and trusting classroom community, then expanding that community to include Phil's classroom, made my students more aware of the need to frame what they knew and of how critical it is to communicate effectively. I also witnessed students' increased willingness to experiment with their creative abilities. I think this creativity derived in part from the diversity of the network they were using, BreadNet. Working with Laguna Indians was a first-time experience for these students, which helped them look at the subject we studied from different perspectives. When they got around to publishing their work in the literary magazine, they had experienced writing about issues close to home and responding to others' writing in ways that helped them grow as writers and people.

The writing these students produced was well thought out. I was often amazed (and always pleased) at what I thought was real quality in their craft. Passionate poetic phrases coexisted alongside essays that explored economic pros and cons. My students became risk takers in expressing their deep belief that we had really messed up in the nuclear arms race both in creative writing and in opinion pieces. They relied on their growing skills, on peer review, and on my feedback to produce quality work that persuades the reader to at least take a second look at the situation we find ourselves in.

A truly important aspect of the writing and the class in which it was produced is that we used the portfolio method of assessment. I never "graded" an assignment until the student felt it was complete. That might take all quarter if he or she felt that much time was needed. We had frequent writing conferences, both between teacher and student and as peer conferences. Times for writing included the 90-minute block during which the class took place as well as time when my computers were free during other class periods. Students could come and go as they needed to. Some of the students who wrote in their own particular style—like René, who wanted to write only poetry, or Beth, who only wanted to write opinion—eventually came around and explored different avenues by the end of these projects.

I firmly believe that keeping portfolios helped alleviate students' anxiety and allowed them the freedom to experiment. David Thornburg, who directs the Thornburg Center for Professional Development, says that the "key" to unlock the potential of individuals is right under our noses on the lower-left-hand corner of our computer keyboards: "[N]estled above each other are two keys that, together, read: 'Shift Control'" (Thornburg, 1999). Using portfolios shifted control from my red pen to the students' own pen and paper. That shift was a major freeing experience for both the students and myself as their teacher. I became more of a mentor for their writing as I moved from "sage on the stage" to "guide by the side." Their portfolios were eventually put together at the end of the year in a bound book. I made myself copies of all their portfolios, and a copy remains on display in the school media center as well.

The work produced by students in New Mexico was equally impressive. In the spring, shortly after we finished the most intensive part of the online exchange, Phil came to visit us in Hampton. He got to meet the students whom his class had been corresponding with and got to talk a little more about the implications of nuclear issues as he saw them. While he was at my school, Phil participated in my students' writing projects, writing prose and poems, and modeling for my students how to transform one's ideas about important public issues, such as nuclear war, waste, or wanton disregard for our natural environment, into personal poetic statements. It seems to me an important step when teachers can write with their students and share that writing to encourage metacognition so that students can see how the thinking and writing process unfolds.

I think we all discovered that healthy people are informed people. When students are allowed to investigate and write about important issues and communicate their findings and ideas to others in their community who share the same concerns, they grow into people who are better able to make positive changes in their world. In *The New Literacy: Redefining Reading and Writing in the Schools*, John Willinsky (1990) claims that this kind of investigative work consists "of those strategies in the teaching of reading and writing which attempt to shift the control of the teaching of literacy from the teacher to the student;

literacy is promoted in such programs as a social process with language that can from the very beginning extend the students' range of meaning and connection" (p. 8). This project allowed two classrooms to network across place and culture in a significant way. It allowed students and teachers to work together in a fundamentally different way as well. Students and teachers alike were co-investigators in this project.

Student responses to working on projects such as Nuke Sites are always positive. They like to get involved in controversy that pits the "little guy" against a larger "enemy." These projects exemplify the "pedagogy of place," and our work illustrates how such a pedagogy ameliorated the tensions in this community between the local and the external, the traditional and the new. Students said that finding ways to describe their own setting to students elsewhere connected them more intimately with their own area and led to its rediscovery.

The final product, Hampton's magazine *Devil's Food for Thought*, which went out to the community, included poems and essays written during the exchange. We gave the magazines away to students at no charge and distributed a number of them to doctor's offices and businesses around town. The magazine was produced with a document design in mind that would engage the community in the same way the students had been engaged initially. A picture taken from an Internet site of an atomic explosion "graced" the cover along with a student's poem. Inside was an explanation of what was in this particular issue, and then the essays and poems followed in a very tasteful layout done collaboratively by the students and me on computer desktop publishing software. By taking the production from rough copy to published product, we showed others in our community what we had learned about the social and emotional impact of living near nuclear sites. The magazine was well received by the student body at large, and other faculty members made comments such as, "How do you get them to write like that?" The answer lies in a different style of teaching that takes a different approach to education from the traditional ones we have been using. In *Education on the Edge of Possibility*, Geoffrey Caine and Nummela Caine (1997) point to this kind of environment, where "learning not teaching is the primary focus." In these classes,

> students and teachers exhibit reflection, critical thinking, and taking responsibility. Self-organization is evident and most clearly demonstrated where students spontaneously organize around provocative projects or ideas and where teachers act as facilitators, continually helping students expand and process what they are learning. Discipline problems, as they are commonly referred to, are absent. The emphasis is on creating commu-

nity. Orderliness and coherence are a natural part of such classrooms, as teachers and students let the tasks and learning drive their behavior. Thus, students know what the basic routines are and how to work in groups, in pairs, individually, or in assembly. The purpose of the activities or tasks also determines what the time schedules are, when to link with sources outside school, and how to find and use appropriate materials and resources. (p. 243)

This describes my classroom in a nutshell. I was able to let go of the control and thus allow students to look at their worlds and see what studies they needed to engage in. I had to begin slowly and build on my experiences, but nonetheless I was finally able to incorporate this kind of activity in every class I taught from Honors English, to Communication for the Workplace, to Writing with Telecommunications, to volunteer projects, or what might be called intentional learning projects.

For example, the Watershed Project (known as the Water Rangers) was a volunteer project. Students had to fill out applications to work with me on the project as well as to volunteer their time and writing to the project. The project attracted 12 students who went on three different field trips to test water and conduct labs back at the school. They kept notes and wrote online responses to others across the state doing the same kind of work. The Water Rangers were led by me and one of my colleagues in the science department. Another colleague of mine who lived in Alaska also took an interest and corresponded with my students. My science colleague and I had a common planning period, so we scheduled the field trips for that time period. He added his expert knowledge of flora and fauna, and I kept track of the writing requirements. We collated and distributed a packet of reading material for the students. I was also responsible for coordinating the students work on BreadNet, sending their writing online and receiving messages from other participants who were involved in similar studies. To stimulate their own thinking about reflective writing, I offered the project participants an example of my own writing in which I reflect on a natural setting that had been in my family for at least four generations:

> While reflecting on these memories, I was reminded of a poem by Gerard Manley Hopkins. It begins, "As kingfishers catch fire, dragonflies draw flame" and goes on to speak of the calling that each of us has to be true to ourselves. Being true to myself means having an alert attentiveness to whatever is there in the present moment. I kind of like to think of that turtle waiting for just the right moment when the water spider is poised on the surface and then—splash!—he has his dinner. Being attentive like those flow-

ers when a gnat jiggles it enough for the enzymes to start flowing. Being attentive to the bob of the float at the end of the line, and to "see," also, when the kingfishers catch fire and dragonflies draw flame.

Let me interject here that while I feel critical analysis is an important writing skill to learn, having a firsthand experience of writing like a great writer is what will produce future great writers. We are short-sighted when we think our only objective is to teach students to analyze a poem but not to write a poem, or to analyze essays but not to write essays. Discovery writing is invaluable if they are to learn about audience and creativity and if we are to continue to have great masterpieces worth reading. Because I was able to interact with these participants by sharing my writing, they could better take the initiative to produce their own valid and important work.

This project produced a number of poems that were heartfelt expressions of inspired moments. I believe with my Alaskan colleague, Tom, that producing these poems may have been easier for my students simply because they bonded with me in our common experience of being outside in a place that offered inspiration. In fact, the main criticism of the experience voiced by the students was that they didn't have as much time to write outside as they would have liked. Such writing seems to me to call into serious question the traditional patterns of instruction and assessment normally followed in the world of academics. Witness, for example, the following excerpt from Byron Loadholt's journal:

> When we first arrived at the site, we could see the river and some trees that we recognized. The weather that day was clear, sunny and cold. While I was observing, I saw many trees that I recognized. The trees that I saw were poplar, white oak, pine, cypress, and possibly magnolia. Also, as I was observing, I saw two other interesting plants. One of the plants was an endangered species named resurrection fern. I also found a leaf that was named little brown jug. If you rubbed the leaves together, it would smell like tea. We also collected water samples from each site. At site #2, we found a purple flower called spider wort. At site #3, we found a dead opossum which might have frozen to death.

When Tom visited our school, he asked Byron how he knew so much about the trees and other plants, and Byron said that he learned to observe things outdoors from his father, who "sees so much more than most people do. I just kind of see it because he taught me."

One student, Jay Parker, wrote a poem that had a meditative quality to it. Jay ended up wanting to be a whistle-blower on the industries that were possibly responsible for polluting our local environment. I found it striking that Jay's wanting to go to battle against the industry was inspired in part by his deep respect for the natural environment described in his "Meditation," which follows:

Deer and raccoon come down to drink
beside the river where I think
sitting on the bank staring at the trees;
the cypress looks back and bends down to me.
I speak to him softly then go my way;
he knows I'll be back later this day.
Around the bend a largemouth leaps,
the willow quivers, a tree frog peeps.
Deeper into the swamp I go,
I dip my hand in, feel the flow;
lives ebb past; my consciousness slips.
I sit here for hours, no words cross my lips,
then I rise to leave this place of rest.
I pass the tree, the kingfisher's nest.
The trees all speak, calling good-bye;
I must leave now or I will lie
under the cypress with my peace of mind
forever and ever until the end of time.

Like the students who worked on the Nuke Sites project, the Water Rangers compiled their work into a magazine, published at school, which included photos, poetry, speculative writing that was done on-line, and field notes. Curriculum integration was also a strong aspect of this project. Reading, writing, scientific investigation, history, geography, culture, and biology were all tied together in one "unit." Often I am asked how a teacher can be expected to move outside the box in which our traditional curriculum forces us to work. As teachers we have to ask our own hard questions about curriculum, how we deliver that curriculum, and then decide what is most important. These projects fostered an expansion of critical thinking and problem-solving skills. But more important for me as teacher, they gave the students and me the opportunity to work and respond as a community of learners. As I said earlier, I no longer had to be the know-it-all, but was rather a co-learner and co-writer with my class. In my experience, project-based curriculum reinvigorates the teachers as much as the student.

This higher quality of learning would not have been possible, however, if we weren't focused as a community on the community. In fact, it became obvious that the larger community was listening in on our study. While my science colleague and I taught the kids about issues of pollution, watersheds, and water quality, the local industry began to show interest. At *their* invitation, we scheduled a trip to tour their water treatment facilities. This trip was the highlight of the project for me because it gave me a broader and sharper perspective on my community. The watershed is important; environment is important; industry allows us to work and have a sound economic base, and so it, too, is important. Both the Nuke Sites and Water Rangers projects provided the participants an opportunity to learn about chemistry, industrial techniques, environmental control, ecology, philosophy, their community, and themselves.

REFERENCES

Caine, G., & Caine, N. (1997). *Education on the edge of possibility.* Alexandria, VA: Association for Supervision of Curriculum Development.

Cazden, C. (1987). *Classroom discourse: The language of teaching and learning.* Portsmouth, NH: Heinemann.

National Action Research into the Military Industrial Complex (NARMIC). (1980). *Acceptable risk? Living in a nuclear world* [slide format]. Palentine, IL: Learning Seed Company.

Savannah River Operations Office and Savannah River Site. (1996). *www.srs. gov.* Retrieved 1999.

Thornburg, D. (1999). *www.pbs.org/teachersource/thornburg/thornburg599. shtm.* Retrieved 1999.

Willinsky, J. (1990). *The new literacy: Redefining reading and writing in the schools.* New York: Routledge.

PART III

Writing for Change

Chapter 11

LOWER 9, DON'T IT SOUND FINE?

Jim Randels with Ebony Carriere

STORM WARNINGS

The setting sun touched the tops of the towering downtown office buildings as tugboats ferried chains of barges down the Industrial Canal. On the Mississippi River levee, six pockets of people gathered around young storytellers. An ancient white horse grazed nearby, dragging behind her the rope attached only to her bridle. The storytellers described Hurricane Betsy and the great flood of 1965 in the lower 9th ward—the horror of watching snakes, shoes, and bodies float down the flooded street in front of their homes. Curious strollers on the levee stopped to listen.

"Run! The water's rising! Find high ground!" Chairs toppled and people scattered as a blue wave descended on the crowds listening to the storytellers. The listeners ducked beneath the crashing "waves" of blue cloth and scrambled to the security of their seats. When the re-creation of the flood was finished, they were summoned up the hill to view scenes enacted from the present life in the 9th ward, which was followed with scenes of the future of the community as the young storytellers envisioned it.

At dusk on six days in May 1998, more than 500 people attended these scenes of *Lower 9 Stories*, one of more than 40 events in Junebug Productions' Environmental Justice Arts Festival. The young storytellers, members of the Positive Outreach Leaders, retold tales they had learned through oral histories they collected in collaboration with Students at the Center, a school-based writing for the community program. More than 2 years in the making, *Lower 9 Stories* sought to reclaim

Writing to Make a Difference. Copyright © 2001 by Teachers College, Columbia University. All rights reserved. ISBN 0-8077-4186-8 (paper), 0-8077-4187-6 (cloth). Prior to photocopying items for classroom use, please contact the Copyright Clearance Center, Customer Service, 222 Rosewood Drive, Danvers, MA, 01923, USA, telephone (508) 750-8400.

history, restore hope, and inspire action in a tenacious historical New Orleans neighborhood that suffered from poverty, racism, powerlessness, and drugs. This chapter recounts the production of *Lower 9 Stories* and describes the coalitions that made the production possible.

STORM GATHERING: TWO STUDENT GROUPS COLLABORATING

Lower 9 Stories emerged from the work of Positive Outreach Leaders (POL), a peer health education theater troupe developed as a partnership among several community organizations in New Orleans with youth as a primary focus: Planned Parenthood; a school-based health clinic at Lawless Senior High School; and Students at the Center (SAC), an elective course at high schools McDonogh 35 and Douglass, which involves students in community-based writing projects.

Funded by the Louisiana Division of the Arts, POL recruited and trained 13 students in an after-school program that met twice a week for 6 months, led by theater educators Kathy Randels and Roscoe Reddix and Planned Parenthood's Carrie Anderson. The POL members, all residents of the lower 9th ward, received training in using storytelling, movement, and theater to communicate with their peers about teen pregnancy, sexually transmitted diseases, and the causes and effects of violence and poverty. The project opened with an intensive week of training grounded in the theory and practice of Brazilian theater activist Augusto Boal. The original 6-month program culminated in performances in neighborhood schools and churches. When funding was discontinued and the three project leaders moved on, POL became dormant for 1 year. Then in October of 1997, eight original POL members and two new recruits met with Kathy Randels three times a week to prepare *Lower 9 Stories*.

This work proved both frustrating and rewarding for Kathy Randels and POL. Meeting after school hours, POL members had difficulty completing the tasks of researching and writing the play at the same time that they were developing their amateur acting skills. Randels claims:

> It was difficult to keep students motivated and obligated to the project. This was because they were all devoting limited free time. We lost many members to jobs, financial burdens, and family obligations. It was also difficult, sometimes, to rehearse after a 6-hour school day. This project would have been much easier to facilitate if it had been executed within the context of a normal, for-credit

class—giving students some credit for their research and using school hours to create the piece, freeing up their time and course load.

Across the Industrial Canal and in the short shadows of downtown office buildings and an elevated interstate that severs Treme, another historically Black neighborhood, sits McDonogh 35, the first public high school for people of African descent in New Orleans. During the 1997–1998 schoolyear, three McDonogh 35 teachers—Joyce Chapital, Warren Johnson, and Jim Randels—were piloting SAC, a course whose curriculum could incorporate the dramatic and writing activities that Kathy Randels and members of the POL were doing with students. Placing these activities within the school's curriculum relieved the frustrations that Kathy encountered due to students' limited available time outside of school hours.

Through pilot funding from a local nonprofit foundation, SAC offers courses for students to become mentors to classmates in writing. SAC students and teachers design, research, and conduct academic and community improvement projects that foster critical thinking, writing, and problem-solving skills. Outside of the school, SAC students collaborate with community organizations and students from other schools on a wide range of writing and community action projects. They have helped establish and maintain numerous adolescent media projects: a citywide teen newspaper, a monthly talk show for teens, a journal of young women's writing, and a series of public service announcements on a local radio station.

The SAC projects bring students into the fields of archaeology, anthropology, and history, with an emphasis on Africana studies, in a variety of neighborhood study projects. Students become involved in studying the community through meeting with visiting scholars, interviewing neighborhood residents, and participating actively in the work of the North Claiborne/St. Bernard Avenue Economic District Association (NCSB). Students also hone their writing and layout design skills by producing a newsletter for NCSB.

The practice SAC students received in such projects prepared them to offer the assistance that Kathy Randels and the POL group sought with *Lower 9 Stories*, and a strong coalition was formed. Students joined the POL group in collecting oral histories from the lower 9th ward, and they reviewed interview tapes and transcripts by SAC students, using this material to develop their play. One SAC student, Tyra Lambert, even joined POL, participating in the thrice-weekly rehearsals for 6 months. In her SAC class, she developed poetry and monologues that formed part of the final version of *Lower 9 Stories*. The POL group invigorated the SAC students' work by providing a public venue in which to share the SAC work.

FISSURES AND CONNECTIONS:
EVERY NEIGHBORHOOD HAS ITS STORM

One of the great joys of teaching is seeing students make connections among various events in history and their lives. Both SAC and POL, like all good educational programs, help students see broader contexts and patterns in the material they study and create. On a balmy October day in New Orleans, about a month after the 34th anniversary of Hurricane Betsy, SAC students from McDonogh 35 High School and Frederick Douglass High School gathered at Black Arts National Diaspora, Inc. (BAND) on North Claiborne Avenue, just three blocks from McDonogh 35. Cheryl Rodriguez, an Africana studies and anthropology professor from the University of South Florida, was leading a discussion about the Central Avenue Legacies Project, her oral history of Tampa's formerly thriving Black business district. Rodriguez explained that her father's law offices used to be on Central Avenue, but like the other businesses in this predominately Black neighborhood, it closed or moved when the federal interstate system carved a new path down Central Avenue, razing the buildings that housed these Black businesses.

McDonogh 35 junior Romanica Guy, whose SAC course work included meeting with the North Claiborne/St. Bernard Avenue Economic District Association and working on that group's newsletter, immediately understood the similarity between Central Avenue in Tampa and North Claiborne Avenue in New Orleans. Sitting in the spacious second-floor exhibition space of the BAND building, Romanica observed, "You know, when Mr. Gant and other people talk about this neighborhood, they describe how successful and beautiful it was before the interstate system came through. They want to restore it to its former glory, and they know it will happen sometime." She admired their determined, hopeful tone despite the anger and sense of powerlessness that accompanies Gant and other neighborhood leaders' recollection of the time when planners decided to place the interstate along Claiborne Avenue rather than the river.

SAC students began to see even greater connections between their city and other cities. Hearing that BAND, a new cultural arts gallery and museum, was located in the building that used to house the Standard American Life Insurance Company, they began to wonder about the disruptions in the neighborhood and connect it to national trends. Students who had studied the life of Ida B. Wells recalled that in Memphis, at the end of the nineteenth century, Black businessman Thomas Moss was lynched for establishing a grocery store that attracted customers from an existing White-owned business. Senior Adrien McElroy recalled that in Tulsa, Oklahoma, just after World War I, the Black business district was destroyed overtly and violently through bombing. He also noted that the advent of integration in the 1960s led to a major reduction in Black businesses. Dr. Rodriguez agreed with this explanation, noting that many factors contributed to shifting fortunes of Black businesses in urban areas.

New Orleans' lower 9th ward, which became one of New Orleans' first modern Black suburbs as veterans returning from World War II and the Korean War built homes along the river on the St. Bernard Parish side of the Industrial Canal, experienced a different type of disruption in its economy. Residents certainly experienced the economic benefits and drawbacks of integration. They had dealt with racism in all its forms. But unlike disruptions in the North Claiborne Avenue and Central Avenue business districts, this neighborhood's displacement came, at least initially, through a natural disaster. In 1965, Hurricane Betsy swept through New Orleans and in its wake left floodwaters that covered the roofs of buildings and destroyed homes in the lower 9th ward. As SAC and POL students prepared *Lower 9 Stories*, this flood became a crucial prism through which to interpret the present and prepare for the future of this historic New Orleans neighborhood.

Students' connection to the past in writing and researching *Lower 9 Stories* also went well beyond the twentieth century. SAC students have done extensive research into the 1811 slave revolt in New Orleans, producing a book that collects their creative and critical writings on the event. Tyra Lambert had learned of Charles Deslondes, one of the leaders of the 1811 revolt, through her SAC classmates' work. When the POL members realized that Deslondes Street, where it dead-ends into the levee, would be the location for their play, they chose Charles Deslondes as one of the play's three guiding spirits. Deslondes organized his community to fight for justice more than 200 years ago just upriver from the lower 9th ward. His story became part of *Lower 9 Stories*, along with the stories of two other guiding ancestors: Black Hawk, an American Indian spiritual leader; and the lower 9th ward's own Mother Catherine Seals, whose Spiritual Church reveres Black Hawk and who has always played an important role in the 9th ward.

Tyra Lambert, studying a poem by Audre Lorde in her SAC class, also made connections with Yemanje, a deity of the Yoruba, an African people of the eastern Guinea coast. She realized that Yemanje's story would provide a context for her to talk about struggles and inspirations for justice along the Mississippi River. Tyra refers to Yemanje in her prologue to *Lower 9 Stories*, in the poem "What Time Is It?" The poem, excerpted here, connects stories of past struggle with observations of present neighborhood problems.

"What time is it?" I ask.
Is it time for Blacks
To step back
Or
Move Forward
And attack
All of the
Dilemmas
That cause their
Neighborhoods to be
Drug-infested,
Violent,
Blights
In their Communities?
Is it time
To stop
Ignoring our problems
And sweeping them aside . . . ?

Is it time
To remember
That once upon a time,
In a community
Similar to our own,
There was a place
Where the rivers
Flowed freely
And
Bore the resemblance
Of the deep blue
Waters
That flowed from
Yoruba's goddess
Yemanje's breast?

Is it time
To look back
And Think of the time
When,
Like Yemanje,
Our rivers have been
Abused—
But not by
Husbands
Of the earth
And
Our children's
Children?

TRACKING THE STORM: SAC STUDENT EBONY CARRIERE'S STORY

In preparation for *Lower 9 Stories*, SAC and POL students studied local and national history and interviewed numerous residents and workers. The stories they heard amplified the broad sweep of history that they encountered in the discussions on the decline of Black business districts. The interviews concentrated on the great flood that came in the aftermath of Hurricane Betsy. But the wide-ranging interviews also covered issues and events such as the civil rights movement, the flight of middle-class residents to more remote suburbs, current problems the neighborhood faces, and adult perceptions of teens in the neighborhood. Many interviewees also discussed the U. S. Army Corps of Engineers' plans to widen the Industrial Canal.

This section highlights one SAC student's experience in conducting her first interviews for this project. She wrote the following essay as part of a SAC course assignment, in which she provided personal reflection and public documentation of school and community writing projects in which she participated. She started the essay as a series of log entries at the end of her sophomore year as a student in Ms. Chapital's SAC class. She completed it in her junior year as a student in Mr. Randels' SAC class.

As Ms. Chapital and I crossed the canal and then drove up Caffin Avenue, I noticed numerous abandoned houses, trash lying in the streets, and people loitering on the corners as if they had no place to be—no bosses to answer to or time clocks to punch. I saw little kids, clearly barely in elementary school, standing at the bus stops alone. It was a frosty and dreary morning, yet the children were draped in light, old jackets, some without any at all. It was quite obvious we had long passed the suburban-like area often referred to as "the East" and had entered into the notorious area known as "The Lower 9."

The lower 9th ward has for so long been New Orleans' own skeleton in the closet: a poverty-ridden, drug-filled, all-black community. You would never see this area advertised in those tourist pamphlets at the Hyatt Hotel. This is the place my Students at the Center class chose to analyze and learn its history.

We pulled into the parking lot of the Lee & Pervis Barber Shop at 9:35 a.m. I walked in and there, waiting, were the three gentlemen we were to interview: Mr. Lee, Mr. Pervis, and Youngblood.

We began with Mr. Lee, the oldest of the three. Mr. Lee stood tall and slender. Hiding behind his beard and mustache dusted with gray was a grand smile. His deep brown eyes were surrounded by lines that resembled rivers. He had a lifetime of experiences written all over his face, and I had my pen and paper ready to record all of them.

While my teacher, Ms. Chapital, set up the video camera, I went over my interview questions and anxiously awaited the arrival of the other students. I was nervous. Although we had practiced interviewing each other in class, I had never really interviewed anyone before. Finally, I could apply everything I was taught and had prepared for in class. In school we often learn new things, but it is rare that students get a chance to actually practice these lessons.

So, I sat quietly running the rules of interviewing in my mind that I had been blitzed on previously. "Never interrupt the interviewee. Make him or her feel as comfortable as possible. Don't ask yes-or-no questions." We had been preparing for this day for weeks—months really when you count all the time we spent in conferences with students from other classes and all the other related activities.

In the SAC class we watched documentaries to give us ideas of what final products would look like and to think about questions the interviewers had asked. We observed one documentary about the Black Panther Party for Self Defense. In it we saw how the filmmaker asked questions that led to strong, vivid stories. We analyzed his technique of asking questions that began with "how," "what happened next," and "what did you think when."

And we studied the way the filmmaker brought together all these different stories, mixing them to let them comment upon and complement each other. We also had the privilege of having guest speakers, such as Dr. Raphael Cassimere, a history professor at the University of New Orleans and long-term native of the 9th ward, discuss with us their experiences in conducting oral histories and making documentaries. Now here was my chance, along with my SAC classmates, to conduct my first interview and gain real experience.

As I waited for my classmates to arrive, I kept running scenes from these documentaries and guest speakers over and over in my head. Then Mr. Lee pulled me aside and secretly expressed to me that he was nervous. He even asked if our interview was going to be used for political purposes. I knew then that he was as nervous as me and that I needed to make him as comfortable as possible.

The camera light came on, and we were ready. We began the interview by talking about the old neighborhood. Mr. Lee told us how everything was segregated: schools, restaurants, and bathrooms. "At one time blacks and whites lived here. We all lived in the same place, but had to go to different schools, eat at different restaurants, and use different bathrooms because some of the whites still thought they were better than us."

He also spoke of Hurricane Betsy, the natural disaster that destroyed most of the Lower 9. Mr. Lee described bodies floating along the flooded streets. He also talked about how Betsy brought the community closer. And he observed with sadness that although Betsy's floods claimed many lives, this catastrophe can't compare to the death toll the floods of drugs have caused.

Halfway through the interview the other students arrived. We all sat around and listened to Mr. Pervis expand upon Mr. Lee's comment about drugs. He described how drug dealers have become the role models in this neighborhood. It was clear Mr. Pervis had lost all hope for the community's future. He lives in a small town in Mississippi and drives all the way to the Lower 9 to open his shop each day. Mr. Pervis was born and raised in the Lower 9 and, like many former residents, had abandoned it for newer homes and "safer" neighborhoods.

Next was Youngblood, whose name perfectly personifies his character. He is young, ambitious and filled with hope. Unlike Mr. Lee and Mr. Pervis, he has not yet lost his faith in the lower 9th ward. He spoke of the reformation of the Lower 9, of community centers, tutorial programs, and scholarship drives. He commented that the rebuilding of any community begins with its children. It was reassuring to come across someone within this community who still has hope for its future. And later, our other interviews revealed a similar mixture of emotions: hope, pride, anger, and despair.

In class we had learned so much about the Lower 9. Ms. Chapital herself used to live there, and her ex-husband grew up there and had been a community leader there all his life. But her stories and our readings and discussions about the Lower 9 cannot compare to actually meeting, interviewing, and fellowshipping with its current residents. We learned about the community not just in our classroom but also from applying skills such as interviewing and observing. Through Kathy Randels, Jim Randels, Joyce Chapital, and all the guest speakers we have learned so much, but the practical experience of conducting interviews gave me something tangible I will remember as I age. I not only learned information, but I also experienced it. Now I can take interviewing and writing with me as a skill I will continue to refine in future academic and community work.

CONJURING THE STORM

[Hurricane] Betsy was only 35 years ago. When people say flood in the 9th ward, they don't hear it like people hear it in other places. When we hear flood, it goes straight to our hearts. I get images of people who have left, of smells that still disturb me. When most people think of floodwaters, they think of touching tires, maybe hitting your engine. This was water over the house that in essence destroyed the will of a community.
—Kenneth Ferdinand (K. F.)

Lower 9 Stories offered an important and interesting challenge to the young people who were putting it together. For the 15- to 20-year-old students who were researching and performing the play, hurricane survivor and lower 9th ward resident Kenneth Ferdinand's use of *only* to modify *35 years ago* seemed incongruous. These students grew up in an age of immediate gratification and fast-paced entertainment. Thirty-five years is twice their age. They faced the challenge of making immediate and visceral something remote in time, if not in place.

Two major factors contributed to these teens' ability to breathe theatrical life into events that happened many years ago. Most important were the courage and generosity of community elders—such as Kenneth Ferdinand and the three men Ebony Carriere and classmates interviewed in the barber shop—who believe enough in educating youth to give not only their time but also their most painful memories. Also important was the SAC and POL working process that encouraged students to make connections between their personal experiences and the events they were researching.

The students initially had difficulty imagining 35 years as near in time, but many of them understood what it meant to have sensory experiences disturb them for a long time. Kente Williams, a 20-year-old freshman at the University of New Orleans and founding POL member, had graduated from Lawless, the public high school in the lower 9th ward. One of Kente's roles in the play was portraying Kenneth Ferdinand's experience in the flood. The pride and dignity with which Ferdinand expressed tragic personal events made Kente understand that his preparation for the play as an honor.

An exercise early in the rehearsal process helped Kente do justice to Ferdinand's story. POL members sat in a circle telling stories about things they had seen in the lower 9th ward. Kente later recalled, "Mostly the group was talking about humorous types of things, like a crack-head going here or 'I seen somebody beat up on his wife,' something like that."

But when Kente's turn came, he realized that the stories had a serious tone. Like Ferdinand, he had witnessed a disturbing event that had stayed with him, just as the smell of the flood had stayed with Ferdinand: "Me and my father were walking down Florida Avenue, and we looked in the bushes. We saw a shoe . . . we looked over in the bushes, and we saw a dead girl. Her body was like turned over. She was like face flat on the ground. She was half or most of her clothes were ripped off. And there was this horrendous stench coming from her body."

Joking stopped as the POL members discussed the meaning of this "discovery" for their neighborhood. They began to understand this body, abandoned in the high weeds on the banks of the Industrial Canal, as a metaphor for the lower 9th ward. The brutality disturbed them and sobered their earlier joking tone. Students may recoil from disturbing, violent events, but such things can also call them to specific action.

Kente's telling of his discovery of the rape victim called the POL members to action. Rather than simply wallow in fear or sensationalize this brutality, they used it as an important motivation for their play. In fact, the young victim would eventually become an angelic spirit that watches over and guides the series of actions that form the "present" section of *Lower 9 Stories*. POL members saw the victim as a symbol of the neglect and isolation confronting their neighborhood. Few people cross the Industrial Canal. Other than residents, the only people who really pass through the neighborhood are those commuting from St. Bernard Parish to jobs in the city. Many landlords live far from the neighborhood. Giving voice to these feelings offered them a way to connect to Kenneth Ferdinand, who claimed that people who did not live through the storm, who did not live in the neighborhood, could not understand the Hurricane Betsy experience. Ferdinand's claim that people in the lower 9th ward have a specific, unique definition of "flood" was beginning to make sense to these teenagers. They were prepared for a more careful viewing of the videotape that their collaborators, the SAC students, had made of Ferdinand and other 9th ward residents' flood stories.

> Our house was about the highest in the neighborhood. It was a raised foundation—on piers. Everybody else lived on slab foundations. We didn't really know anything about flood or hurricane; we just knew the water was rising. We thought it was just the street backing up, though. My mom told us to get the broom and sweep out the water.
> —K. F.

The POL group members seized on this image of using a broom to sweep away water that's climbing up the steps. They had already decided to use brooms as props and symbols throughout the play. Ferdinand's story enhanced their vision. The image of 17-year-old Kenneth Ferdinand following his mother's instructions to sweep rising water from the front of the house struck them as a powerful mixture of courage and futility, of employing simple tools in the face of uncertain disasters. The broom became more than a prop in *Lower 9 Stories*; it formed an image of dignity, hard work, and hope. And it echoed with the magical African and Native American roots of the land down river from New Orleans and of the ancestors of students in the play. It reminded them of the creative transformation of simple objects. In the "past" section of the play, ancestral ghosts use brooms to try to clean up the current messes in the lower 9th ward. In the "present" section, the broom represents a weapon and serves as a percussion instrument. Patrons of a corner bar use it as a pool stick, and a crack-head uses it to clean up a neighborhood store for money. In the "future," the actors pay tribute to enslaved Africans in America who "jumped the broom" to signal a marriage ceremony. In this use, the players and community members form a covenant to work to improve their community as they honored teens killed in the 1990s as well as African American ancestors who struggled for freedom.

> Mother told us to go next door to get grandfather. As my brother Keith and I started down the street, the wind was so strong that sheets of plywood and corrugated tin blown from buildings and backyard piles hit us and knocked us down. So we knew we couldn't get him. My dad said, "Come back. The wind's too strong, and he'll be OK. Grandfather's too old, his heart's bad, and the wind will make it too difficult to bring him over." We didn't have water at that moment. By the time we got to our house, water had risen to the porch—4 feet off the ground.
> —K. F.

At this point in the play, Kente Williams and his four fellow cast members have summoned the audience to join them in the performance area. Pockets of audience members gather around each cast member, listening to tales from the past that the performers have gleaned from SAC students' interviews of community elders. Kente tells Kenneth Ferdinand's story of surviving the flood during Hurricane Betsy. Preparing this portion of the script was especially challenging for Kente. Watching the taped interview of Ferdinand gave Kente the impression of "a proud man, a strong man" who had lived through "a terrible experience for him and his family but one he would never forget."

Kente knew from telling cast members the stories of finding the raped girl's body and of learning that his uncle had been robbed at gunpoint—both of which became key motifs in the present and future sections of the play—that such memories are precious and painful. He wanted to do justice to Ferdinand's words and spirit, so he watched the tape repeatedly. Sometimes he would simply study vocal inflections, facial expressions, and hand gestures. Other times he faithfully transcribed the 1-hour interview. "I'd watch for a few seconds, then I'd write. I wrote every word he said. Then when I showed [the first draft of the monologue] to Kathy [the director] the whole monologue was five pages long." Kente had difficulty condensing Kenneth's words because "there was so much of the story that was important, so much that needed to be told."

> When we realized grandfather was better off not moving in the wind and rising water, we thought all was OK. But we assumed the water would only be to the door. When it reached 4 or 5 feet, we knew we were in trouble. Neighbors started coming to our

house, since it was so much higher. The water rose rapidly,
though, unlike anything we'd ever seen or could imagine. We
stacked furniture to the ceiling and got into the crawl space in the
attic: 36 people—1 pregnant, 1 amputee, 1 broken leg, kids—all
escaping the water which had risen to the ceiling. My brother
Keith and I spent all night looking between the water line and the
hole in the ceiling to see if any rescuers were coming. Snakes were
crawling in from what was essentially a river outside. I was sop-
ping wet. I had on my white band bucks, a pair of white shorts, a
T-shirt. I saw two people drown trying to swim out of St. Mau-
rice and Law to go get help. Those heroes drowned.

—K. F.

Kente and his fellow POL members hurl these stories at the audience like a furious storm. The actors all speak at once, mimicking the
fury of the storm in their urgency to let audience members learn what
they have learned from these interviews. Audience members strain to
hear in the cacophony of competing monologues. The audience quickly
realizes that to understand the stories, they must enter the performance
space, circle around a performer, and move as close as possible to the
speaker. The audience movement parallels the process students followed in researching and writing this play, the process of listening intently and even aggressively to a community's history.

We had spent the first night in the attic. In the morning, we had
to break a hole in the roof and climb out. People in boats from St.
Bernard Parish saved us. The boat parked at the gutter. We
walked off the roof shingles onto the boat. From there they drove
us to Hardin School. We stayed on the roof of the school, at least
500 of us, the whole next night. . . . Finally we had to take boats
to the Claiborne Avenue Bridge, 3 miles away. You had to walk
up to the highest point of the bridge to get on the public buses.
One old man had a robe on, the newspaper tied around his feet
for shoes, and an electric cord tied around his dog for a leash.

The stench when we returned was horrible—decaying animals
and bodies, sewage. When we went back you had to have
National Guard with guns. I tried to go back to get my grandfather's body, but we couldn't get it for a week. My dad had to
return to the morgue, and the body was awful.

It was cold in September. The movies paint an accurate
picture in disaster movies somewhat. It's like fight or flight; you
know what you've got to do and you do it. Your hand's cut, and

you wrap it with whatever you can and keep working. Everything is automatic pilot. Nothing will ever be about that. The time spent focusing on emotions of the moment is much less than the time spent trying to survive. After it was over, then there was a lot of deep depression in the community, and then a lot of people lost their sanity.
    —K. F.

Broad blue cloths wash over the audience, breaking up the story circles and sending the audience up the grassy field to the crown of the levee, where they'll watch the "present" and "future" acts of the play in which Kente and his fellow cast members will dramatize their own stories and invite the audience to share their dreams for the future of the lower 9th ward.

AFTER THE FLOOD

I don't have a photograph—my whole family doesn't—of before 1965. I can remember some: my brothers and I in football uniforms, opening gifts of little safes under the Christmas tree, Mardi Gras day in cowboy costumes.
    —K. F.

Kenneth Ferdinand sat with Ebony Carriere and Jim Randels 5 months after the *Lower 9 Stories* production. This meeting had been rescheduled: Six weeks earlier, a hurricane and its floodwaters had again threatened New Orleans, this time prompting the weather service to recommend evacuation and the mayor to open the Superdome as a shelter for city residents. In his eloquent, complex way, Ferdinand was explaining what seeing the play meant to him and why unexpected tears came to his eyes during the performance. He says that the interviews and play have made him realize that there are memories and issues that he and his neighbors must continue to process.

Going up to the levee for the production was kind of frightening. I told my wife, "Let's hang back." I didn't want to be involved in a mistake. It's kind of like having a baby—it's painful. I hold the flood that way. I don't want anyone to make light, to make comedy. So when these kids said they'd do a play about Betsy, I thought it wouldn't be much—that they couldn't know what they were talking about, that they couldn't come near replicating my experience.

But those kids had obviously learned about the neighborhood and the flood. I have to tell you, I cried. My cynical expectations were totally undermined by their honest, serious portrayal, and by their attempt to connect with the neighborhood/community that was then and that now remains. Their production wasn't about entertainment, but about capturing the essence of somebody's life and about making it real at that moment.

—K. F.

Ebony and the other SAC and POL students who hear such accounts of the play have begun to think of their class work in a new way. No longer are they merely completing exercises, developing skills, and learning history; they are contributing to a neighborhood in their own small way. The educational missions of the two groups, the Positive Outreach Leaders and the Students at the Center, allow students to extend projects from year to year. Ebony, through her interview with Kenneth Ferdinand almost a year after her initial interviews for *Lower 9 Stories*, was not only able to see that the skills she acquired in this project will continue in her future work; she was also able to see that the interviews themselves have taken on a life of their own in the hands of POL and community members.

Such work has a powerful, transforming effect on students. Centanni Clark, a founding POL member and sophomore at Lawless High School during the *Lower 9 Stories* production, now represents his school on *Teen Expression*, a monthly teen talk show created by SAC students and 16 local high schools in the New Orleans area. With support from the Institute of Women and Ethnic Studies at New Orleans University, students wrote, researched, and produced nine of these shows during the 1998–1999 schoolyear. Centanni brings his concerns about the lower 9th ward to shows on topics such as teens and violence, careers and goal setting, and drug abuse. His acting and writing skills also contribute much to the topical skits on each month's show. Centanni sees his work on *Lower 9 Stories* as a catalyst for much of this work. "All that we did was for a purpose, a message to give to the community. It doesn't just go for the lower 9th ward. It goes for the 6th, the 7th, you know, the 8th, the 3rd, all that stuff. You know what I'm saying? Everybody needs to do the same thing we're doing—take pride in our community, instead of destroying it." Centanni's words echo the lyrics penned by fellow Positive Outreach Leader Adrian Ford, which *Lower 9 Stories* audience members chanted each balmy May evening in 1998: "Lower 9, don't it sound fine/It gets hard sometimes, but you've got to shine."[1]

Kente Williams, who never took any leadership roles in high school and who joined POL only because he was a ham who loved to perform, now plans to work with Centanni Clark to continue a young theater troupe based in the lower 9th ward. "I would love to keep the POL going, to do some more pieces based on research on the lower 9th ward, to do more storytelling. I would like to take a leadership-type position if I have to, because it's the type of positive group we need in this community." POL has recently received a grant to continue its work in the lower 9th ward. And on September 9, 1999, the 34th anniversary of Hurricane Betsy, POL joined with SAC, Kenneth Ferdinand, and Hartzell United Methodist Church to produce a community conversation about the continued effects of Betsy.

In Kente's case, reactions by both his father and Kenneth Ferdinand immediately following the performance solidified his desire to continue building a 9th ward–based theater company. "When my father realized where the story of the dead body came from, he was like shocked. He couldn't believe that something that really happened—that we witnessed—was being portrayed on stage. He was proud of me for having the courage to tell that story, to play that story as true as possible."

Kente recalls Kenneth Ferdinand's wife, Melba, telling him after the play that Kenneth was speechless. All he could do was hug Kente and repeat, "Thank you. Thank you." In the interview 5 months after the play, Ferdinand articulated his pride in the youth of the lower 9th ward, the POL members.

> I always have high expectations for our students. I taught at Lawless. We have schools we constructed in the lower 9th ward. But I've always thought our kids were perceived as second-class. These kids blew that image. One kid, I know, had a speech defect. The lead kid is at University of New Orleans. It was so moving to see them do something they feel strongly about. You don't often find that in our kids' education—something that makes them passionate.

NOTE

1. From the lyrics to the *Lower 9 Stories* theme song, written by POL member and Lawless Senior High student Adrian Ford.

Chapter 12

BETWEEN SACRED MOUNTAINS

An Interview with Rex Lee Jim

Chris Benson

Editor's Note. Rex Lee Jim is a Navajo Indian who was born, raised, and still lives in Rock Point, Arizona. As a boy, he attended Rock Point Community School for several years. For high school, he went to schools off the Navajo reservation, in Asheville, North Carolina, and Carbondale, Colorado. He received a degree in English from Princeton University, and is currently pursuing a master's in English from the Bread Loaf School of English, Middlebury College. Of his teaching philosophy, Rex says, "I try to address student needs through student interests, tapping into their background and what their future may hold for them. Most of all, I want them to experience joy through learning and hard work." Rex's philosophy is evident in the book *Between Sacred Mountains*, an unusual compendium of Navajo knowledge, a text to which Rex contributed for many years as researcher, writer, and translator when he was a student at Rock Point Community School. The writer N. Scott Momaday has called *Between Sacred Mountains* "a small encyclopedia of Navajo country," suggesting "one can learn a good deal about the Navajo people and their world by looking closely into the pages of this book, and that learning is very valuable, of course."

Sam and Janet Bingham, teacher/journalists who initiated the work on *Between Sacred Mountains*, asked Rex to work with them because, as Rex recalls, "I was not shy and talked all the time. I was also doing well in my academic work. At one point, I asked them if I could do

Writing to Make a Difference. Copyright © 2001 by Teachers College, Columbia University. All rights reserved. ISBN 0-8077-4186-8 (paper), 0-8077-4187-6 (cloth). Prior to photocopying items for classroom use, please contact the Copyright Clearance Center, Customer Service, 222 Rosewood Drive, Danvers, MA, 01923, USA, telephone (508) 750-8400.

anything for them that would be academically challenging for me, and I began to work on the book in my junior high school years. Later, when I returned for the summers during my high school years, I earned some cash for helping out. *Between Sacred Mountains* is about a way of life. Navajo people share their belief systems, their history through their own eyes, how they interact with the natural world, and how they face and deal with concepts and practices not traditionally Navajo. It's a book that lends itself to history, philosophy, technology, anthropology, and contemporary trends because it is about a living and growing people."

Rex Lee Jim teaches at Diné College in Tsaile, Arizona.

CB: Tell me about the community of Rock Point, where you lived when you began working on the book *Between Sacred Mountains*. Tell me a little bit about the culture and the people there.

RLJ: Rock Point is in northern Arizona, about 45 miles north of the famous Canyon De Chelly. It's red rock country, with mesas sticking out of the landscape and lots of deep-cut canyons and high plateaus. Much of the area is desert, but there are mountains in the distance. It's a wonderful place, harsh and usually hot in the summer but very cold in the winter. The people there are friendly; open in many ways. I think their openness and willingness to try new things is evident in the book.

CB: In what way?

RLJ: The elders in some American Indian communities will not go to great lengths to interact with the young people. The elders in the communities surrounding Rock Point did and still do: sharing knowledge, inviting students to their homes, cooking for them, eating with them. Without such openness, the knowledge that is passed on is often just passed within families. This community was like that at one time; some elders and the community people didn't share with all the young people. But that has changed now that we have developed a community school, which means we invite parents into the school and the school is central to community life. There is constant interaction between the community and the school. The purpose of creating *Between Sacred Mountains*, at least for me, was to connect the education of our young people to the community, to make the community our classroom.

CB: What kind of school was Rock Point School when you created this book?

RLJ: For many years the BIA [Bureau of Indian Affairs] controlled Indian education. Rock Point was a BIA school until 1971; then it became a contract school. Not long after Rock Point became a contract school, Public Law 93-638 was passed, which promoted Indian self-determination. Now there are many contract schools that enable Indians to assume control from the BIA. In a contract school, the local people elect their own school board. That local board is empowered to run the school, to develop and improve curriculum, to hire and fire people. So, indirectly, a contract school allows the community to be much more intimately involved in such things. The school board that was elected in Rock Point had several goals: It wanted local knowledge to be taught in the school; it wanted Navajo students to be fluent and literate in Navajo first, then English; it wanted to unify the school and community. The curriculum was set up to accomplish these things. Eventually, the community became very involved in passing on traditional knowledge to young people. The best way to do that was to bring the people of the community into the school and to let students go out to learn in the places where people lived.

CB: Tell me a little bit about the curriculum of the school. How does it differ from the typical public school or the typical BIA school?

RLJ: Much of the instruction at Rock Point is done in Navajo. From kindergarten to sixth grade, there are two teachers in each classroom. One teaches only in Navajo. The other teaches only in English. For example, students will learn a math concept in English, and then the next time it will be taught in Navajo. The same goes for the other subjects. Instruction alternates back and forth in both languages. The amount of Navajo and English instruction remains constant from kindergarten through sixth grade. Later, in junior high and high school, the prevalence of Navajo in the curriculum is reduced. In order to graduate high school, though, students have to take at least one course in Navajo. Everything is taught in both languages, and that dual focus on language makes it very different from the typical public school.

CB: So language is an important component of community knowledge?

RLJ: Very important. What holds the whole curriculum together is the emphasis on language and thinking.

CB: What were some of the community-oriented aspects of the curriculum besides the language?

RLJ: Well, students focused on lots of cultural things. There was a program called Foster Grandparents, which brought elders into the school. In addition to the two regular teachers in each classroom, the school recruited an elder from the community to work with students in each elementary classrooms. These "foster" grandparents assisted teachers in teaching specific local knowledge, like plant life, for example. That topic was covered by grandfathers. The school sought to bring in many people from the community who had specific local Navajo knowledge to share with students. We looked to the community out of necessity because when Rock Point became a contract school, a lot of the BIA teaching staff left because they didn't believe that six Navajo elders who weren't schooled in Western ways would run a school. But the elders believed they could do it. And when many people left, the board of elders looked around at who was left and saw some were recreational aides, some were dormitory aides. The board told them, "You need to go back to school, to develop your teaching skills, and we will give you a contract to teach here." The board was able to do that because it was a contract school that had made the decision to be self-determined. So that's what my school did, and eventually my old dormitory aides finished their schooling; now they have master's degrees and bilingual endorsements and they teach at the school. The elders wanted to achieve this kind of unity. It was a great accomplishment.

CB: So you were a young student, approximately 11 years old when these changes were made in the school. And you worked as one of the primary authors of *Between Sacred Mountains*, a book of Navajo knowledge, which was published in 1982. You worked on the book, gathering information and interviewing Navajos and translating their words into English. How do you categorize the book? Is it an encyclopedia, a natural history, an interdisciplinary reference book? How do people use the book?

RLJ: I'm not really sure how to label the book. I think it presents knowledge. You could use it many different ways. For example, I use it in my social studies methods class at Diné College as an example of how to obtain and validate local knowledge. I ask my students to interview elders in their communities to learn for themselves how elders think about knowledge and why it's important to pass it on. I also encourage my students to invite the elders to the classroom, where they can talk to other students. I encourage students to take their classmates to the elders' homes to learn about the environments and landscapes in which they live. In this regard, the book offers many ideas and examples of how to discover important cultural points of instruction and discussion. In Rock Point, students were awed and encouraged to do more of such learning in the community when they learned the value of their grandparents' knowledge, which was valued and placed in a book.

CB: Tell me about the other contributors to the book and the parts they played. How did the idea for the book start?

RLJ: Sam and Janet Bingham were the ones who were really behind it. They were two journalists who were traveling through the Navajo Nation and saw an advertisement at the trading post for jobs at Rock Point School. They applied and got the jobs. After they began working at the school, they acted on the school board's vision and hoped that students could learn from books about local knowledge, produced by local people.

CB: The title page of the book lists the Binghams as "listeners, learners, and scribes," meaning that they were listening to your stories and learning as you did?

RLJ: Yes. Sam and Janet used the byline "learners, listeners, and scribes," rather than calling themselves "authors." I think that byline says something about Sam and Janet; that is, the fact that they didn't claim to be the "authors" of the book and relegate the rest of us as mere helpers. They knew that the knowledge belonged to the people. And they honored the people's knowledge by calling themselves learners, listeners, and scribes. Sam and Janet were really interested in documenting this kind of local Navajo knowledge. They wrote about the Chairmen of the Navajo, the ultimate leader of the tribe. They also wrote pamphlets and small books on Navajo forestry and government. Through doing this kind of cultural and historical documentation, they came up with the idea to do a book on Navajo knowledge and involve the students and the elders in the process.

CB: In the book, you and Judy Apachee are listed as "seekers who asked and understood." Were you and Judy the main go-getters for the information? The interviewers?

RLJ: Yes. I did most of the interviews in Navajo, and then I did a translation and a transcription. I did a lot of that. Judy did also. There were others, too. It was a community effort.

CB: As a young boy, you were fluent in Navajo. Did you learn anything through these extensive interviews about the language of the Navajos? I imagine talking to many elders was an intense language experience.

RLJ: It certainly was. I'm a writer today, I believe, because I was able to speak to and learn from elders like George Blueeyes. I loved the way those elders talked, and there are still many who speak in that same custom. Their Navajo is descriptive and accurate. It's like a mother cat playing with its kitten—poetic, playful, fun, new, and gracious. The elders are good storytellers. They get your attention just by the way they talk. I could sit and listen for hours. So I thought, "I would like to speak like that. I would like to write like that." So I listened. I learned a lot of vocabulary most Navajos my age don't have because I listened and talked to these elders. They have a certain way of talking to people, and I acquired some of those customs in speaking—their reasoning and how they put things together. And a lot of things were not only philosophical but extremely practical. Yes, I did learn a lot.

CB: A lot of knowledge in the book comes from elder Navajo George Blueeyes. Tell me a little bit about him. Where did he live? How old he was when you met him?

RLJ: He was at least 80, and he lived about 3 miles south of Rock Point. He was a medicine man. He was a student of my grandfather, and some of the ceremonies he knew he learned from my grandfather. He was a great medicine man. He was funny, humorous; he kidded all the time, cracked a lot of jokes about himself. You don't meet many people who can do that. He had a way to deal with people, and he was very knowledgeable. Because he was a medicine man, he knew the stories, the songs, the prayers; the names of the plants, how to use them, when to use them. With that knowledge, he was very open, very willing to share.

CB: Did he sense an urgency to document or record this information and knowledge?

RLJ: Yes. He demanded I be there to meet him at a certain time; he expected me to stay for so long. We did sense an urgency. We worked weekends and evenings. He had his way of agreeing to meet with me: he'd say,

"Well, I'll give you the interview, but you'll have to drive me to Farmington to get some things." So we would drive all the way to Farmington, about 2 hours from Rock Point, and during the ride he would tell me stories, and point out places along the way, and tell what happened there a long time ago. It was an experience! He was intense. His words were fluid, like water: It seems not to be moving, but it is *always* moving. That's how his words were.

CB: The artistry and the drawings in the book are beautiful. The artists— Rudy Begay, Wayne Charlie, and Hank Willie—were they Navajos?

RLJ: Yes, all professional artists. Wayne Charlie was teaching at Rock Point at the time.

CB: Navajo culture is based on oral history, and storytelling is a primary method of passing on traditions and knowledge. Does the book, as a compilation of *written* accounts, contradict the custom of orality in any way? How do you feel about the fact that the stories, which were previously passed along by storytelling, are now written down?

RLJ: I think that cultures change, and Navajo culture is open to change. Our openness and ability to change are reasons why we are still here and why we still have a lot of our cultural ways. The answer to your question depends on what you mean by "written." For me, the sun paintings, the body painting, the ritual paintings are writing. A lot of Navajo people would agree with that. It could be called "ceremonial" writing. Now we would probably accept what's written down as nonceremonial writing if it reinforces our culture. It's a good thing. As a people, we are beginning to write more. We are beginning to write about traditions, experiences, and some stories.

CB: So things change.

RLJ: Yes. Things are changing. People are accepting the written word and literacy.

CB: One thing that struck me when I read the book is that it's not like a history book that tells a reader exactly how it was or how it is; instead, there are a lot of open-ended stories. For example, in many places the text asks the reader questions like "Was this right?" or "How did the Navajos survive this?" A lot of questions like that pop up. I was wondering if you made a conscious effort to include that open-endedness, and if so why.

RLJ: It was conscious effort. That open-endedness is the result of our intention that language and thinking should guide the creation of the book. The open-endedness raises questions about Western and Navajo interpretations of history and facts. In some way, the questions are a way of getting at the truth. The book not only questions the Navajo version of the truth but all other versions as well. Our stories are as much alive as the stories that non-Navajos tell about us, and Navajo children need to be aware of that in order to try to get to the truth of what happened; we have to listen to several stories and ask the same questions. That way we get closer to the truth. By doing that, we will become better seekers and therefore better people.

CB: Though the book is in large part an oral history, some of the research for the book came from other texts. Did you have to travel long distances to libraries?

RLJ: Yes, we did have to travel. There were texts at the Rock Point School, some in the library in Diné College in Tsaile, Arizona, and some at the University of New Mexico. And some historical texts were supplied by Sam and Janet.

CB: One of the goals of writing for the community projects is to find ways for communities to take control of vital issues that concern them. The latter half of *Between Sacred Mountains* raises questions about the reservation's natural resources and who gets to use them. Can you talk a little about those kinds of issues as they relate to the Navajo community?

RLJ: The natural beauty and the resources on the reservation are extremely precious because the land is very arid. Water is scarce, plant life is scarce; and so it's very easy to exhaust the resources and even the beauty. Some traditional Navajos believe in the philosophy of using the land, raising lots of livestock, but sometimes they end up overgrazing. There are traditional ceremonies attached to raising livestock, which encourage this use of the land, and yet on the other hand, we must realize that resources are scarce. How can we balance those views? When you talk to the traditionalists about reducing their herds, they may get mad at you. They don't want to let go of their livestock because that means letting go of prayers and songs that are associated with animals, rooted in the land, and which have traditionally allowed us to be stewards of the land. On the other hand, overgrazing actually hurts the land, and *Between Sacred Mountains* points out this dilemma. Another issue for the community is learning to deal with the modern way of governing land use. The government now issues grazing permits that mandate livestock reduction in some cases by limiting the number of head of cattle or sheep that a rancher can sell. Theoretically, limiting sales will limit the number a rancher raises on the land. But people often get around the permits by taking their livestock to the small border towns, reservation towns, and selling them there. Land use is an important issue for our people to look at.

CB: So for Navajos, *Between Sacred Mountains* raises community issues that hang in the balance: mining, grazing, farming, and the bureaucracy that governs these things. What are the answers? How do you hope it will work out? If you were to write an epilogue to the book, what would it say?

RLJ: I think *balance* is the right word. For example, my family has cattle, horses, goats, and sheep. But we have just enough. We don't have many sheep, but we have enough to allow the younger children to learn responsibility to take care of their own sheep. We have several horses, too. We love our horses, but we don't allow them to graze outside their corral. Every now and then we let them out for a short time, but we bring them back in and buy hay and grain for them. By taking care of their own livestock, children learn the responsibility of taking care of the rest of the herd. In so doing, they learn to take care of and respect the property of their family members and others. There's a balance between what the individual or family needs and what is respectful to the land. Learning this balance keeps the young people spiritually connected to the land. We are trying to strike that balance. That way we maintain our culture and, at the same time, we take care of the land. At least in my family, that's what we're trying to do.

CB: Another issue in *Between Sacred Mountains* is the way the coal mining companies have used, or perhaps abused, the land. Is it possible for mining to be done in a balanced way?

RLJ: I think it could be done.

CB: But doesn't the book make the point that most of the profits from mining went off the reservation and that it was very unfair?

RLJ: Yes, but I think that situation has changed since the book was written. Since then, the government of the Navajo Nation has been in a position to negotiate with the mining companies. A lease is expiring in a few years, and negotiations are in the works, and some of the companies probably won't renew the contracts. Some of them will be closed down. Now the companies are required to repair and replant the mining areas, whereas before, fewer demands were made on the mining companies. It's much harder for me to speak about mining because I don't come from a community where there are mines, but I think the people who actually live there would rather see the mining companies go. I think if they did not have the problem, they would celebrate. I think if local people had true control, they would let the companies go. Yet at the same time, the mines have a certain economic value not only to the local people, but to the people as the Nation. So again, balance is the way, but it would take a lot of hard work by people willing to work together: locals, Navajos, people as a nation.

CB: What was the most vital issue of the community when you were doing this book?

RLJ: I think the main issue was, and still is, to ensure the strong participation of young people in the community. Most of the Navajo elders who helped the students create this book did so because they wanted young Navajos to understand their history, culture, and the traditional knowledge and skills. The main concern of the elders was to help young Navajo people appreciate this knowledge, maintain their language, and learn to create a balance among all aspects of life: the natural resources, the Navajo culture, the American culture, prosperity, and spirituality. Passing this knowledge and way of life on is important, but if it's going to happen, it has to begin with individuals. As young people read the book, they should be encouraged to feel a strong sense of community and purpose, one that balances their individual families' interests with those of the community.

CB: The last chapter of *Between Sacred Mountains* is a poem by a tenth-grade student named Thomas Littleben. This final "chapter" to this very detailed, almost encyclopedic, book is stunning in its simplicity:

My Land

I am sitting outside my hogan.
I am thinking,
Looking at the red rocks,
  the ridges, the sheep,
  the plants,
  and all in my world.
I look at my parents.
They are getting old,
  weak, and limping.
There aren't any of my
  sisters and brothers
  around.
I am thinking
What it will be like here
In the future.

CB: Like much of the book, the poem communicates a sense of open-ended-ness, perhaps an uncertainty.

RLJ: Thomas Littleben was my classmate. His poem concludes the book with the idea of a person thinking about his future. As long as people are thinking, we are all right. As long as young people say, "I am thinking," action will come afterwards. If they are thinking about the land, if they are thinking about the family, if they are thinking about the environment, if they are thinking about their future, then there will be action. There will be a strong sense of hope, a strong sense of commitment to the land. As a tenth-grader, Thomas Littleben was thinking about these things. His thinking in the poem led to action, and now he teaches Navajo literacy in Rock Point. In that sense, his poem is a good ending.

REFERENCE

Arthur, C. et al. (1982). *Between sacred mountains: Navajo stories and lessons from the land.* Tucson, AZ: University of Arizona Press.

Chapter 13

WRITING A FUTURE

African American Teen Mothers Finding an Identity in Charleston, South Carolina

Elizabeth Coykendall Rice

INTRODUCTION

Several summers ago, while at the Bread Loaf School of English in Vermont, I received a grant to conduct a writing for the community project on health issues in Charleston, South Carolina. My family and I were just moving to Charleston, so I saw it as a great way to get to know the area and its people; I wanted to work with high school students, and through writing, I wanted to affect policy, procedures, and society. I wanted to make a difference; I had big plans. I imagined working with a teacher and his or her students in a downtown high school, doing action research and publishing our "real-world" writing on health issues of importance to teens. What I found instead were "real-world" problems and issues in a very real situation that didn't necessarily have easy solutions.

In preparing myself for my writing for the community project, I read countless articles and books on action research, and then I came across Fred Hechinger's book *Fateful Choices: Healthy Youth for the 21st Century* (1992), which had just been published. In his book, Hechinger stresses the importance of getting students involved by writing about health issues. He explains that "much can be done to prevent health and education casualties" when students gather information and

Writing to Make a Difference. Copyright © 2001 by Teachers College, Columbia University. All rights reserved. ISBN 0-8077-4186-8 (paper), 0-8077-4187-6 (cloth). Prior to photocopying items for classroom use, please contact the Copyright Clearance Center, Customer Service, 222 Rosewood Drive, Danvers, MA, 01923, USA, telephone (508) 750-8400.

learn about topics that are of vital concern for them. Hechinger refers to *Code Blue: Uniting for Healthier Youth*, the 1990 report by the National Commission on the Role of the School and the Community in Improving Adolescent Health, which indicates that the current state of adolescent health in America today constitutes a national emergency. Hechinger and others suggest that the "challenge is to enlist all available resources of the home, the school, the health profession, the community and the religious organizations to reduce the risks" (p. 68).

THE SECOND CHANCE CLUB

Armed with my new knowledge and Hechinger's book, I went in search of a project. As an outsider to Charleston and its culture and ways, I found it impossible to "get in" anywhere to conduct my "meaningful" project. I wrote several letters to local high schools and to the various universities in the area. Remembering the suggestions by Hechinger and others to enlist all available resources, I also contacted the Pediatrics Department at the Medical University of South Carolina (MUSC), which is located in downtown Charleston. Much to my delight, Dr. Charles Darby, head of pediatrics at the Medical University of South Carolina, contacted me and said that he had passed my letter to Dr. Janice Key, head of adolescent medicine at MUSC. She later wrote me and explained that MUSC had recently started two new projects at Burke High School in downtown Charleston. One was a school-based health center, and the other was a counseling and support project for parenting adolescents who were students at Burke High School. She was very interested in my working with either group, but she was most interested in having me work with The Second Chance Club: A Family Centered Intervention for Adolescent Mothers. Dr. Key, who also was the project director for the Second Chance Club, gave me a copy of the project's abstract. In the abstract I learned that:

> The pregnancy rate for adolescents is higher in the United States than any other industrialized country in the world. Adolescents who already have one child have a particularly high rate of pregnancy. South Carolina has one of the highest rates of adolescent pregnancy nationally and a rate of 54–57% repeat adolescent pregnancy. Infants born to adolescent mothers have many medical and developmental consequences such as low birth weight, prematurity, and developmental delays. When they become school age, these children have poorer school performance. Adolescents who have a baby often drop out of school, have lower paying jobs, and have medical complications if they have inadequate prenatal care. These medical and

developmental risks are compounded if the adolescent has a second child while still a teenager, close in timing to the first pregnancy. (Key, 1994, p. 87)

In the interviews with Dr. Key, I learned that the Second Chance Club was formed in 1989 by Jann Owens, assistant professor of nursing at MUSC, and that the club was intended to "target adolescent mothers and their families by providing health education and counseling both in their homes and in groups, and in a culturally appropriate, multigenerational approach" combined with medical services in the Burke High School–based health center (Key, 1994). Burke administrators and MUSC staff work together to identify approximately 40 to 50 girls per year who qualify for the program. "The Second Chance Club and programs like it," Dr. Key (1994) explained, "not only address the health care needs of vulnerable populations but also help to improve the relationship between communities and health providers like MUSC." Teenage pregnancy is a concern for public schools and the community, and although it is important to encourage teens to wait to have children, if they don't, the teens need proper prenatal care. Participation in the club is voluntary, and members must have a signed consent form from their parents. The club is "administered" by an interdisciplinary team of counselors, nurses, social workers, health educators, and community workers. Dr. Key thought that getting club members involved in writing about health issues that were of importance to them would be "exciting" and might also generate support, recognition, and, specifically, a brochure for the Second Chance Club. Dr. Key informed me that the club had been asked to participate in an upcoming Maternal Health Fair at the Citadel Mall. In addition, the American Academy of Pediatrics' Healthy Tomorrows Technical Assistance team, one of the sponsors of the grant, was to visit the school-based health center and the Second Chance Club, so the creation of a brochure would help publicize the club and its purpose.

Dr. Key referred me to the project coordinator of the Second Chance Club, Thelma Aiken, a trained social worker. She told me a little more about the club and invited me to a meeting in March. Aiken told me that the Second Chance Club consisted of approximately 40 young women (I'm still not certain whether to refer to a pregnant 16-year-old as a mother, woman, or a girl). All members were current Burke High School students, and at the time all were single African Americans who were either pregnant or already had at least one small child.

Aiken explained to me that many of the girls were ostracized at school and in their home communities because of being teen mothers.

At Burke, the girls were not allowed to compete for homecoming queen or the Miss Burke contest because they were teen mothers. The administration was concerned that the participation of teen mothers in such contests might have given the appearance of condoning teen pregnancy. In the face of such discrimination, the club offered these girls a peer support group in which they could learn about good nutrition, baby care, and parenting skills. Moreover, the club provided a medical and academic support system for them as teen mothers and high school students determined to earn their diplomas.

March came, and I drove to Burke and parked in the cyclone-fenced teachers' parking lot. Two Charleston police cars cruised by. I headed to the main office and asked the secretary where I might find the Second Chance Club. She had never heard of the club, so she sent me to the school-based health center. From there, I was directed to the band room. The Second Chance Club uses the band room after school as long as the band or any other school-sanctioned club doesn't need it. The Second Chance Club meets after school not because it is convenient for the teen mothers or Ms. Aiken but because all "unofficial" clubs meet after school.

From my first meeting with Aiken and the club members, it was clear that Aiken and a few of the girls were eager to have me work with them. Many girls didn't show up for the meeting, and a few who arrived late seemed more intent on the snacks offered. I explained that Dr. Key had asked me to help the girls create a brochure for the club and that we could also focus on health issues of particular interest to them as adolescents and mothers. All was quiet, and then Lattita announced that she wanted to create a brochure on "safety practices to follow with small babies" because her 8-month-old boy was beginning to get into things. Shaquetta wanted to tell the real story about being pregnant—things like having morning sickness, feeling really tired, and gaining weight. Another girl wanted to write a brochure on labor and delivery and what it is "really" like. All the girls liked these brochure ideas, but we decided first to create and publish the brochure for the club members and for the upcoming maternal health fair at the Citadel Mall; later we would work on the other brochure ideas.

Because many of the girls didn't come to the club meetings, the girls decided to create and distribute a questionnaire so everyone could participate in the creation of the brochure. This would allow Aiken and the "active" club members to gather information from the members on a variety of topics—what they liked most about the club; how the club could better serve their needs; what speakers, activities, and education the girls wanted; and when and where the club should meet to allow for more participation. Sending out a questionnaire would allow each member to personally contribute to the brochure.

Only after being with the girls and Aiken for a while did I begin to "see" and understand the girls, teen pregnancy, and the club more clearly. Club attendance was not sporadic because of a lack of interest; many of the girls could not regularly attend the meetings because there was no child care or transportation available. Some of the girls' parents or grandparents took care of the babies while the girls were in school, and once school was over, the parents or grandparents had to go to work. Here was a group of girls who were trying to get an education, raise healthy children, and make a life for themselves. They had busy, complicated lives in a society and world that offered them little compassion and support. Creating a brochure or being nice to a well-meaning White educator wasn't really a high priority for them. Therefore I learned to take my "cues" from the girls. They accepted that only a few members could attend meetings; that was real life. They also understood when one of the girls got pregnant again despite the education and services offered.

Two weeks later, Aiken called and said that some of the questionnaires had been returned—12 out of 40. When I returned to the meeting, the girls were enjoying reading over the completed questionnaires, looking for quotations and ideas to extract and include in the brochure. One of the major tenets of the club is to act as a support group, so the girls wanted to include how the club helps a young woman who is "beginning to feel confident for herself" and how "knowing that what you did as a teen is not actually wrong, but it can be good as well as bad." The club members also wanted photographs of the mothers and babies and actual quotations from the members. Yet many of the girls showed hesitation and resistance in revealing their "identity" as teen mothers to local high school students and administration. Just as the girls were beginning to positively define and realize themselves as teen mothers and as members of the Second Chance Club, the very nature of identifying themselves to "outsiders" was frightening. As a group they decided that only those teen mothers who felt "secure" in being photographed for the brochure would have their pictures included.

A few months before I began the writing for the community project, Aiken and the girls had written a constitution and bylaws for the Second Chance Club. The girls suggested that the philosophy, scope, and 5-year objectives of the club needed to be included in the brochure in addition to quotations and pictures. The philosophy of the club is "to believe in myself so that despite my shortcomings in life, I can accomplish my goals; to be a responsible individual, both as a student and as a parent; and to improve the betterment of my livelihood as a parent." The scope of the club is to provide high self-esteem, increase knowledge of good health habits for mother and child, encourage members to attend school, increase knowledge of human sexuality and the importance of practicing abstinence, and provide an opportunity to develop career goals.

When the girls decided to use these quotations in the brochure, they began to look closely at the words and make meaning of them and how they related to their lives and the Second Chance Club. One young girl thought that some of the phrasing sounded a little like punishment. "Despite my shortcomings" and "practicing abstinence" raised questions. Was it a "shortcoming" to have a baby as a teen or out of wedlock even though many of their friends and some of their own mothers had themselves lived those experiences? Why was Norplant provided if one of the main tenets of the program was to practice abstinence? Composing the brochure raised serious questions for these girls.

Some of the girls felt that the philosophy, scope, and objectives of the club needed revising so that the statements had real meaning to them. They sounded "good," but some of the girls didn't really know what they said or meant. Some of the girls admitted that they didn't really know what the philosophy, scope, and objectives of the club meant prior to our discussion. We talked about how the club helped educate and counsel and how it provided access to medical funding and medical care through MUSC and the school-based clinic. Given the short time frame before the health fair, the girls decided to go with the text as it read and to revise it later when there was more time. We added some pictures of storks, baby clip art, and a photo of one young woman with her baby.

At the health fair, we field-tested the hot-pink and hot-blue brochures (the girls' choice of color). The girls enthusiastically handed out their brochures to passersby and to the other maternal health care providers present at the fair. The girls obviously enjoyed being a part of the fair and telling people about their club; they felt proud of their accomplishments and the brochure. They also liked being spokespersons for the club, talking to others about how the club had helped them. Dr. Key came to the fair and praised the girls for their participation at the fair and on their brochure.

A few weeks later we worked on the final brochure, adding additional quotations from the members as well as photographs of the club mothers and their babies. The philosophy and scope changed a bit so that "other girls could read and understand it." A friend who is an art director at a Charleston advertising firm offered to work with the girls to fine-tune the brochure. By the end of the schoolyear, the girls had a club brochure, two other brochures on the myths of sex and conception, and a poster that outlined home safety tips for parents of small babies. The brochures about labor and delivery and teen pregnancy were put on hold so more research could be done. These brochures were published and distributed at the Burke High School clinic, the health department, local Charleston high schools, and clinics in the Charleston area.

WRITING LOGS AND INDIVIDUAL AND COLLECTIVE WRITING

Another activity I did with the club members was to create writing logs. Writing was not a component of the Second Chance Club before I introduced writing for the community concepts to them, except to fill out myriad medical forms each month. I bought notebooks and asked the girls to begin keeping writing logs (journals) to record their ideas for the brochure, thoughts on upcoming presentations, and thoughts on parenting and other related topics. With regular practice in writing in the logs, club members, Dr. Key, and Aiken began to understand that writing, either as an individual act (writing logs) or as a collective act (generating ideas and lists and creating brochures and questionnaires), served an important part in self-discovery.

Using the objectives and philosophy of the Second Chance Club as our guidelines, we brainstormed a list of possible topics for writing. The list included such topics as effective parenting, self-esteem, safety, human sexuality, fathers and fatherhood, mothers and motherhood, health care, nutrition of the mother and child, responsibility, teen pregnancy, relationships, abstinence, teen parenthood, childhood, peer pressure, and career goals. When we were jotting down our ideas for the journal topics, Lattita had written down fathers. The father of her child was helping raise their child and sometimes came to the club meetings, but some of the girls didn't want Michael to come to the meetings. Many of the girls wanted to write about their own mothers but couldn't quite begin to write about or define themselves as mothers. We talked about how they could write down their hopes and fears, joys and frustrations, and that years later they could look back and read about their early years (literally and figuratively) as parents and as high school students. For those who took it seriously and wrote regularly, the journal offered a reflective environment, which seemed lacking in the club and in their own lives.

In the individual act of writing, the journal became a place to imagine, explore, and change thinking or attitudes or to try on new roles. It was where one could begin to learn from experience, distinguish past behaviors from current ones, and, ultimately, take charge of life. In the collaborative writing the girls did related to club brochures and the bylaws, the writing activity created, defined, and solidified the club, projecting a positive rather than negative identity to the school, to the larger community, and, most important, to the girls themselves. The experience of writing together became a validation of a "sisterhood," as Aiken put it, to the previously fragmented individuals who all shared a common "problem." Through writing and discussion, and as members of the Second Chance Club, many of the girls have begun to create a new place and identity for themselves, one that is active and involved rather than passive and detached.

AFTERWARD: THE SECOND CHANCE CLUB TODAY

After a couple years, my family and I moved from Charleston. When I left the writing for the community project and the Second Chance Club behind, I knew that the journal writing and the creation of the brochures were just the beginning. The girls wanted to put together a regular newsletter that would cover adolescent health issues, and they wanted to write a play about teen parenting and visit at-risk middle school students.

I returned recently to Charleston to see Aiken and the girls. It had been almost 3 years since I had worked with the club, and I learned from Aiken that many of the girls I had worked with had either graduated (about two-thirds of them) or dropped out of school. Aiken and the girls had revised the brochure several times and had rewritten some of the text and tenets to make them more accessible. Instead of meeting after school, the club now meets every Thursday at lunchtime for group sessions, but occasionally they have speakers or programs after school or on the weekend. Currently, there are about 20 active members, a much greater number than when I was working with the girls, although attendance is still sporadic for some of the same reasons. About 50 girls at Burke qualify for the program because they are either pregnant or have a small child or children. Aiken said that meeting at lunchtime allowed for more participation and more involvement. Transportation wasn't a problem either.

Another new direction for the club is that the members have been trained as teen peer educators in two new programs, "Reducing the Risk" and "STAND: Students Taking a New Direction," and through role-playing they help educate at-risk girls in the Charleston public middle and high schools. Last spring, the Second Chance Club members went to several Charleston middle schools and talked candidly and openly with at-risk sixth- through eighth-grade girls about dating; pregnancy; labor and delivery; and the effects teen pregnancy and teen parenting have on the teen, the family, free time, participation at school, the community, and society. Aiken and the club members said that it was a dynamic and wonderful program and that many of the at-risk girls shared personal stories with the club members. The guidance counselors at the various middle schools also thought it was a wonderful presentation. Aiken and the girls are planning to sketch out and script the program more for the next visit; the first one was quite spontaneous. Aiken would also like to include role-playing and reflective writing in this year's program.

In January 1997, Aiken and ten of the club members wrote a grant to Youth Services of Charleston requesting funding so that they could take the SAT preparation class offered through MUSC's Office of Diversity. Eight of the girls took the class and two of the girls scored over 1,000 on their SATs. One of the girls is attending the University of South Carolina and another is at Charleston Southern this fall. Ms. Aiken thinks that the girls are experiencing the power of the written word.

In May 1998, Channel 5 News in Charleston did a segment entitled "Mean Streets: Sweet 16 and Pregnant" and featured a segment on the Second Chance Club. Channel 5 gave some staggering current figures on teen pregnancy in South Carolina. They reported that every day 31 teen pregnancies occur in South Carolina and that South Carolina has the tenth highest teen birthrate in the nation. Eighty percent of the teen pregnancies are unplanned, and many of the fathers are at least 3 years older than the girls—many of the fathers are between the ages of 18 and 25. Two-thirds of the teen mothers in South Carolina drop out of school and never graduate, a figure that shows how successful programs like the Second Chance Club really are. In the segment on the Second Chance Club, Shawnqua recounted her rather quick and terrifying labor and delivery at home and explained how she was afraid to tell her mother about her pregnancy. A MUSC psychiatrist interjected in the TV segment that teen parenting is an "isolating situation" that often divides families.

Aiken said that, in general, things are better for the girls. With the brochure, newspaper article, and TV segment about the Second Chance Club, the school and community are more accepting of the club and of the girls. They have a better image, Aiken knows, but she thinks that much could be done to improve overall social issues in the state. Aiken and the girls are continuing to look for grants for funding for SAT courses and for improving writing skills for South Carolina's high school exit exam. Child care is still an issue for most of the girls; many can't attend school because of lack of child care. Aiken and the girls are researching potential funding in the community to contract with local child-care providers to care for the babies while the mothers are in school. In addition, through a letter-writing campaign, the girls are developing contacts with local businesses to create shadowing and internship opportunities for career development. Aiken also wants to improve the mentoring program and possibly create a video and follow-up program for presentation to the at-risk middle school girls. Aiken understands the need for more community involvement, including schools, parents, MUSC, local churches, child-care providers, and local businesses and agencies.

In learning to take charge and in staying actively involved and conscious of their bodies, babies, and futures, the Second Chance Club members are learning to become active women, students, parents, and citizens. As Hechinger (1992) explains:

> Health issues and choices which face young adolescents today are ours as a society as well, for, given sufficient attention and support, young people can have the chance to grow up healthy and whole both in body and mind. What is at stake are not only the precious individual lives of our young people, but our national health and our future as a nation (p. 22).

One of the overall goals of the Second Chance Club is to reduce the rate of repeat adolescent pregnancy. Medicine can "fix" certain problems, but language and writing (individually and collectively) can help youngsters make discoveries about themselves that can actually prevent risky health behaviors. Through projects like the Second Chance Club, adolescent mothers (and fathers) can become better students, parents, and citizens, and grow healthy and whole. Then healthier futures occur.

In the conclusion of his book, Hechinger (1992) urges that "young adolescents at crucial crossroads in their lives must be helped now to avoid risks to their health and future well-being. To safeguard their health is not an act of charity; it is a reaffirmation of a humane society and an investment in the nation's future" (p. 215). The women of the Second Chance Club have worked hard to define and create an identity for themselves in their club, school, communities, and society, and they are certainly at a crucial crossroad in their lives. Therefore, we must affirm these new identities and invest in a humane society and our nation's future.

REFERENCES

Hechinger, F.M. (1992). *Fateful choices: Healthy youth for the 21st century*. New York: Carnegie Corporation.

Key, J.D. (1994). *The second chance club: A family centered intervention for adolescent mothers*. Unpublished manuscript.

Key, J.D., Barbosa, G.A., & Owens, V.J. (1999). The second chance club: Repeat pregnancy postponement using a high school club intervention. *Journal of Adolescent Health, 24* (2), 87.

National Commission on the Role of the School and the Community in Improving Adolescent Health. (1990). *Code blue: Uniting for healthier youth*. Washington, DC.

Chapter 14

A LICENSE TO THINK

Writing for Change as Privilege, Obligation, and Professional Journey

Tom McKenna

In 1995 I took a year's leave of absence from teaching to pursue my own writing and to explore models of experiential education. Prior to my year out of the classroom, I attended the Bread Loaf School of English at Middlebury College in Vermont. There I worked closely with Dixie Goswami, head of the Program in Writing at Bread Loaf and director of Write to Change, a nonprofit agency that supports teachers and students whose writing projects are designed to benefit the community beyond their classrooms. With an endless spring of evocative questions from Dixie, and a grant from Bread Loaf and Write to Change, I began to develop a focus for the year. What were other teachers doing to expand the scope of their classroom work beyond the walls of their classrooms? In what ways were they able to use writing to effect actual change?

Through a series of conversations with members of the Bread Loaf Teacher Network (BLTN), I was able to develop a partnership with Janet Atkins, who taught at Wade Hampton High School in Hampton, South Carolina. In March of that year, I visited Janet's home, community, and classroom and spoke with her students, their parents, and several of her colleagues. Even now, years after my visit to Janet's class, I am still affected by my partnership with her and the culture of her classroom. In the Internet age, as education rhetoric about "classrooms without walls" and "virtual communities" builds to a fevered pitch, I

Writing to Make a Difference. Copyright © 2001 by Teachers College, Columbia University. All rights reserved. ISBN 0-8077-4186-8 (paper), 0-8077-4187-6 (cloth). Prior to photocopying items for classroom use, please contact the Copyright Clearance Center, Customer Service, 222 Rosewood Drive, Danvers, MA, 01923, USA, telephone (508) 750-8400.

often ground myself by remembering the kinds of values that Janet's students attached to things such as their impact on involved adult listeners, their shared sense of community and group identity, and their opportunities to explore and to make change.

In ways that I could not fully anticipate, this project became an apprenticeship for me as a beginning teacher researcher and as an educational "networker," and in this apprenticeship, I've found a lesson in professional development. In the process of studying what happens to young writers when traditional classroom structures open up, allowing students to write for social change, I found myself in the midst of a form of professional development that, through its authenticity and complexity, would work real change in me.

At the end of the 1994 summer session of Bread Loaf, I decided that I would set up a computer conference on BreadNet called "Experiential Education." This conference would be a place where I would begin to gather data about what was happening in various project-centered approaches to teaching secondary English. That summer on campus, there was much talk among teachers in the Bread Loaf Teacher Network about collaborative projects centering on local communities and environments, projects about place. Dixie and I looked for a question to ask students, parents, administrators, and co-teachers, a question that might help us better discuss what was happening in these place-based classes. The questions that I originally posed to four BLTN members included:

- What did the students actually do in place-based projects or curricula, since they were not doing many of the things that students typically do in traditional curricula?
- What difference did it make that use of language, with its emphasis on personal, expressive, and imaginative writing, was intended to be practiced across the varied disciplines that are inherent in place-based projects or curricula?

Although these questions did remain central to the dialogue, the shape of the project changed fairly radically once the school year began. By October, the "Experiential Education" conference was renamed "Place Project Notes." It would be a forum for teachers to share insights about the various versions of place-centered studies. And for me, it would be the place to focus on a case study of the work of two teachers (Janet Atkins and Scott Christian) and their students.

I began the project with a "weekend warrior" approach to teacher research and telecommunications. I chose to spend my "workweeks" living alone in a driftwood cabin, a few hours' hike from Unalaska, the Aleutian community that I was trying to understand as my own and my students' home. There I was doing work that in many ways paralleled the students' work—using a journal to come to know my local environment, reading local and natural history, and trying to shape significant personal writing in response to my surroundings. On weekends I trudged back to town, weaseling my way into some friends' kitchen, plugging into their phone line, and trying to resume my place in various electronic conversations. The eventual collapse of the "Experiential Education" conference was partly a result of my guerrilla telecommunications tactics and the sporadic conversation patterns. In retrospect, I realize I had tailored the project to my own specific agenda, rather than to the realities of what busy teachers were doing in *their* day-to-day lives.

By late September, Janet had emerged as the strongest voice in the crowd, perhaps because she was both determined to clarify the goals of the conversation and well set up to shape what we were doing with the realities of her classroom life. Here's an excerpt from a September 27 entry in the computer conference discussion:

> I'm really interested in two aspects of nature writing/community inquiry. One is how it can truly become writing for the community, and the second is how it can be of impact on the students' lives. I teach in a county that is bordered to the south by a major river which is polluted with, among other things, mercury from the nuclear waste site up river. To the east is the ACE basin—a national wetlands preserve which is a political hotbed. . . . To the northeast is the county which includes Edisto Island and a number of other barrier islands. We are mostly swamp (excuse me, wetlands) and pine forest. The environmental issues here are preservation, tree farming, agriculture (especially irrigation), hunting and trash.
> —Janet

Janet's conviction to study how students' "nature writing" could affect their community and their own lives, as well as her willingness to share the context of her place, began to shape our discussion and move it in a direction that became more relevant. The South Carolina members of BLTN were in the process of designing an interdisciplinary study of wetlands. They collaborated on their students' field-based studies using BreadNet. Alaska teachers were similarly arranged, dividing into groups to share accounts of fall happenings in their communities. I didn't interact much with either group, and my project developed its own focus more by default than by design. At the end of October, I wrote online:

> My goal, however fuzzy right now, is descriptive. I'd like to be able to describe those "aha" moments where students, teachers, colleagues see some larger connections than they had prior to these experiences. And I'd like, also, to be able just to describe what kids are doing in these projects that they might not be doing in a more traditionally defined language arts class.

Scott Christian, an experienced teacher researcher, later suggested that we leave off the "aha" moments and just see what comes from these interviews. His work in Nikiski and other aspects of the Teacher Network ultimately kept him away from the conversation in the ensuing weeks. But as my project began to focus solely on Janet's work, Scott's suggestion was influential in helping me clarify further what my role would be. I would simply talk to people—young people and older people—and read their impressions. Further classification or analysis would take its shape based on those primary impressions.

A few other strands came together during this phase of the project. After finishing my cabin stint, I was invited to join several other Bread Loafers and a host of distinguished natural historians, educators, and writers at the Roger Tory Peterson Institute's forum "Writing and the Natural World." Conversations there gave me a powerful glimpse of the possibilities for young people to move from observation to action. I began to think of Janet's question about how her students' field work and writing would truly become "writing for the community" as my own question as well. I also received encouraging notes from Dixie Goswami, who shared her experiences planning the wetlands conference in South Carolina. She suggested that I come down and visit Janet and her students. Prior to my visit, Dixie, Janet, and I kept up a lively conversation about all aspects of the project. Writing to us online about the work of South Carolina teachers in collaboration with university people from several disciplines, Dixie helped me conceive of a paradigm, and some utility, for my own work by describing the novelty of what we were doing: "It's been hard and invigorating work with lots of discussion (debate). Having a scientist with us has really changed everything. So what have we got here—a unique kind of 'do-it-yourself' professional development."

The do-it-yourself model of development, through interaction with people in different contexts with mutual concerns, would describe my own introduction to teacher research. It also became a fitting description for the kind of self-education that Janet's students were involved in. From the time when Janet and I began to anticipate my visit to her classroom, we exchanged several notes about the contexts in which we each work. And while Janet, I believe, was simply trying to convey information about—and to reflect on—her own teaching experience, she was also giving me a model of her journal-writing process.

MESSAGE 1 NOVEMBER 3

Hi Tom, I read your message, and thought I'd write about something that happened in my classroom today and send it to you. What follows is sort of a teacher journal entry. I thought you'd like to know about an idea that my students came up with today. I asked them to do a proposal for a writing for the community project, and suggested a number of options. Among these options were a video/brochure for rising 9th graders, an anti-smoking brochure, a new community center, and a career manual. Most groups selected from the list and set about writing their proposals and subsequent progress reports. Today, however, one group in my 8:00 class decided that their options were too limited. All but one student in the group knows what he plans to do after graduation so the career booklet didn't suit them. They didn't think they could get funding for a community center, and they felt an anti-smoking brochure would be thrown in the trash can. When they called me to their tables, they explained these thoughts and asked why they couldn't write a proposal for a program to help high school students quit smoking—sort of like Alcoholics Anonymous. I asked them to tell me what their final product would be, and they agreed to write letters to several agencies to get support. I also suggested they might have to promote the project once it became a reality. So we'll see what they can come up with.

Another group is doing a modified proposal on the community center. Instead of building from scratch, they are proposing to renovate an older building and staff it with volunteers who would care for and tutor latch key kids. The renovations would be done by the building construction students here at the high school. I'm not sure about the legal ramifications of this project, but I like their idea.

I don't have an educational utopia in my classroom by any means; however, I question the traditionalists' approach to 12th grade English. The reason I question their approach is the same reason my kids question it. What exactly is the point of learning how many lines make up an octave or quatrain anyway? I'm glad I learned that material in high school, but I went on to make a career out of it, and most people—even teachers I work with in other fields—couldn't tell me the definition of an octave!

Well that's enough about pedagogical philosophy for now. Write back if you can. Play devil's advocate or ask questions for clarification. I'll answer sooner or later.

—Janet

When I reflect today on my response to Janet's note, I see the seeds of what would become perhaps my most important discovery or affirmation from Janet's students. Janet's kids would remind me not to forget the value of that tired term, *ownership* of their learning. Here's an excerpt from my reply to Janet, which conveys what I was learning in November, through online communication, about Janet's pedagogy. It also provides a fairly typical model of the kind of journal-like text that we often exchanged.

Hello, Janet. First of all, having never done a writing-for-the-community project like yours in the classroom, I'm very impressed with the context you have put your students in. From the sounds of things, you have students who are coming forward to tailor their education to their own sense of what is right, what might work. As your description of that one day last week has bounced around in my head this week, I keep seeing your students in a posture of modifying things—most notably the group who thought the teacher-provided suggestions were "too limited" and who went on to propose an AA-style support program for smokers. The community center group also sought to modify circumstances (in this case, also, literally a building) before acting. Dare I use the word "ownership"? It does seem that you have kids in a context that empowers, motivates, or demands them to modify the circumstances of their education until it somehow feels right.

. . . Seems like we're both interested in what kids are doing (in this case, to me, modifying the constraints of their "assignments"), how they're affected by contexts which present language use at least as much as a tool as a subject of study, and how students move from observation/discussion/personal experience to taking action.

—Tom

Some time between the date of this response to Janet and her reply, I became the self-dubbed Sub-from-Hell. From a crowded urban middle school classroom, where, as a substitute teacher, I was becoming schooled in the art of coercion, I had sent an exasperated note to Janet, wondering if she had discovered any insights about student ownership and initiative through place-based projects. This was Janet's cue to explain the development of her team of voluntary wetland students, "The Water Rangers." In a classroom where four adults (myself plus two aides and the sub from across the hall) patrolled to keep kids reading their textbook, I began to think about the power of voluntarism and about how, with the Water Rangers, Janet and her students were expanding the bounds of their "assignments." Here, too, Janet's mentoring role takes on another dimension, as she refers me to the work of James Britton.

THURSDAY, NOVEMBER 17

Janet: I'm wondering whether any of this place-based learning and teaching has caused you to think about issues of initiative, ownership of work, etc.?
    —Tom, the Substitute from Hell

And here is Janet's response:

THURSDAY, NOVEMBER 17

Hi, Tom! I just thought I'd let you know that I received my first two applications for our wetlands project today. Since I don't teach a class that fits the plans we made at our S.C. October conference, I'm recruiting kids to do the wetlands enterprise as an extracurricular project. We have a twenty-five minute advisory period daily that I plan to utilize for our meetings. I'm not sure when we'll actually go out on a field trip, but it should be soon. I'll put their first field notes up as soon as I get them.
    Today, I had a speaker in my Applied Communication class from DHEC (Department of Health and Environmental Control) who spoke to the class about the negative implications of smoking *and* what they need to do to proceed with their brochures and proposals for their anti-smoking campaign. I thought he gave the students a lot of good information including the fact that they need to study the Big Book of Alcoholics Anonymous in order to find out what they have to do in their Smoker's Anonymous group.

I've made out lesson plans for my next unit in this class, but I've pushed them aside due to the interest in these projects. It's a risk because it's going to take time to complete the projects—time the curriculum doesn't really allow. In James Britton's (1987) "A Quiet Form of Research," the following passage strikes me as pertinent to this conversation and to the Tech Prep (Applied Communication) movement:

> I remember one enthusiastic researcher who, in a prestigious conference, expressed the hope that "by this time next year" his thoroughly researched social studies program would be in use in every school in the state. To think in this way is to ignore totally the teaching/learning context—the minutiae of behavior of a particular teacher in moment-by-moment interaction with a particular group of students in a particular school and locality on a particular occasion. However well a program may have been researched, it can achieve its objectives only as a result of the full participation of both students and teachers. . . . I believe the notion that teaching is interactive and not unidirectional has been with us long enough for us to realize that what the teacher does not achieve in the classroom cannot be achieved by anybody else—by a department head, a principal, the writers of statutory guidelines, or anybody else. (p. 15)

In the normal run of Applied Communications, the curriculum is about as canned as a curriculum can be. That's why I do projects like this Writing for the Community one. It allows me to meet the "competencies" for the class (an occupation-ed imposed term), while experimenting and then reflecting on what my students have done and can do. But that's curriculum. I suspect what you are dealing with is a lot deeper than just what you have to teach. I think I hear a little about who you have to teach as well . . . and perhaps who you are when you have to teach those students. If Britton is right, "good" teachers really have their hands full. I've only just begun to think of the implications of this passage in relation to your substitute-from-hell query, but let me know if I might be on the right track. I'd also like to know a little about your own classroom at Unalaska.

Anyway, I'll put this letter and other ones I've written in the place-notes folder for others to read. Until later.

—Janet

In this note, Janet is living Britton's "interactive and not unidirectional" model of teaching. In reflecting on her practice out loud for me, she provides an instance of the interwoven lines of communication between teacher and students, teacher and fellow teacher, and teachers and those teachers' teachers. I began to realize that, like most good teachers, Janet naturally finds a way to do many things at once, to structure her activities so that they are useful and instructive in many dimensions.

In answer to some of the questions I had asked, Janet provided me with ethnographic data on her students, and she described the more traditional syllabi that her general-level students would follow without these projects. She then stated in very clear terms what she saw as the source of her students' desire to take some control of their learning: "As for the students who modified their projects last week, I think their motivation came partly from the fact that they are practical, and partly from the fact that I give them license to think."

The next significant event in the chronology of our exchange demonstrates how the Teacher Network gives teachers license to think in ways that are at once personally meaningful and practical. I mention this not so much to celebrate the accomplishments of the simple structures of online communication, but to continue to articulate how the metaphor of network, with its multidimensional possibilities, might matter to teachers like myself, who have found that traditional "training" models, disconnected from the context of my teaching, fall short.

To begin the wetlands exchange, South Carolina teachers posted pieces of writing to introduce the wetland they were to lead students to study. In a mid-November entry, Janet described a spot on the Salkehatchie River that her students would be studying. Recently I've returned to her introduction to this piece, and a response that follows, as examples of fellow teachers' struggles with this difficult genre. Chris Benson's reply to Janet, in addition to helping everyone involved try to define the genre of nature writing, illustrates a function of a network that I would later learn about from Janet's students: the value of the strangely paradoxical listener, an outsider (in this case a colleague, but one from a different region of the state and removed from the high school grind) who somehow cares.

THE SWAMP
BY JANET ATKINS

What I remember the most about my father's wetlands property is the strange looks I would always get when I told my friends that we were going to The Swamp. That's what we called the place. I also remember the long, boring rides from Greenville to Hampton, and later from Summerville to Hampton, when we would just go to the swamp and sit and admire the land. We children got out and explored, but my dad and mom just sat on the hood of the car (an Oldsmobile "Land Yacht"), and shared dreams of a time when they would build a home and live on this land for the rest of their lives.

The water was what we call black water, and this particular river, the Salkehatchie, is the headwaters of the Combahee River, which combines with the Ashepoo River and the Edisto River to form South Carolina's ACE Basin. On a recent visit there I noted how high the water was. It swirled in eddies as it headed toward the ocean. A turtle just under the water's surface snapped at bugs floating above it, and I noted with a certain pleasure that the old cypress tree now reaches at least half way across the run. A patch of small yellow flowers (yellow-eyed grass, I think) was at the water's edge. When I looked up a description of this plant in the Audubon's Wetlands guide I was reminded of the "violence" of nature. This plant happens to be carnivorous—but then I really don't mind how many bugs it "eats."

Another memory from childhood is of the many fires one could see along Fisherman's Trail in the dusk. From the bridge looking down the run, the fires dotted the bank telling the location of each man or woman who was spending quiet time catching a mess of redbreast or catfish. In my teenage years, I spent many quiet moments with my grandfather, cane pole held out over the dark water waiting for something to pull the float under. Even now I can feel the excitement of seeing the first nibble at my bait, knowing that some delicious catch (all too often that old turtle again) was just about to strike.

While reflecting on these memories, I was reminded of a poem by Gerard Manley Hopkins. It begins "As kingfishers catch fire, dragonflies draw flame" and goes on to speak of the calling that each of us has to be true to ourselves. Being true to myself means having an alert attentiveness to whatever is there in the present moment. I kind of like to think of that turtle waiting for just the right moment when the water spider is poised on the surface and then—splash!—he has his dinner. Being attentive like those flowers when a gnat jiggles it enough for the enzymes to start flowing. Being attentive to the bob of the float at the end of the line, and to "see," also, when the "kingfishers catch fire and dragonflies draw flame." Come in person, and I'll introduce you to the Swamp anytime!

And here is Chris Benson's response:

All I can say is "WOW." Janet accomplishes in her writing something that is so difficult, so very difficult, for even gifted writers to
accomplish when contemplating a natural scene or experience. I
have been trying to write a nature poem (as well as prose) for
about three weeks. And the biggest problem is that I keep asking
myself "so what?" It's so hard to get the observations, the
detailed facts and description, to amount to something that takes
the reader beyond the surface of the natural scene or experience.
That's the key in all writing, I know—to take the reader beyond
the details toward some pleasing or disturbing revelation, but it
seems especially hard in nature writing. Why is that?

I think it has something to do with the fact that nature gives
the appearance of being static. I know that the natural world is
not static; it's in a constant state of symbiosis and flux, but it's
the constancy that makes it seem static. And it's hard to break
past the surface details of the appearance of a natural scene to
find what it means. Really, I find it hard to be a part of a natural
scene; I'm an outside observer. Usually having such distance helps
a writer toward insight, but with natural scenes, that distance
seems exclusive, and I end up using too many adjectives and just
writing descriptive prose about the blue sky, the feathered hem-
lock limbs, the wrinkled crawling surface of the lake, etc.

So I appreciate Janet's Swamp piece, which is really not about
the swamp or the river but rather about the thrill of living in the
moment and anticipating *something about to happen.*

Chris's response not only helped me articulate the symmetry between what was happening with Janet's students and among her online
colleagues; it also helped me approach my students' writing efforts in a
way that a writing rubric certainly would not. Nature writing is a difficult genre, and no amount of competency-based curriculum or stan-
dards-based instruction will change that. But when colleagues examine
a difficult genre as fellow writers, we may heighten our sensitivity to
our students' frustrations and successes.

By late November, the format for my research had almost completely changed. The idea of a conference to evolve standards for judging project-based programs had fizzled because it was not useful to the
teachers who were asked to pitch in; they didn't need it. What emerged

instead was a dialogue that shaped itself to meet the needs of two teachers. From this point until my visit in February, our talk centered around my visit to Hampton. In late February, I finally made it. I showed up in South Carolina with a brand new tape recorder, with long lists of questions for students and with a ton of anxiety about being in such a distant place. After a morning of observing Janet's classes and meeting many of her colleagues, I talked to groups of students. Among other things, I asked kids to describe what they had been doing and why they were doing it, and I questioned them on the following topics:

- What differences the various settings made for their writings
- How writing for the electronic exchange might be "different" from other kinds of writing
- How they felt they might be making some kind of a difference
- How they might use the things they had learned
- What, if anything, they might have learned about how they learn during the course of these projects

We had three tape-recorded conversations: one with many of the kids from the writing for the community projects; another with three students from the Water Rangers; and a third with a gathering at Janet's home of Water Rangers students, parents, and another teacher. Within a couple of days, I had enough data to warrant a book, but I also had some especially clear and intriguing observations about students' learning contexts, about their notions of audience, and about their impetus toward activism.

CONTEXTS

From my first step inside Wade Hampton High School, I was struck by contrasts. I heard the usual furious pace of joking conversations amid slamming lockers, saw youthful smiles and serious morning frowns. Unlike our little carpeted school that is in many ways the center of town at Unalaska, though, this school was fenced in, with hard surfaces everywhere, brick and tile. I needed to obtain a "visitor's pass," and en route to the office I couldn't help noticing teachers stopping students from going to lockers in restricted parts of the buildings. Yet teachers were also welcoming me at every turn, interested people questioning me about Alaska. Still, these friendly folks were addressing others formally as "Mr." and "Mrs." Inside Janet's classroom, at the bell, I took note of the usual spirited smilers and sleepers, and I began to take solace in the similarities of our teaching situations. However, I also noticed students' choice to segregate themselves by race at the classroom's tables.

A woman came in with the results of a survey that listed students' vocational interests. I heard the inevitable laughter and chiding accompanying her findings for the choreographer's career, for the beautician's. Yet some students were intently studying the document, apparently amazed to recognize themselves in the continuums of interests and preferences. Over the next few days, I would take a less quantitative approach to learning about Janet's students' backgrounds and interests. While I formally interviewed students in several of Janet's classes, I also traveled with the Water Rangers group and entered into a rich genuine context for discussion. I'd chat and listen in the van, I'd meander through the Salkehatchie wetlands with groups of students, and I'd explore the inner and outer workings of the Westinghouse plant with them.

I joined the Water Rangers on the day of their third outing. Student Lee Norman, one of the most vocal of the Rangers, gave me this account of the chronology of the wetlands study and the Water Rangers' voluntary role in it.

> First we had to write an essay describing why we think wetlands are important. Ms. Atkins put together a pamphlet with some basic features of the wetlands and why they're important. . . . Then Ms. Atkins and Mr. Thomas [Lee's science teacher] pretty much told us how they wanted our notebooks to work, about how they wanted us to write down the temperature and just describe the area we saw, and if we saw anything interesting to write that down. Then they told us about the testing and what we would test for, and that we'd have to write on what we saw, that we'd have to make some kind of creative effort afterwards. And then they pretty much loaded us up and took us out to our first site. We walked around with the group for a little while, and they just let you pretty much go and just look on your own if you wanted to. Then we just wrote down all that, and after that we wrote our essays and poetry and whatever else. The next few days, usually the next three or four days after we came back, we tested the water in Mr. Thomas's lab during our advisory period. We did that for each of the trips, and today is our third trip out in the wild.

How did the contexts for writing in both the wetlands project and the problem-solving projects seem to matter to these kids? The comments of the kids who studied the wetlands suggested that there was a productive balance between a context that is open enough to allow the activity to be *exploration* (a word that I feel is very important for this whole project) and yet structured enough so that students will feel guided. When I asked members of the Water Rangers an open question about what they had been doing, Lee responded quickly by saying that they had been "exploring," and Rebecca Young and Rebecca Hall responded immediately to Lee's assessment.

TM: If you had to tell someone what this Water Rangers business is all about, where would you start?
LN: I would almost say "explore." (*Others agree.*) But you have to know a lot about something. The wetlands are not unexplored, plenty of people have [explored them], it's just really a learning experience I'd say. [We're] trying to figure it out, how it works and why it happens like it does. . . . Then there's the other end of it, the lab part, where we do tests.
RY: It's interesting.
LN: That's just to make sure, just to make sure our wetlands are OK. We're doing everything we can to keep them safe.
RY: Protecting.
TM: So you're interested in exploring, you're testing, you're protecting. Anything else on this? Anything else on what your mission is?
LN: Maybe to increase public knowledge. I'm not sure exactly.
RY: Awareness.
LN: And we attracted some attention, apparently, from Westinghouse.
RH: Yeah, we were testing the water above and below the plant.
LN: They might think twice about, maybe, dumping something in the water.
RH: They know people are checking to make sure that they aren't.

In several situations, students contrasted the context of writing in the classroom with that of writing outdoors. Students spoke about how ideas tend to flow more freely and easily outdoors (where they themselves can move around more freely), whereas in the classroom they often felt stifled or somehow watched by others.

TM: How about your process of writing when you go out there? How do you decide what you're going to write, and when do you decide what you're going to write? What's it like to go out there and write about what you do?
LN: It's different than most other classes and most other experiences.
RY: I'm more relaxed out there than sitting in a classroom. I'd rather just sit down in the grass or some place and just write because my mind is cleared of other things.

LN: Yeah, like in a classroom, you're so distracted, sometimes you can't
   really be as creative as you would be if you were somewhere else.
RH: Sitting in a desk doesn't exactly spark your imagination. (*Laughter
   flows from the three students here.*)
LN: Sometimes you see things out there and you're just like, "Aw, gotta
   write about this," or "I gotta write about why we should protect this,"
   or something like that. It just hits you.

In an unprompted conversation with Nicole, a student in Janet's
classroom, she talked about the importance of the freedom in this context for learning. I asked her why she wanted to be part of the Water
Rangers, and she quickly began speaking about how it is different from
the monotony of school. "Outside, you can be more relaxed, you don't
have to be, like so intense. . . . And you end up sometimes noticing
more. . . . The school is like that; it's just the sameness of every day. It
drives some people to leave." Nicole felt that if the Water Rangers
course were to become a graded part of the curriculum, there would be
a danger of its also becoming monotonous, like other aspects of school,
and that there would be more of the kind of tension that in her view
made it harder to notice things.

As my conversation with the students moved to their idiosyncratic
writing processes, drawing from their outings, the importance of freedom to choose methodology in this context was underscored by Rebecca Hall's discussion of a recent poem she had written following one of
the Water Rangers outings.

TM: Could you each tell me a little bit about your process?
RH: Well, let's see. This last time I wrote a poem, and I just went back
   through my notes and saw what all—tried to remember what I had done
   and what I had seen. Then my mom walked into the room, and I had
   been looking at cypress trees, so I just made the comparison between the
   cypress trees and my mother, and how the cypress trees, they protect
   what's underneath them. When I would sit in my mom's lap, that was
   my sort of safety, and how the cypress trees tower over the stuff underneath it, that was their protector.
LN: When I sit down to write it's usually two or three days afterwards,
   when I've had time to think about it. And I read over my notes again and
   I try to picture the image of us walking around, and what I saw and
   what I looked at and didn't understand. Sometimes I write descriptive
   pieces. I've written one descriptive essay and then I turned in a couple of
   poems last time. But on the poems I tried to relate what we saw to other
   people.
RY: I just look back at my notes, about where we went and everything and I
   have to envision it for myself, what I saw, what people said about it,

what I thought first, whenever I first saw it, and it makes me get a feeling for it. And then I just write. . . . I like to write about animals that I was seeing, or the tracks, and about the different kinds of trees—descriptive stuff mostly, describing what I've seen.

During an evening meeting of Water Rangers students and parents at Janet's house, Byron, a Water Ranger, talked about the writing context as it has been set up for them in terms of choice of genres. He acknowledged that he had come to see *narrative* accounts of outings as a choice that would allow you to capture what happened out there, whereas poetry would give you the "real meaning." While each student's process differs, and as each will undoubtedly differ from the whole Water Rangers cohort, it is clear that the license to think—to wander, to explore, and to mull over his or her findings—allows each of these students to take a Wordsworthian path toward a completed product, conjuring powerful feelings and associations from actual wanderings and more tranquil recollections.

Just as the license to think divergently—after a common, purposeful experience gathering information out of doors—promoted a wide range of response among Janet's writers, so these experiences also seemed to transform group dynamics. During several conversations, I talked to students about their observations of group dynamics within the Rangers. The word *diversity* came up several times, as in this exchange with Lee and the two Rebeccas.

TM: Tell me about this group as a whole, the Water Rangers. How would you describe the characteristics of this group? Is it—
LN: Diverse.
RY: Yeah.
TM: In what ways?
LN: Just the cliques we all hang out with are quite different.
TM: Are they really?
RY *and* RH: Yeah.
RH: Think about it. People who otherwise wouldn't—
RY: Hardly ever be together.
TM: Really?
RY: And I think all of our personalities and everybody comes together. You get a variety of writings and thoughts and perspectives.
LN: Yeah, a lot of different perspectives because of the different attitudes toward things in general.
TM: Is the group chemistry evolving as you go along?
RY: I think we're getting closer than we were whenever we were first together, because I remember our first ride out there. Everybody was so quiet. They didn't say anything. They just rode in the van until we got

there. And you could tell after our first lab or whatever you want to call it, our trip, the next one was a lot . . . Everyone was talking; we were joking around with each other. We were having fun and getting to know each other.

In fact, on the day that I traveled with the Water Rangers, conversation was more than a little animated. I clearly recall talk ranging from friendly speculation on the causes of deer mortality to a fierce but respectful debate between a lone anti-hunting vegetarian and a mixed group of others who were offering alternative viewpoints on deer management. The diversity of the group combined with the openness of writing choices to allow writing for change to be a two-way street. Students, in writing with the notion of possibly effecting change, are themselves changed by their common mission.

AUDIENCE AND ACTIVISM

Janet's students seemed especially affected by the peculiar writer–audience relationships in the hybrid context of writing for change and sharing that writing over BreadNet. Her students articulated a desire to turn their experiences into action, to have an impact on others with their work.

Almost all the students agreed that the computer network (in this situation) set up a nonspecific audience. Together, they came to a generalized sense of this audience: people who were not necessarily familiar with their area, but who might have some common interest. In our informal conversations, several students spoke about how writing for the computer conference was challenging because they had to think about how to make writing clear to someone who did not know much about the places and subjects they were writing about.

Lee Norman, in relating his choices of genre after the field outings, revealed his internalized concern with audience, saying that when he writes poems he tries "to relate what I saw to other people, where they can understand it."

TM: There's a phrase that you just said that really caught my attention and that was "trying to make it clear to someone else." Who do you imagine that "someone else" to be as you're writing? Do you imagine that "someone else" to be a real person out there that you're writing to? Do you think about your audience at all when you're writing this stuff?

LH: I try to think about what—not a particular person—but what most of the people that read it could understand it, like most of the people in the

world, most of the people, wherever, that would read it, could understand it.

RY: Yeah, I agree. More for a group of people than for one specific person.
Because everyone's gonna perceive it in a different way. I think it's kind
of neat knowing that other people are going to be reading what you've
done.

In our evening discussion at Janet's house, I asked the group what
was different about doing English this way and how it mattered that
they used BreadNet. Byron noted being surprised to get a response from
someone on BreadNet: "It was cool to see that there were people out
there who actually *cared* about the work that we were doing." Several
members of Janet's Tech Prep group also responded in this regard, saying how surprised they were that professionals from "as far away as
Beaufort" would care enough to come to speak to them about their
work.

A crucial component of these comments—one that separates Janet's
work from that of others who claim to be expanding students' audience
with electronic tools—is suggested by the simple word *care*. In these
cases, perhaps because of the relatively small size of the BreadNet network and because of the carefully orchestrated, community-oriented
structure of Janet's projects, the voices that came across the wires could
be heard as caring ones. In less carefully orchestrated telecommunications work, the effect of the anonymous audience is often exactly the
opposite. Responses on the faceless Internet can be callous and un-
thoughtful.

One of the questions that Janet raised early in our online correspondence was whether these projects would seem, from her students' perspectives, to have any impact on their education and lives. As I have
mentioned, one method for observing the impact such projects might
have on the intellectual development of students was to listen closely to
their impressions of the experience, to keep an ear tuned to revealing
comments as students speculated on a variety of issues that related to
the project only tangentially. I found this open-minded approach en-
lightening. I also took a more direct route and simply asked them the
awkward question of whether they might "do" anything with what
they've been learning. (I tried to leave that question as general as possible.)

Responses ranged from silent shrugs to Jay's wanting to figure out
a job in which he could do exactly what he'd been doing in the Water
Rangers project. Lee, who envisioned himself as a history teacher some
day, had a very pointed sense of how he would bring his future classes

to places where history had happened, or at least bring them outdoors. Rebecca Young talked about becoming a camp counselor, and my sense was that this was a plan she had had before this project, but one that something in this project might have affirmed. Others from the Water Rangers group talked about just being more aware, spending more time outdoors learning to see more of the places that they go to.

Eric, from the Tech Prep group, talked to me about how he might approach problems differently in the future, how he now realized that you have to take opposing viewpoints seriously and consider them in solutions. Some students acknowledged that they didn't think their own work would make a difference, but Russ was careful to point out that he still preferred this kind of project because he saw that "the potential was there" to make a difference. In one of the most moving sections of these conversations, Al, a guy who admittedly had no great attachment to Wade Hampton, was emphatic that even if they did not get a new youth center, or actually form a working smokers' support group, their efforts would make a difference. Al noted that all their brothers and sisters and friends would be coming up through the school. If they could leave the legacy of their *attempts*, he felt, then the next group would be that much further along. And if they could influence just one or two underclass students, that could still have an impact on their school.

What did Janet's writing for the community students actually do, since they were not doing many of the things that most students do most of the time? They did not, to my knowledge, establish the teen center, radically clean up the Salkehatchie, or reform effluent regulations in the low country. I might be tempted to say that they met all of the objectives for the Tech Prep curriculum (or, in the jargon of today's environment, perhaps all of the "performance standards") at Wade Hampton High School. And indeed they may have. I might also claim that each student was led to a doorway to some kind of personal change that might make lasting positive changes in his or her life. But my interest, for now, is not in these systemwide kinds of assessments. I will say that these students were given what Dewey (1938) refers to as an "educative experience," a carefully crafted engagement with the real world, in all of its authentic complexity. But they were not abandoned there either. Through the various types of experience, networking, and conversation—ranging from guided instruction, to direct observation, to opportunities to volunteer, to opportunities to engage in informed dialogue with interested parties—they learned through the process of making sense of their experience.

What difference did it make that the experience of an English class, with its inherent emphasis on personal, expressive, and imaginative writing, was centered around these experiences related to the students environment and community? An especially interested parent during a dinner conversation at Janet's house spoke about what he had heard from his daughter and from the discussion among the Water Rangers about both their field work and their online work. "What I see," he said, "is that you're teaching awareness. So how do you grade awareness?" Certainly this kind of work does not fit easily into the necessary—and not so necessary—structures for conducting business in our contemporary public schools. Several years later, I'm still composing my answer to this parent, and I may be revising it for the remainder of my teaching career. My simple answer is that you seek to describe awareness of the learning environment, to honor it, perhaps even to celebrate it, and you conspire, as Janet and her colleagues have done, to promote it.

Conducting English classes in this way in these unlikely places made some very tangible differences for individual students. Some students had the rare opportunity in a school setting to experience a choice of writing topics as liberating rather than paralyzing. In contrast to the thinly engaged work that most of us have seen at one time or another in open-ended writing workshops, applying English methods to the science-style field trip allowed some of these students real license to think about genre, about form, and about significance. Loosening classroom structure enough to allow these kinds of risks is not always appropriate, and it is never easy to do productively. But the voices of Janet's students—like the dutiful kids who never let me forget an idle promise—remind me that if I'm interested in promoting personal engagement and sophistication among writers, I have to strive to build contexts that keep kids accountable, that motivate them, and that give them the opportunity to say, as Al did, that they had a chance *to try* to make a difference.

Small-scale networks (both electronic and face to face) can facilitate a kind of growth that is sustainable because they are rooted in the complex daily lives of both teachers and students, and such networks often give rise to unforeseen events. In a way that I could not have anticipated, this project placed me in the middle of an important network of interdependence—students tied to students, teachers to fellow teachers and community members, students to teachers, and teachers to students' parents. Certainly Janet's informal mentorship, my first step into learning from students through classroom research, does not amount to "training" any more than Janet's experiences with writing for the community may amount to definitive social or personal change. But this interaction with Janet and her students has moved me much farther than all of the school inservices I've ever attended toward readiness for the "hundred and one decisions" that Britton (1987) recognizes—decisions that "can only come from inner conviction . . . by consistently applying an ever-developing rationale" (p. 15). I've arrived at this place of readiness to learn more not because I've learned a new bag of tricks but because the support of a small-scale network has given me license to think.

REFERENCES

Britton, J. (1987). A quiet form of research. In D. Goswami & P. Stillman (Eds.), *Reclaiming the classroom*. Portsmouth, NH: Heinemann.
Dewey, J. (1938). *Experience and education*. New York: Collier.

Chapter 15

READER REFUNDS

J. Elspeth Stuckey

I directed the South Carolina Cross-age Tutoring (SCCAT) project for 8 years. As it happened, during the final phase of the project in the mid-1990s, I was asked to share what I had learned with two professional reading associations. Full of education and myself, I gave two speeches.

I have been haunted by them ever since.

The first occasion, actually, was a speech that Shirley Brice Heath had been requested to give, and Shirley asked if we might share the podium. (Shirley is a longtime advocate of cross-age tutoring, and, to kick off the project in South Carolina, she provided the model and research history, not to mention my salary.) I said "yes" as if sharing a stage with brilliance was what I usually did when not scrambling around on my hands and knees in a dark, dusty school closet filled with ancient audiovisual equipment, looking for a discarded Apple IIe.

The plan was simple. Shirley would develop a set of questions about cross-age tutoring, and I would develop a set of answers. She would respond to my answers, and I would respond to her responses. We would refine and modify to fit the time span, and she would write the introduction and conclusion. The gist of the discussion was how well such a program worked to teach reading and how to gauge its effectiveness relative to other programs.

Shirley lived on the West Coast, and I lived on the East Coast, and so we Fed-Exed diskettes back and forth to each other, feeling, at the time, very high-tech and collaborative about the whole thing.

I knew that Shirley would begin the dialogue once we got to the microphones, and I was happy to trail in her wake. Frankly, it had not

Writing to Make a Difference. Copyright © 2001 by Teachers College, Columbia University. All rights reserved. ISBN 0-8077-4186-8 (paper), 0-8077-4187-6 (cloth). Prior to photocopying items for classroom use, please contact the Copyright Clearance Center, Customer Service, 222 Rosewood Drive, Danvers, MA, 01923, USA, telephone (508) 750-8400.

even occurred to me to ask the title of the speech prior to our giving it, and I saw the title only a few minutes before we actually began to speak. That's when I also heard the introduction for the first time, and the light began to dawn.

The title was "Cross-Age Tutoring and Research: Before or After Policy," and the audience, about whose jobs I had not sufficiently inquired either, were high-profile, nationally regarded education professors specializing in research and policy making. Before 2 minutes had elapsed, Shirley posed the critical question: "If we have the gut feeling that something is working for the kids, should we use the time, staff, and funds to do an assessment and to authorize research on the process?"

At that point I had my own "gut feeling"—that I was about to be ground up and spit out like odd numbers in a standard deviation. Shirley and I, friends in the regular world of ideas and goals, were about to take opposite sides.

Which we did with zing.

I said that assessments and research projects designed to discern the felicity of reading projects—in the presumed interest of discovering something new about children and reading and school—were total wastes of time. "Who are you kidding?" I asked. Many assessments—their staffs, their *treatments*, their jargon, their shelf-lives—ruin the very thing they contrive to measure. They are too far up the food chain, I said, to know if what they do produces a greater or lesser number of school kids being eaten alive.

Shirley, who is way up on the food chain herself and is single-handedly responsible for millions of dollars of funding for education, was just as blunt. "Fine," she said. "Don't assess but don't expect to get any foundation grant money to fund your programs."

And so the repartee went. Needless to say, I lost. At the end of the speech, everyone in the audience applauded enthusiastically, a few professors signed on to the South Carolina project, Shirley went to Europe, I went back to the audiovisual closets, and the second invitation arrived.

This next invitation was to speak at Clemson University to South Carolina public school reading teachers, folks to whom philanthropic funding does not often accrue (or did not in those days) and whom I knew in a more up-front and personal way.

I was relieved, also, because it gave me a chance to reorient the perspective that, I thought, the previous speech had skewed. Indeed, to my mind, the real problem between Shirley Heath's position and mine was not whether to do research. The real problem was that the disagreement did not matter. Shirley could advance the cause of scientific rigor in reading research, and I could bash theory, and we could both be right, but the failure of children to learn to read in school would persist.

I had personal confirmation.

In the 8 years that I worked in South Carolina schools, the same kids continued not to be taught to read, the same kids continued not to learn to read, the same brothers and sisters and sons and daughters of nonreaders became nonreaders, and the nonreaders occupied the same socioeconomic class. These were the kids who dressed the same, ate the same lunch, lived on the same block or on the same road, rode the same school bus, and dropped out of school on the same schedule. They were the kids who said "There go Dr. Stuckey" as I walked down the hallways of their schools, a phrase I learned to cherish as much as I cherished the children who said it because they were the ones who never failed to remind me of the astounding consistency; that is, the failure of the schools to stop failing these children.

What many good teachers suspected—and I understood their suspicion—was that no amount of language theory *or* instruction was going to alter the landscape for a significant number of the children in their classrooms. No matter what the teachers did, based on this or that theory (or this or that fight about theory), nothing seemed to transform certain nonreaders into readers. What the teachers suspected was that curriculum—that thing theorists call the synthesis of theory with practice—did not drive change at all.

So what did?

That, I decided, was to be the subject of the Clemson speech. Whereas I happened to agree with the teachers (that more reading research and/or test cases in a classroom were not going to change the kids), I also did not think South Carolina's solution of the day was going to work, either.

At that time in South Carolina, the State Department of Education [SDE] had embraced a compelling, if unexamined, theme to guide the profession. Paraphrasing the African proverb, the SDE declared, "It takes a community to raise a child." Though not necessarily appreciated as such, this was a radical notion in a profession that staked its validity on form and content. Yet the theme was heartily embraced.

Although I esteemed the effort, I also found it hollow. It would not do, I believed, to acknowledge on the one hand that "pure teaching" (blood kin to "pure research") did not work, while on the other hand locating the solution in no-man's-land. Let's face it: The communities of the children who did not learn to read were not the communities in which their teachers lived. Was it fair or reasonable to presume that teachers were supposed to teach the children's communities, too? Moreover, I had begun to see more frustrated teachers who relieved themselves of the responsibility to reach the unreachable kids and the ratification of that decision by the society from which most of these teachers came.

Yet how was I, staring at a sea of faces of reading teachers, supposed to engage them in this conversation? Telling teachers how wrong they are—yet another definition of researcher—is not, as I have said, particularly effective or accurate. So, I started with what I thought teachers knew best: the community of school. The most consistent feature of schools, I said, that I encounter everywhere I go, is rampant, insistent fragmentation. No real community could ever work this way.

Everything in schools was always divided: grade levels, subjects, gifted, remedial, wealthy, poor, Black, White, stay-ins, pull-outs, 20 minutes in the computerized instruction lab, 20 minutes on worksheets, 20 minutes of silent reading. Among students, there were cliques, clubs, gangs, isolation, optimism, depression, happiness, and misery; among teachers, there were classroom neighbors who had little idea of what the other was doing, workloads involving twice as many students or preparations as others, activities so frighteningly different that sleep in one setting was as predictable as chaos in another. In effect, matriculation proceeded from grade to grade and teacher to teacher with little front-end work, comprehensiveness, or continuity, except at the very top or very bottom of the heap of children who either benefited from or lost out to standardized tests.

But, I added, without missing a beat, do not get the idea that I found public schools unique. At the time of the reading conference, Clemson University was trying to reorganize itself. The only community not subject to academic bickering was athletics. Where should the School of Education go—to Arts and Sciences or Nursing? Where should the School of Performing Arts go—to Architecture? And what about departments within schools? Curriculum and Instruction had little love for Counseling, and both are broken into elementary and secondary, and neither is Ed. Psych. I was in the department of English. Do you know what professors of English say about professors of education? The same thing that professors of education say about professors of English. Do you know what professors of English *and* education said about me, someone who, in their wide experience, was doing business *without portfolio* in both their fields? (Tell me the last time you remember an English professor showing up in a third-grade classroom or an education professor claiming responsibility for teaching composition.)

But here was the rub. Not only did I direct a program whose chief reason for being, I believed, was community but whose great contribution to education was its manifest ability to show how community and reading were transparent. Just as there is no pure reading, I wanted the audience to understand, there is also no pure community. Each is always and only about one thing, and that is content. In other words, we read and we have communities for the same answer. We want something.

What, I asked, is the common sticking point between failing schoolwork and children—and communities? (Or, to put it another way: Why is it that even teachers who want to cannot achieve communities in their classrooms?) The answer that I posed was that we subscribe to nostalgic ideas of community and school—ideas that not only never were that but contradict cardinal notions of who we are and what we want.

If you think I am off base—who, you might ask, is ill spirited enough to question a notion as lovely as community?—consider the idea of "commune," which, after all, is the root word of *community*. How comfortable would the parents of the children in the typical classroom be if teachers sent home a note to request permission for sons and daughters to go on a "communal" field trip? How comfortable would you be?

This discomfort is why, in a tangled sort of way, I believe we had to steal and to paraphrase the proverb from Africa, the proverb whose original words are, "It takes a *village* to raise a child." The African country and its village society that once existed—and never was as glamorous or homogeneous as we might like to think—existed in conditions of plenty. That is, there was enough to go around. Among villagers there was, if not equality, then parity. Everyone had enough food, enough housing, enough communication. Everyone participated in food gathering or preparation, children were parented by enough of the adults, there was leisure time to go around, disputes were settled and rules changed as needed. Neighbors did not necessarily like each other, but they lived together and they respected one another's right to be ornery.

In sum, the community functioned not because it was full of comfortable people but because it was built on an economy sound enough to permit relative comfort. This is not how it is today in Africa, or, if we are honest about it, how it has been in the United States, whose history includes decimating the native community and importing and enslaving another—as it happens, the very community whose proverb we also came to appropriate.

The point is that in schools, children come from communities that are so economically strapped and fragmented that they cannot feed, house, or clothe their members. Worse, children who attend the same schools arrive from communities of opposites. How difficult is it for a child from dire economic deprivation to negotiate a world in which other children live in communities that are not deprived?

The central issue, in other words, is not that there are rich and poor communities, but why some communities seem to solidify along school lines while others founder there. Moreover, for teachers the crucial question is why, or *how*, they are expected to know what to do. After all, if reading theorists are a dime a dozen and communities cannot even spare their children from neglect much less find the time to read them bedtime stories, then what's a reading teacher supposed to accomplish in five 50-minute periods a week?

At the risk of overstatement, I think the value of the SCCAT program was that it answers that question.

Cross-age tutoring looked like a literacy program, although, by the time it ended, it included academic subjects from Spanish to biology. The practice was simple. On a regular basis—usually twice a week—classrooms of older students merged with classrooms of younger students to work together. For example, on Tuesdays and Thursdays, during second period, eighth-grade middle school English students in Estill, South Carolina, would tutor first-grade students at the elementary school. This program was different from other cross-age tutoring programs in the writing component it included. The older students would read *and write* with the younger students. They used library books, in-class books, and, eventually, stories that students had written for each other. In other words, they used the materials they had on hand or produced, not materials systematically purchased or tied to grade criteria.

The tutoring sessions lasted from 20 to 40 minutes, and they occurred in classrooms, cafeterias, libraries, or gymnasiums. Many times, the students walked down the hall or from building to building to reach one another; in some settings, a school bus provided access.

Another distinguishing feature was that after each tutoring session, the student tutors wrote letters about what they had done and sent them to those of us who were the adult project participants. The tutors were asked to write about the books they had read, the responses and behaviors of the younger children (and their own), their insights, questions, observations, and so on. And we wrote them back.

"We" were educators and university students involved in field-related, academic coursework. In the responses to the tutors, we asked questions, made observations, gave suggestions, and so on. The letters were regular and collegial, and they focused on the academic dimensions of the tutoring relationship. We told the students that what they were doing was important, that their actions and observations mattered to our understanding of education. We asked them to tell us in their letters how to make their time in schools better.

We were telling the truth.

A final distinguishing feature of the SCCAT program was that it trained the at-risk, remedial, incorrigible, disabled, exit-examined, self-contained and uncontained, and resource students to be the tutors. These were the kids who were rarely viewed as academically adequate or suitable students, much less teachers or leaders, but we felt from the outset that if the principles of the SCCAT program were sound, the program would work successfully with these students. Eventually, of course, based on the success of the at-risk students, the entrance requirements were loosened to welcome other-labeled students such as the "gifted and talented."

Most tutoring programs are set up to improve the work of the children being tutored. The SCCAT program sought improvement in the work of the tutors. What we found was that as a result of tutoring, writing letters, and receiving consistent feedback, the tutors improved their own knowledge and ability. Their correspondence with the outside adults was a form of writing to learn. (Teachers sighed with relief when the tutors did not do worse on standardized tests at the end of the year.)

Other things improved as well. Whereas an eighth-grade student may read quite poorly, even in a class of poor readers, he reads quite acceptably to a second-grader who, as it turns out, is terribly nonjudgmental about the linguistic prowess of an older child who spends time reading to her each week.

Behavior changed. Students for the first time in their school lives acquired tags such as "responsible," "excited," "proud," and "patient."

Boundaries changed. Chapter I reading students were joined by Chapter I math students. A rural elementary school that began the project with two classes looked, several years later, like a beehive on certain days as every class catacombed its way to tutoring sets. A middle school, whose most incorrigible class was taught by a teacher who brought cross-age tutoring into her students' lives for 3 years, began a gardening project that, over another few years, turned the front lawn of the school into a small farm and the bean seeds into projects among tutors and tutees. And a class of high school students taking Spanish tutored sixth-graders using Spanish storybooks written by Cuban American fourth-grade children in Miami, children who were learning to write in Spanish and English.

Technology changed, too. Tutors and correspondents originally wrote to the outside correspondents and posted letters in brown manila envelopes. One day, the project purchased modems for the computers that had proliferated in at-risk classrooms across the state. E-mail among isolated, rural schools was born. Although the tutors had been accustomed to using computers as a mere skill-and-drill exercise machine, a kind of worksheet on monitor (whose programs cost thousands of dollars to develop and to buy), they quickly adapted to using the computers as tools for communication and began to write and send long, informative letters to one another across the state. One of the last electronic links in the project was between adult education students at a technical college—whose correspondence urged tutors to stay in school—and high school students on the verge of dropping out.

School events changed. Each year, students from across the state converged on a college campus to hold their own miniconference, which served as public forums for the knowledge they had gained and generated through tutoring and writing to one another and correspondents. Students in the first grade assembled with students in college in auditoriums, classrooms, and lunchrooms to present their findings. Students held seminars to discuss cross-age curriculum and, as they put it, "things that work with the tutees." Students who in the past had never been perceived as leaders made impassioned, rehearsed speeches to hundreds of their peers and not a few adults. During the project's last year, two miniconferences were held to accommodate the number and geographic location of schools and school buses.

Significantly, literacy changed as well.

Although, on the face of it, the project appeared to be a reading-based literacy drive, it produced massive numbers of letters, and many students who participated as they matriculated wrote volumes over years. Although students in the past had been asked, and often failed, to write in school settings, they succeeded in this writing because of the real audience of peers and interested educators who were listening and responding to their ideas. Elicited was a kind of writing that had not, in most students' (and teachers') experience, appeared before.

The number of letters the tutors wrote over the several years of this project was astonishing, amounting to thousands, as the South Carolina Cross-age Tutoring program was instituted in as many as 35 schools simultaneously over many years. I could not have responded to such a mountain of letters, even though I would have enjoyed doing so, and so I recruited advocates of literacy wherever I could find them (and I found them everywhere, from secretaries in schools to graduate students at various universities) to correspond with the tutors about their experiences. I had the great privilege to respond to many of these tutors myself and to read the letters they had written to other correspondents, and I became intrigued with the depth of thought, emotion, and sense of advocacy for learning that was expressed in the letters.

In virtually all the tutors' letters, I found a deep appreciation for the opportunity to be involved in tutoring younger students. I must admit that their appreciation alleviated any fears I may have had initially that I was involving them in a program that would be overly task-oriented and simply not much fun. To my delight, I discovered the kids enjoyed the activities of tutoring. I was glad they were having fun, but their appreciation, I believe, attested to the effectiveness of the tutoring model for learning: I was convinced then, as I am now, that when learning is fun, it must be effective.

I know the tutors' appreciation for the program attested to its effectiveness because they told me so. Countless students remarked spontaneously without being prompted that the tutoring experience was increasing their abilities not just to teach another child but also to learn more complex applications of literacy for themselves. Tutors told us over and over again in the letters that they, the tutors, were learning to read better, learning to speak foreign languages better, learning to do math better. This improvement was not hard to understand for one very obvious reason: Practice makes perfect, and increasing the amount of time the tutors spent practicing the skills (of reading, writing, thinking, etc.) with the tutees would likely improve ability of tutee *and* tutor. But I began to see another phenomenon at work: Heightening feelings of improvement in ability were often correlated to the extent to which tutors reflected on tutoring as a learning experience for themselves. Students who reflected at length about the learning process of their tutees and of themselves felt they were making improvements in their academic ability. I have no hard scientific data to support this claim, but I do have boxes of reflective letters from students who claimed that the experience was affecting them in this positive way. I am inclined to believe them.

I am inclined to believe them because the letters are written with wit and insight, and the expressiveness of the letters was a delight to me and other correspondents. These students, who were predicted by their previous scores on standardized tests to do poorly in reading and writing, were writing engaging, thoughtful, and detailed letters. Their reflections ranged from extolling the literary value of comic books, to recording insights about the learning process that would astonish professional educators, to attempting to persuade me to bring more pencils, paper, and books on my next site visit. These children expressed them-

selves with clear voices, not always in grammatically correct or stylisti-
cally appropriate sentences, but they were adept at expressing themselves as individuals with knowledge to share.

Their letters expressed a strong sense of commitment to the project,
to their schools, and to the tutees. This pleased me as a program administrator because it refuted some of the negative press given to schools
and schoolchildren. Perhaps their commitment increased because as
members of the lower economic classes, the tutors rarely got opportunities to express a sense of altruism, and many were finding out for the
first time that they indeed had something to give to others. They liked
tutoring others simply because they enjoyed being kind, but I also
closely observed the self-esteem of some tutors improve as they realized
they were providing something needed by a younger child.

Other qualities associated with the tendency toward altruism included pride, dedication, and thoroughness. Students who expressed
pride in helping others also expressed dedication to continuing in the
program and an inclination to do the tutoring as thoroughly as possible.
Some letters described how the tutors began, without prompting, to
discuss the tutoring experience among themselves in an attempt to tease
out some of the problems they encountered and to discover how different tutors attempted to solve the problems. The sense of commitment
of the tutors to the program was no more touching for me than when
one student expressed a sadness or fear that his tutee might not remember him once the program was finished. Other tutors expressed a similar poignant sense of care, even love in some cases, for their tutees, and
I found this a remarkable and unexpected effect of the program, an
effect I'm reluctant to try to quantify. I'm still uncertain about even
how to write about this effect.

Even though people reacted to these letters according to the roles
they played in the education of children, most readers of the letters
were dumbfounded by the overarching sense of responsibility tutors
expressed and their keen attention to academic (some researchers prefer
literate) detail. This from students who clearly lacked some of the finer
graces of punctuation and paragraphing.

I would recast the observation.

I believe that what students expressed in their letters was a sense of
"community." In fact, writing the letters was a way of "community
building" because the project ensured access to those strengths that
allow communities to work. This insurance, in fact, was granted by the
schools, the teachers, and the administrative willingness to free up
enough time during enough days to let students read and then write to

one another. In other words, economy and infrastructure were not a problem.

The students supplied the strengths—the collection, assimilation, and distribution of cohesive skills that make the community function. To put it metaphorically, the students provided the cup of sugar, the plumber's helper, the drive to the emergency room in the middle of the night, the neighborhood trip to the ice cream shop, the grandmothers and fathers and aunts and uncles who say "Hello, and what have you been doing today?" Cross-age tutoring gave students what they—and we—want *right there in the relationships and right there in the books.* Why do we have to do research to tell us this?

In *Rules for Radicals*, Saul Alinsky (1971), a writer who was tired of the status quo, enumerated the qualities of the people in his experience who had fomented change. To my eye, many of these qualities emerged in the letter writing of the cross-age tutors. Change-makers, he said,

- Use personal experience as the basis for teaching, and they invite others to do the same
- Have almost unlimited patience and are able to listen
- Are curious about others, and share their own knowledge in order to get new knowledge
- Are not daunted by surprise; they like surprise
- Have imagination and empathy; sometimes they work so hard because they can't live with themselves if they quit
- Have a deep reverence for life
- Have a sense of humor
- Have a better vision of the world that they look toward even as they go through many of the deadly, monotonous details of the day
- Have a healthy ego; they believe they can do what must be done
- Have an open mind; they know they haven't learned it all
- Realize that the greatest joy is in allowing others to create

Who, I asked, has a healthier ego or imagination than seventh-grader and tutor Ralph, who successfully attempted to flatter and charm me into bringing him more pens and paper for his schoolwork? Who has a reverence for life and shares his knowledge more than fifth-grader George, who really likes to help children read, write, and learn words? Who is willing to put up with the monotony of details but demands accountability more than Gregory, a serious sixth-grader who fears his tutee may forget him if he doesn't give him his best effort?

Who has a more open mind and lovelier sense of humor than Adam's tutor, who in his letters expressed doubt that he could even do what he was asked to do as tutor?

On the other hand, the qualities that Alinsky attributed to people who change things really are radical. Today, 3 decades after Alinsky's book came out, "radical" students may be the best hope we have to do what needs to be done to make changes in education. We need to ask them.

In asking children how we should change schools for the better, I've learned how little has changed in the way education is administered. Witness the last decade in South Carolina, which has seen the *funded* legislation of newer, tougher, and more standardized tests, uniform exit exams for public school courses, higher cutoff scores on teachers exams, and the creation of a supraeducational bureaucracy to oversee the already massive State Department of Education.

But some things have happened, and I can illustrate them by two examples.

The first involves a story Shirley Heath told.

One of the neighborhoods in which Shirley did her seminal work for *Ways with Words* (Heath, 1983) was a community in South Carolina where she had continued to return and offer support. Shirley's research indicated that schools must connect with the linguistic community of minority children if these children are to acquire the communicative skills of mainstream America—that is, access to economic stability. To those of us who thought language was a key, the power of writing was the virtual guarantee that children can and will acquire unlimited ways with words if they are provided appropriate conditions and tools.

On her return visits, which were as steady as the years, Shirley watched the fates of the young community members spiral into dropout rates, drug use, unemployment, and so on. Nothing—most especially nothing in the schools—seemed to change or to make an impact.

There was one child, a male African American, Shirley said, who failed to follow this pattern. He had displayed a greater determination to "make it"—he had been more of a reader and a writer than his peers, and he spent more time by himself—but Shirley was puzzled about this child's choice. What, she asked him, made the difference?

"You did," he replied.

That was a testimony to something that, at the time, I did not fully appreciate.

The second thing that happened occurred immediately after the speech that I gave to the educators at Clemson. After the niceties at the podium were concluded and I began to thread my way through the emptying room, an attractive, bustling teacher with a big handbag stopped me. She was digging in her bag, and she looked nonplussed but expectant.

"Isn't this you?" she asked, pulling from her bag a black-and-white photograph, the kind taken in the 1950s in the public schools I attended. The children were arranged in rows, their faces looking like postage stamps.

"I knew when I saw your name in the program this had to be you," she said. "I have never had another Elspeth."

I flashed back to the speech, to the pronouncements of failures to teach, to indictments of mainstream communities, to public schools that don't seem to care enough to create the communities that would change the status quo even when they embrace the ability of their students to do it.

And then I looked into the eyes of my first-grade teacher who had taught me my first letters.

She laughed, "I look a little older now."

"So do I," I said.

The time that has elapsed since both of those occasions has tempered my zeal. It began to make sense for me to leave education. I had begun to realize that the teachers who taught kids to read or who did not needed far more than supportive communities and decent theory. Indeed, for the most part, they had both. My first-grade teacher was *still* teaching. She did not need me. What she and others like her needed, more than anything else, was a society that did not select them for their willingness to go to the mat day after day to save a losing child. As long as that society exists, education will continue to sacrifice most of its "different" children while championing heroines who manage to break the fall of a few.

In the end, I had to agree that Shirley Heath is correct. Undocumented change in the midst of a world of failure is unfundable.

Certainly, the South Carolina Cross-Age Tutoring program stopped when the money ran out. The infrastructure supported the old things. Researchers got a good story. I learned humility.

Of course, there was the child who stayed with the program from the time she was in the sixth grade until she graduated from high school, first as a "tutee" then as a tutor, writing to me the entire time. During one of her tutoring sessions, someone discovered that she couldn't read because she couldn't see. She needed glasses.

She telephoned the other night, about 2:00 A.M. This time, she was in Montana, just shipped in from Kosovo. Prior to that she was stationed in Korea for 2 years, and, before that, in Germany.

In the Air Force, she is an emergency computer programmer. She recently signed on for her second tour.

Nobody needs to tell her the value of cross-age tutoring. She tells everyone she meets.

So, maybe we've got it backwards.

Maybe it takes a child to raise a community, or a village, or a whole educational structure.

REFERENCES

Alinsky, S.D. (1971). *Rules for radicals*. New York: Random House.
Heath, S.B. (1983). *Ways with words*. New York: Cambridge University Press.

ABOUT THE EDITORS
AND THE CONTRIBUTORS

Janet Atkins is an eighth-grade literature teacher at Northwest Middle School in Travelers Rest, South Carolina. She previously taught at Wade Hampton High School in Hampton, South Carolina. Her curricular interests include environmental and social justice issues. Janet was a DeWitt Wallace Fellow at the Bread Loaf School of English for 3 years and currently serves as the coordinator for Bread Loaf in the Cities program funded by the Carnegie Foundation. Janet is married and has two teenaged children.

Evelyn Beck teaches English at Piedmont Technical College in Greenwood, South Carolina. In 1996, she was named the Educator of the Year by the South Carolina Technical Education Association. She is also a freelance magazine writer specializing in business and education issues.

Chris Benson is editor and publications coordinator for the semiannual *Bread Loaf Teacher Network Magazine*, which contains articles, book reviews, interviews, and classroom stories written by and for teachers. Special issues of the magazine have reported on teacher research, school reform, community building, rural communities, changing policy, and teaching with technology. Chris is a research associate at the Thurmond Institute at Clemson University, where he has taught writing and literature. He is an active associate of Write to Change, a nonprofit agency promoting literacy and social action. He co-edited *Electronic Networks: Crossing Boundaries/Creating Communities* (Heinemann, 1999) with Tharon Howard, Dixie Goswami, and Rocky Gooch.

Scott Christian is director of the Professional Education Center at University of Alaska Southeast in Juneau. He has a master's in English from the Bread Loaf School of English and taught for 12 years in Alaskan schools. He has conducted research in education for the Spencer Foundation, Harvard University, and Middlebury College. His book *Exchanging Lives: Middle School Writers Online* was published in 1997 by NCTE.

At Clemson University, **Carol Collins** is the director of Writing and Performing Across Communities, a project sponsored by Write to Change which uses improvisation as a learning tool for creative writing and to strengthen learning skills. Carol is an adjunct faculty member in playwriting for the South Carolina Governor's School for the Arts and Humanities and director of Celebration! Ensemble, which performs stories and poems written by K–12 students. Her latest play, *Ropes*, premiered during summer 2001 at New Plays Premiere at the Brooks Center for Performing Arts in Clemson.

Walter H. "Rocky" Gooch is the director of telecommunications for the Bread Loaf Teacher Network, a professional development program of the Bread Loaf School of English at Middlebury College. He provides support, guidance, and training to public school teachers who are Fellows in the program. Rocky also serves as secretary for Write to Change, a national community-based, nonprofit organization that promotes literacy in many schools and communities.

Dixie Goswami is Professor Emerita of English at Clemson University and longtime faculty member of the Bread Loaf School of English. She directs Write to Change, a national, community-based literacy nonprofit organization, which sponsored many of the projects reported on in this book. Presently, she coordinates the Bread Loaf Teacher Network, a professional development program that awards fellowships for graduate study to teachers from across the United States. Dixie has published articles on writing, teaching, and learning, and co-edited several books. She is on the editorial boards of *Changing English*, *Writing Teacher*, *Journal of Written Communication*, *English Education*, and *Issues in Writing*. Dixie co-edited *Electronic Networks: Crossing Boundaries/Creating Communities* (Heinemann, 1999).

Rex Lee Jim was born and raised in Rock Point, Arizona. He lives there on his family ranch and commutes to Tsaile, Arizona, where he teaches for the Center for Diné Teacher Education at Diné College. He loves horses, acting, traveling, and writing. He enjoys teaching as well, which he considers a hobby.

In high school, **Lauren Kocks** was a student of Marjorie Kleinneiur Morgan, who introduced her to several writing for the community projects. Lauren is currently a student at Texas A & M University in College Station, Texas.

Bernadette Longo is an assistant professor with the Rhetoric Department at the University of Minnesota, Twin Cities. She recently won an NCTE ACE award for a sustainable schoolyards project integrating a college horticulture class and a middle school class—an important community-building experience for the participants. Dr. Longo is the author of *Spurious Coin: A History of Science, Management, and Technical Writing* from SUNY Press, as well as numerous journal articles and conference papers.

Currently Assistant Professor of Education Technology at the University of Alaska Southeast in Juneau, **Tom McKenna** specializes in literacy and technology and learning. He has taught English and computer technology in K–12 schools ranging from the remote community of Unalaska in Alaska's Aleutian Islands, to Barcelona, Spain. Tom received his master's in English from the Bread Loaf School of English in 1996.

Susan L. Miera has a master's in English from the Bread Loaf School of English and teaches at Pojoaque High School, Pojoaque, New Mexico, where she is also the English Department chair. Susan is an active member of Bread Loaf Teacher Network and enjoys researching and writing about the use of computer conferencing in the classroom as a tool for teaching writing, editing, and publishing skills.

Marjorie Kleinneiur Morgan is a veteran high school English teacher in Dallas, Texas, in the Richardson Independent School District. She has a master's degree in English from the Bread Loaf School of English. Marjorie has been doing writing for the community projects with her students since 1991 and considers technical writing and service learning the highlight of her students' work.

Jim Randels teaches elective writing courses at two New Orleans Public Schools: Frederick Douglass and McDonogh 35. He founded the Students at the Center program, which he co-directs, with students Erica DeCuir and Kenyatta Johnson. Jim is also active on executive and coordinating councils for Community Labor United, Louisiana Research Institute for Community Empowerment, and United Teachers of New Orleans.

Elizabeth Coykendall Rice received her M.Ed. in English from Clemson University in 1988. She has taught writing and literature at both the high school and college level. In 1997, she developed and directed the America Reads program at Clemson University. She currently lives in Genoa, Italy, teaching English to Italians, translating Web sites, and raising her three sons.

Rosie Roppel received her master's degree from the Bread Loaf School of English in 1998, where she received the DeWitt Wallace-Reader's Digest Fellowship. She taught English at the middle school level for 17 years and now teaches English and Spanish at Ketchikan High School in Ketchikan, Alaska. Rosie served as the Director of the Alaska State Writing Consortium for 8 years and has published many articles and chapters chronicling research in her classroom.

An English teacher at Beloit Memorial High School in Beloit, Wisconsin, **Beth Steffen** enjoys researching and writing about literacy and its intersections with students' and teachers' lives. Her *English Journal* article "Bad Boys, Bad Girls, Whatcha Gonna Do? Teenage Outlaws Create Curriculum" won NCTE's Paul and Kate Farmer Writing Award.

J. Elspeth Stuckey directed the South Carolina Cross Age Tutoring Project between 1990 and 1995. The project served over 60 rural schools in three states and involved students from pre-kindergarten through graduate school. Stuckey is a former Fulbright scholar and recipient of a Rockefeller humanities fellowship at the UNC/Duke Center for Research on Women. Currently, she is the Senior Vice President for Excellence at Eckerd Youth Alternatives, Inc., in Clearwater, FL.

Laura Schneider VanDerPloeg has taught language arts in middle and high schools in Boston, Wisconsin, and New York, and worked as a staff developer in Brooklyn, New York. She received a master's degree in English Education from Teachers College at Columbia University and has done graduate work at the Bread Loaf School of English. As a teacher in Wisconsin, she was a member of the Write for Your Life project, a national student writing project that promoted adolescent health and well being. In 1999, she and Marcella Pixley received a Spencer Foundation Practitioner Research Communication and Mentoring grant to conduct the research presented in this article; in 2000, they were awarded an NCTE teacher research grant to further support their work.

INDEX